BROMOIL
A FOUNDATION COURSE

DEREK WATKINS

photographers'
pip
institute press

First published 2006 by
Photographers' Institute Press / PIP
an imprint of Guild of Master Craftsman Publications Ltd
Castle Place, 166 High Street,
Lewes, East Sussex BN7 1XU

ISBN 1 86108 333 5

A catalogue record for this book is available from the British Library.

Managing Editor: Gerrie Purcell
Production Manager: Hilary MacCallum
Commissioning Editor: April Sankey
Photography Books Editor: James Beattie
Managing Art Editor: Gilda Pacitti
Designer: Ian Hunt

Set in Meta and Eurostyle

Colour origination by Altaimage Ltd
Printed and bound by Kyodo Printing (Singapore)

Contents

Introduction

The bromoil process is not just a fascinating and enjoyable technique for producing beautiful prints, it is a method that is steeped in the history of photography itself.

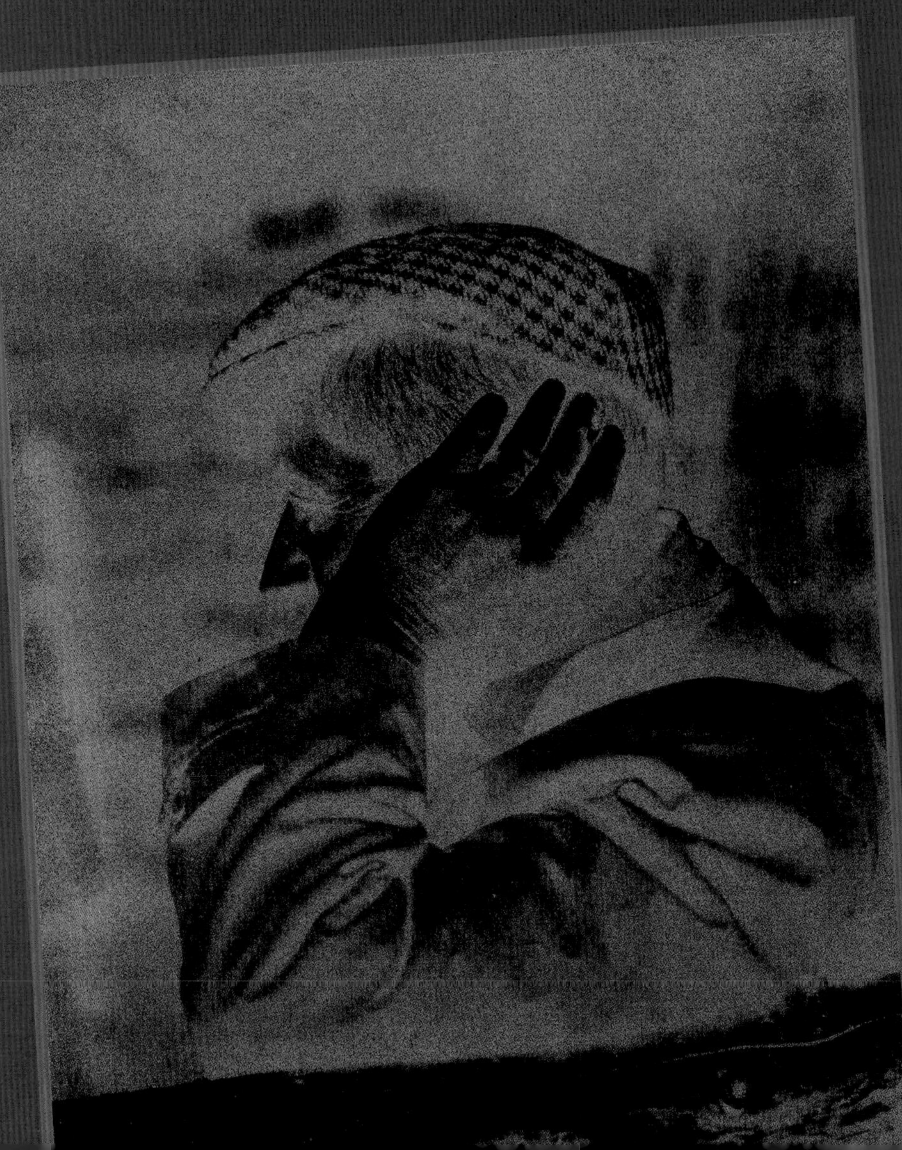

My earliest recollections of the bromoil process are of the mid-1950s, when I first became seriously interested in photography and joined a photographic society. One or two of the members were producing very beautiful, often delicate, prints that looked more like etchings than photographs. There was a great mystique surrounding the process, which these workers tended to promote, making the process seem far more difficult and complicated than it really was. At that time the vogue was moving away from the soft, almost romantic pictorialism that had dominated photography for the previous fifty years or more. Replacing it was the hard, gritty photorealism and the sharply defined images of the 'f/64' school of straight photography – a movement to which I subscribed for some forty years and, indeed, still do for much of my photography.

As a result the bromoil process and its practitioners were rather scorned, and the art began to die out. There was, however, a small group of workers dedicated to keeping the process alive, most of whom were members of the Bromoil Circle of Great Britain. The Circle, which was founded in 1931 by Sam Weller FRPS, is still very active today, and it is largely due to this group of enthusiasts that there is now a bromoil revival taking place. The Circle runs workshops where small groups of photographers can learn the processes by watching demonstrations and gaining hands-on experience. Thanks to enthusiasts in the United States, Europe and Australia, interest in bromoil and other historical processes is also increasing around the globe. The Internet has also been influential in opening up the lines of communication between bromoilists and has led to the foundation of the International Society of Bromoilists.

The bromoil process was invented in 1907 and it is pleasing to see that 100 years on there is a renewed interest in this historical process that not so many years ago seemed doomed to obsolescence.

So what is a bromoil print? Quite simply, it is a normal bromide print from which the silver image has been removed and replaced by an oily pigment image. But why would anyone want to replace a perfectly good silver image with an ink one?

There are three reasons. The first is that, while a silver print will deteriorate over the years, even if it has been archivally processed, an ink image is completely permanent. It will last as long as the paper on which it is formed. The second, more important reason is that the bromoil process offers a great deal of control; during the application of the ink there are limitless opportunities to manipulate the image and create a true work of art. Finally, every bromoil print is unique. It is these three features that make the bromoil process so attractive to creative photographers.

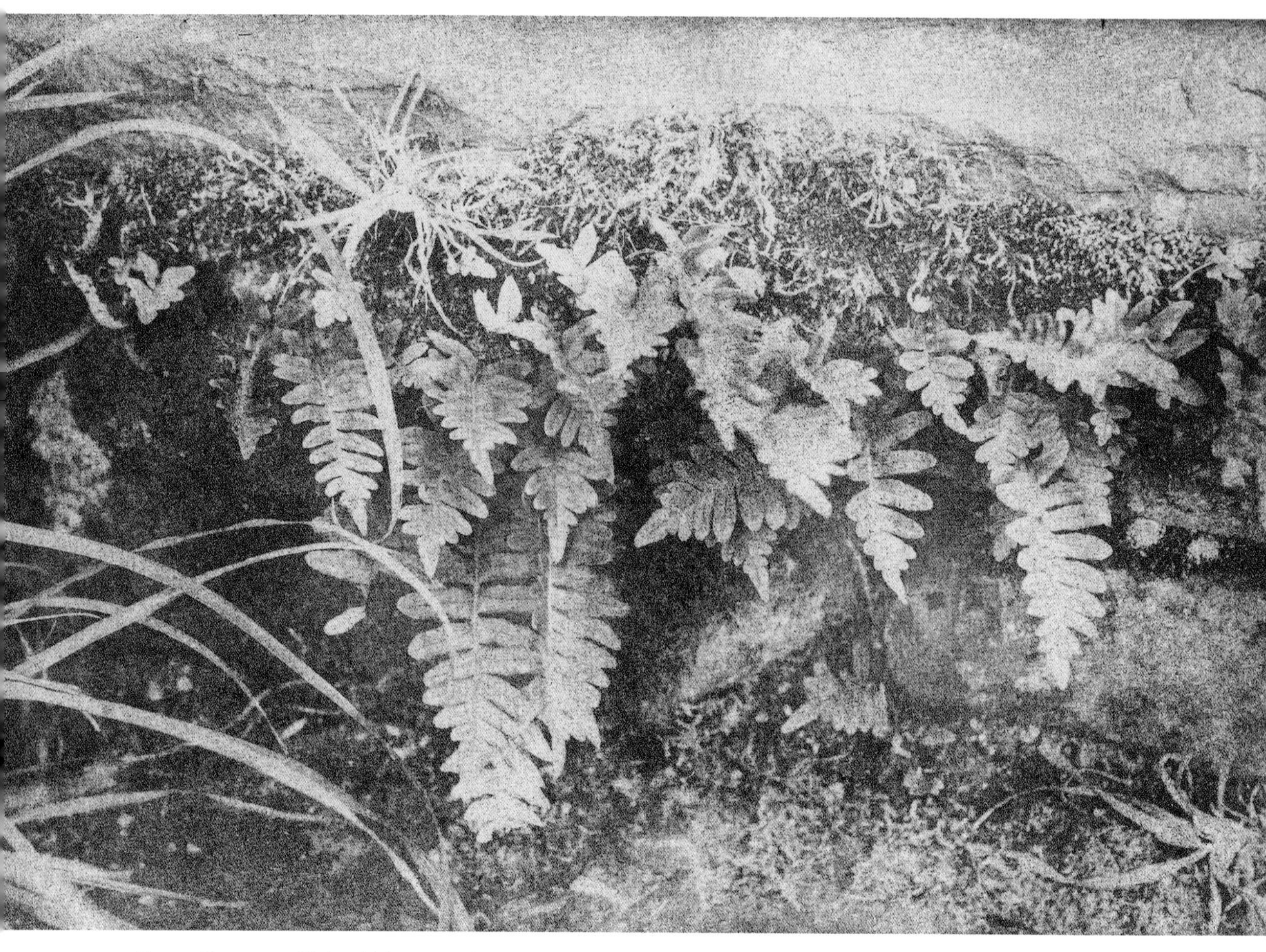

Ferns, Glyngarw, Wales. Taken on Olympus OM-1 camera with 50mm lens using Ilford FP4 film and Microphen developer. Inked with GC&I 1796 ink on Kentmere Art Document paper.

A LITTLE HISTORY

The history of the bromoil process can be traced back as far as 1855, when Alphonse Louis Poitevin patented a method of producing an image in greasy ink on gelatin that had been sensitized by potassium dichromate. However, Poitevin's description, contained in Patent 2815 of 1855, was too vague to be of any practical value.

Nearly 50 years later, G. E. H. Rawlins wrote an article in the 18 October 1904 issue of *Amateur Photographer* that described a similar process, which became known as oil printing. Rawlins applied the ink to his prints using a composition roller, but further experiments showed that greater control of the pigment image could be achieved by applying the ink with brushes. These brushes were similar to stencil brushes and the ink was applied with a gentle dabbing action. However, the main drawback of the oil process was that the speed of the dichromate-sensitized gelatin was slow, much too slow to allow prints to be made with an enlarger. As a result, oil prints could only be made successfully by placing the negative in contact with the paper and exposing to sunlight. This meant, of course, that a large negative was necessary. Although this was not a major problem at the time, because most photographers were using large-format cameras, smaller-format roll-film cameras were starting to become popular and the smaller negatives they produced needed enlarging to give a reasonably sized print.

Then in 1907, C. Welbourne Piper, a leading pictorial photographer of his day, wrote an article in *Photographic News* detailing a method of turning bromide prints into oil-pigmented prints. This method was based on a suggestion published earlier that year by E. J. Wall and became known as the bromoil process. Its main advantage was that, because it was based on a print made on bromide paper that had a speed many times that of dichromate-sensitized paper, enlargements of any size could be made from the negative. Over the following years the bromoil process gained in popularity. Materials manufacturers produced special bromide papers without a gelatin supercoat, which made the inking-up procedure easier. Several companies produced ink, in a variety of colours, designed especially for the process, and specially shaped brushes were sold by photographic retailers for applying the ink. These brushes had what was known as a 'stag-foot' shape and had been devised by F. J. Mortimer FRPS, sometime editor of *Amateur Photographer* and *Photographic News*, and described by him in his book *The Oil and Bromoil Processes*. Indeed, these brushes became known as 'Mortimer' brushes and were subsequently produced for many years under that name by James A. Sinclair & Co of London.

The demise of the bromoil process in the 1950s and 60s meant that the materials and equipment necessary for the process slowly disappeared from the market until materials made specifically for the production of bromoil prints were no longer available. Those photographers still producing bromoils were doing so under increasingly difficult conditions, continually experimenting with various bromide papers and inks in a constant struggle to keep the process alive.

Bromoil and Pictorialism

Towards the end of the nineteenth century, many photographers became bored with the detailed and accurate reproduction produced by the camera. They hankered after pictures that were more impressionistic, believing that this would make photography more of a true art form. The advent of 'high-art' photography in the early 1850s saw photographers begin to use new techniques among which were combination printing, differential focus and what we now call 'alternative processes' such as gum-bichromate and oil printing – the forerunner of bromoil.

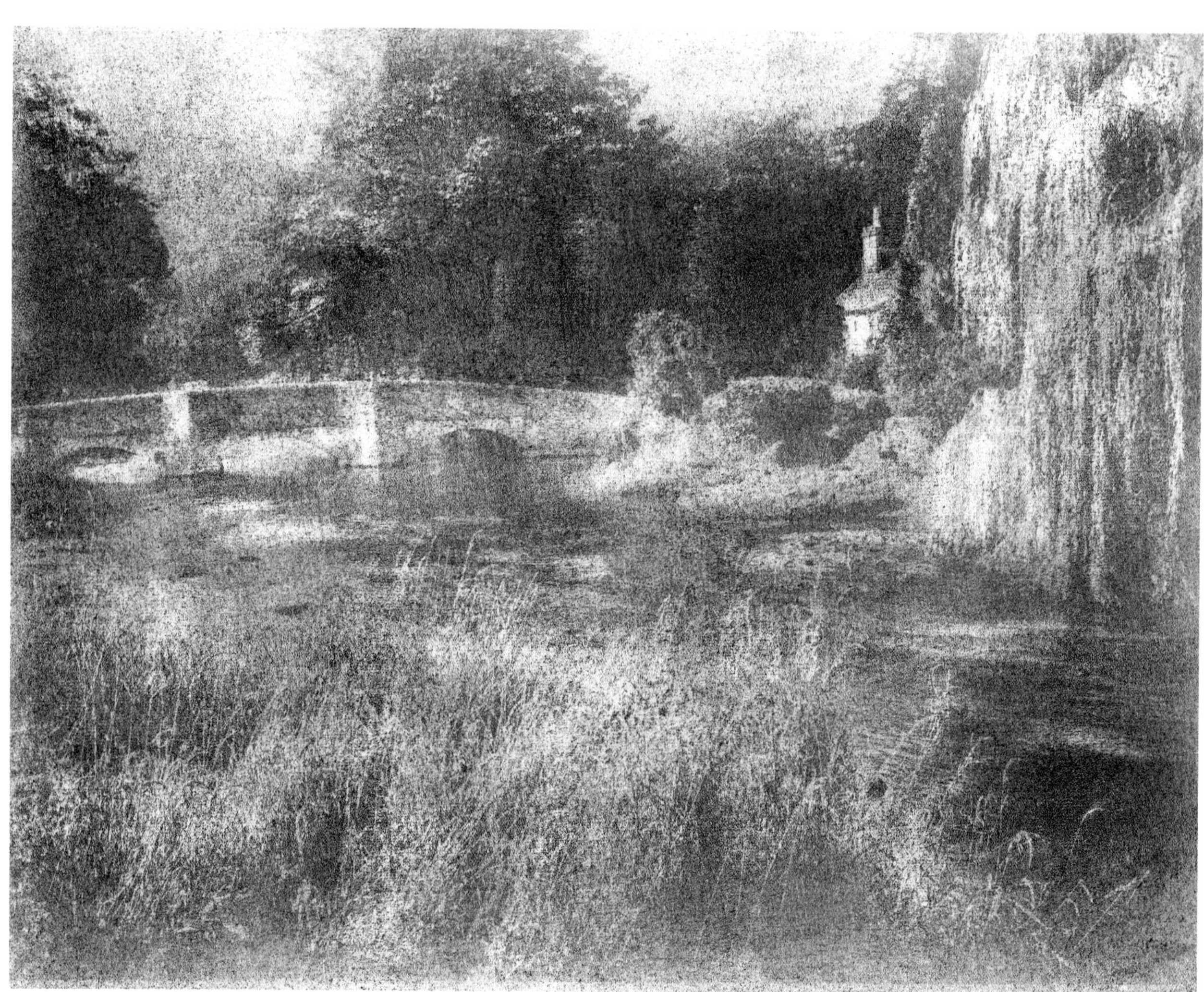

Ashford-in-the-Water, Derbyshire by Colin Ivison

As these techniques became more popular, the term high-art photography was replaced by Pictorialism. The pictures that were produced tended to follow the styles made popular by the paintings, drawings and etchings of the time. Indeed, the subjects depicted in the pictures were often secondary to the perceived artistic quality of the image. So when the bromoil process was introduced in 1907 it was natural for Pictorial photographers to embrace the process, offering the high degree of control that it does.

Pictorialism was always a controversial idea, right from its inception. By the 1890s, several members of the Photographic Society – later to become the Royal Photographic Society – became disenchanted by what they saw as the Society's exhibitions ignoring their artistic work in favour of the more detailed reproduction of 'straight' photography. The argument became so bitter that in 1892 several members resigned and founded a new group called the Linked Ring to exhibit and promote Pictorial photography. This was followed a few years later in America by the formation of the Photo-Secession, which had broadly similar aims. Members of the Photo-Secession movement included such well-known and influential photographers as Edward Steichen, Clarence White, Gertrude Kasebier and Alvin Langdon Coburn. Many of these practitioners used pigment processes in their work, though not necessarily bromoil. Steichen, for example, was wellknown for the gum-bichromate prints he made at that time.

The Linked Ring was disbanded during the first decade of the twentieth century to be replaced by the London Salon of Photography, which remains today as one of the most influential Pictorial exhibitions in the world. Its stated aim is to 'exhibit only that class of photographic work in which there is distinct evidence of artistic feeling and execution'.

Bromoil today

Today, with the renewed interest in bromoil, the outlook is a lot brighter. Several papers are now available without a gelatin supercoat, which makes them especially suitable for the bromoil process, and it has been discovered that several supercoated papers are also suitable. In the late 1990s, the manufacturer Kentmere produced an experimental batch of bromoil paper in collaboration with the Bromoil Circle of Great Britain. It has proved to be highly effective and is now available in limited quantities from the London-based retailer Silverprint.

Although special bromoil inks and brushes are now available again from a few specialist suppliers, they are by no means essential for success. Inks designed for lithographic printing and relief printing are equally suitable, and a wide variety of brushes for oil painting can be put to alternative use as bromoil brushes.

The reason for the renewed interest in bromoil – and, indeed, other historical processes – is not difficult to understand. My own belief is that it is a reaction to the automatic-everything, technology-led mentality that manufacturers promote for obvious commercial reasons. Quite simply, cameras with automatic focusing and automatic exposure control in countless different modes have removed a large measure of the skill from photography. And the advent of digital imaging has brought manipulation and the production of reasonable-quality colour prints within the reach of anyone who can operate a computer. Although this is, perhaps, a good thing as far as the casual photographer is concerned, it has left many more serious photographers frustrated. There is very little challenge any more; photography has become altogether too easy. So photographers looking for a challenge are turning to processes that will stretch their abilities and give them a picture that really has something of themselves in it. Bromoil is one of those processes. It is a unique blend of art and craft that allows you to produce results that simply cannot be achieved in any other way.

It is my aim in this book to introduce you to the process, to show you how to produce good results quickly and without too many failures, and to start you on the path to discovering your own individual style. And, above all, to show you how you can really enjoy making pictures using the bromoil process.

***The Flat Cap*. The original was taken many years ago at a New Forest pony sale on a Prakticamat camera with a 135mm lens. The film was Kodak Tri-X developed in D76 developer. Inked with GC&I 1796 ink on Kentmere Art Document paper.**

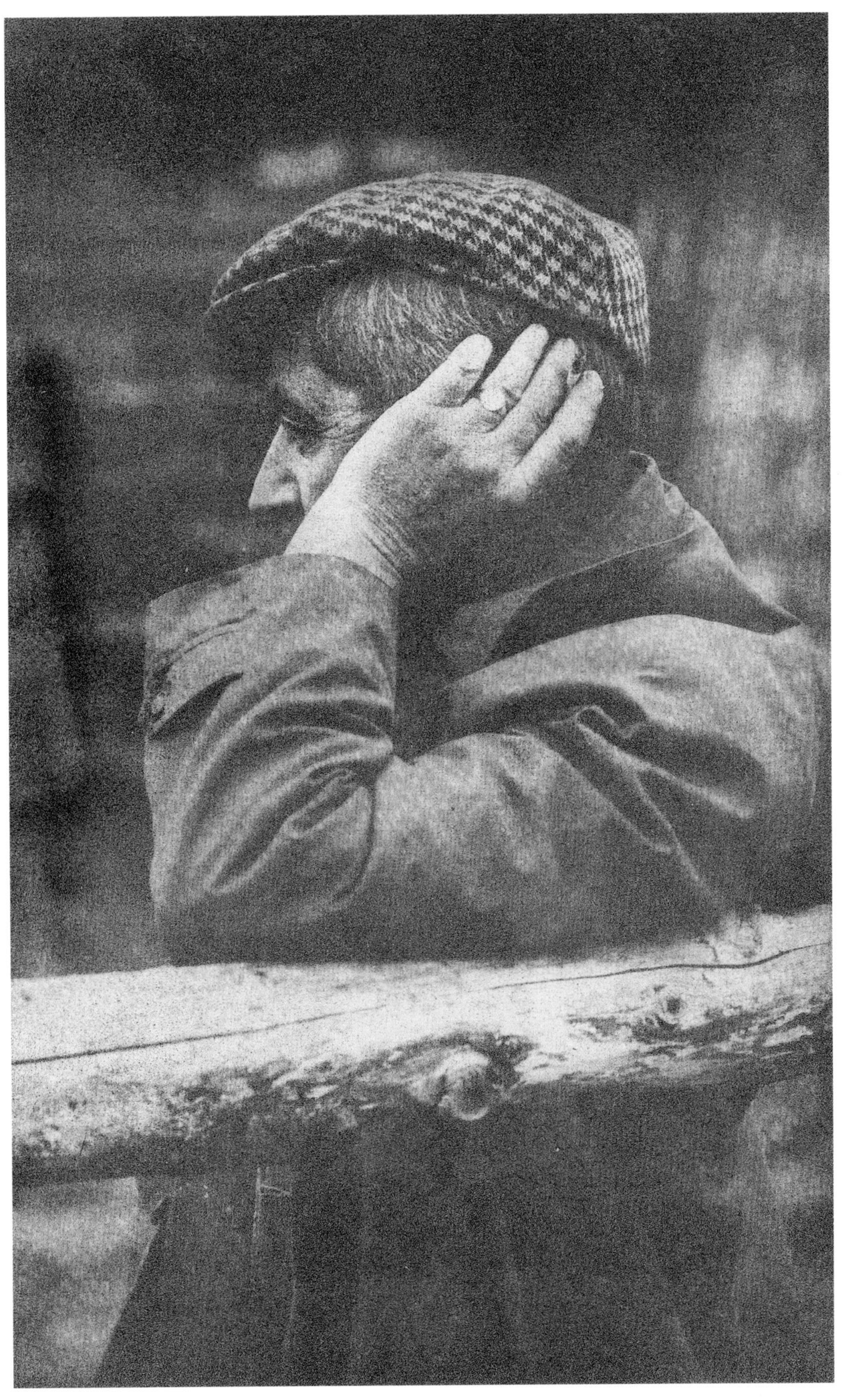

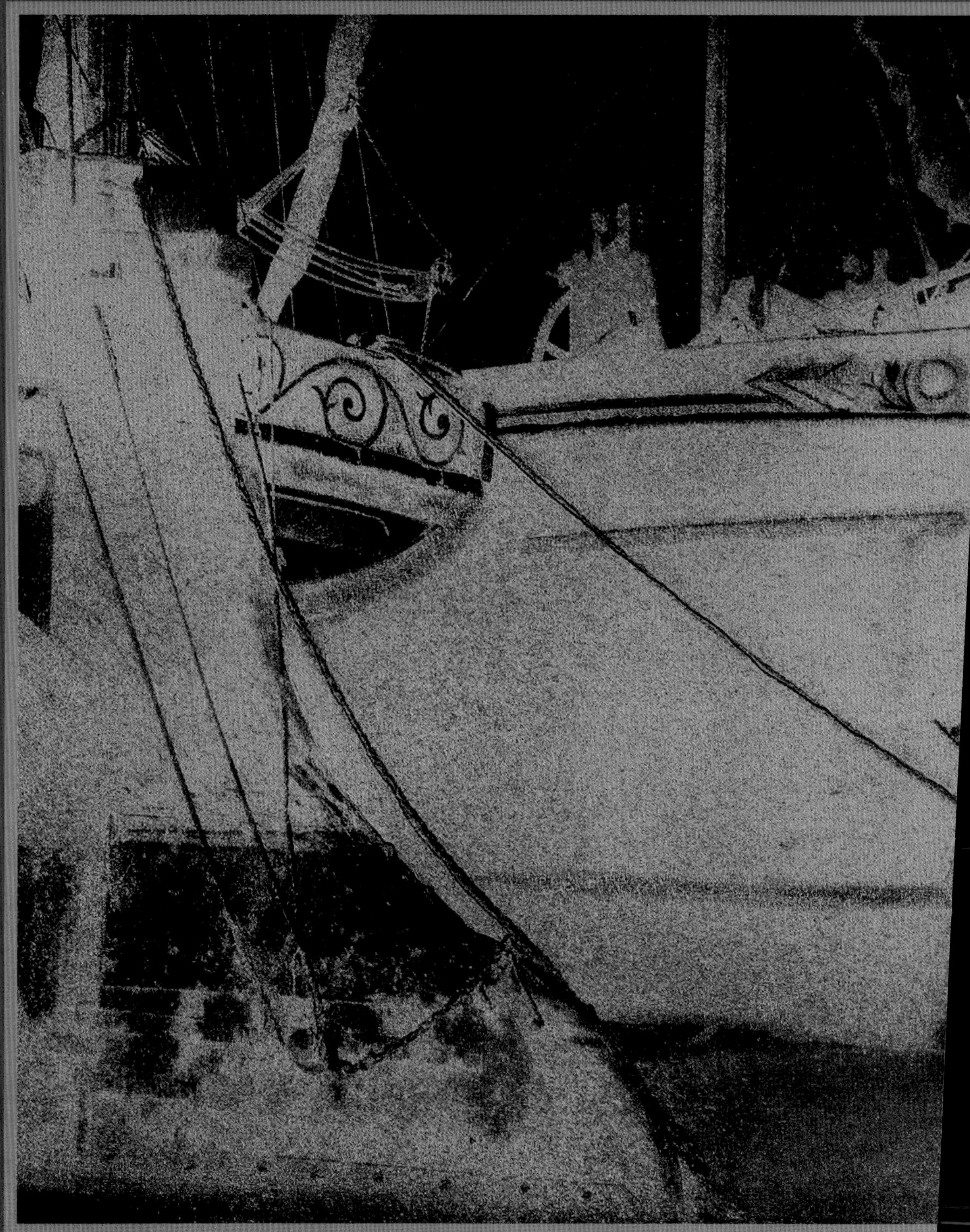

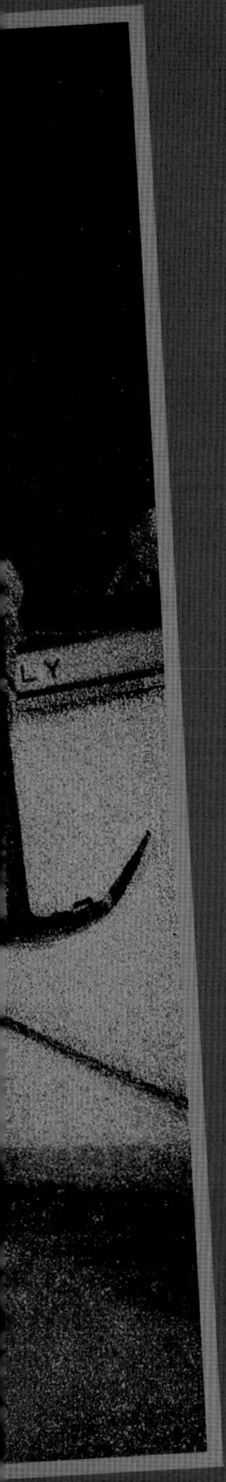

Part I
The bromoil process

The bromoil process consists of a number of different stages and Part I of this book will guide you through the process, from taking the photograph to mounting the print.

1 The process in outline

Making a bromoil print is essentially a conversion process, changing a silver image into an ink image. This chapter provides you with an overview of the process before each step is explained in greater detail in the following chapters.

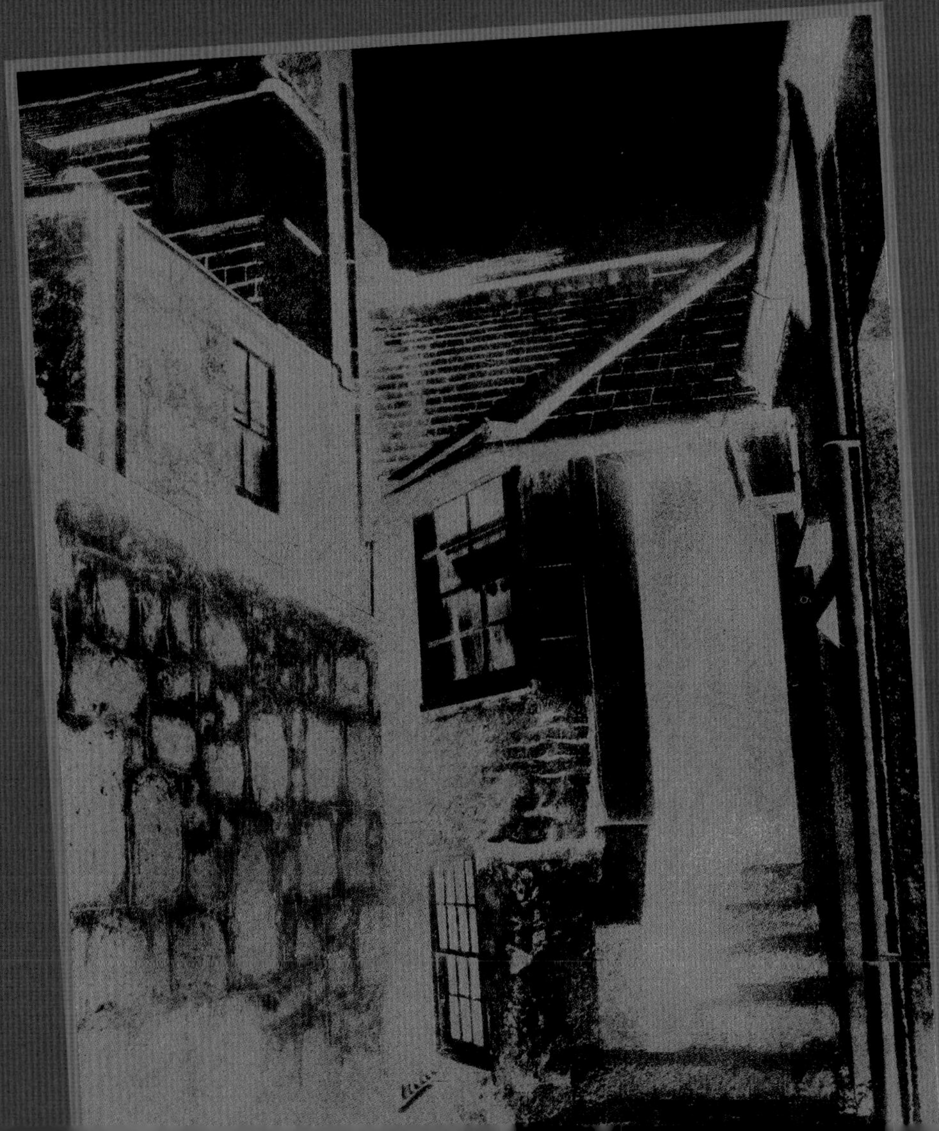

A bromoil print is created by first making a black & white print on chlorobromide or bromide paper in the usual way. Non-supercoated papers, such as Kentmere Art Document, are easier for those new to the process to work with. However, many modern supercoated papers have also been found suitable for making bromoils, such as Ilford Multigrade Matt, Forte Polygrade and Agfa Multicontrast Classic 118. You will find more about suitable papers in Chapter 4.

When you have made your print, the next stage is to turn it into a matrix that will absorb water in proportion to the silver image in the print. There are three operations involved in this process.

1 Bleaching the silver image to convert it to a form that reacts proportionally with the tanning solution.
2 Tanning, which produces differential hardening or tanning of the gelatin holding the image, so shadow areas are strongly tanned, mid-tones proportionately less so, and highlights are not tanned at all.
3 Fixing out the bleached silver image, which plays no further part in the bromoil process.

Some bromoilists use a combined bleach and tanning solution, others use separate bleach and tan baths. Both methods work equally well, so it is simply a matter of choosing which best suits your particular way of working.

tip

Although it is possible to use resin-coated paper, it is not really advisable, especially if you are a beginner. Resin-coated papers need an extremely delicate touch with the inking brush, and it is very easy to wipe off the ink accidentally. It is also better to use a matt-finish paper rather than glossy, because it will take the ink more easily. It also, in my view, looks much better; the sheen of the glossy paper does not seem completely natural when contrasted with the matt finish of the ink.

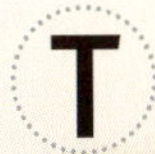

TERMINOLOGY / Tanning

Part of the job of the bromoil bleach-tan or separate tanning solution is to tan or harden the gelatin in the paper emulsion. The action of this tanning is directly proportional to the amount of silver forming the original image. After tanning the image is called a matrix.

TERMINOLOGY / Matrix

When the silver print has been bleached and tanned it is known as a matrix, and consists of an almost colourless image in slight relief. This relief absorbs water in varying degrees during subsequent soaking and allows the ink to be accepted or rejected depending on how much water is absorbed. The less water absorbed, the more ink is accepted.

When you have bleached and tanned the print, rinse it in water for a few minutes then fix it again to dissolve the silver converted into colourless compounds during bleaching. Follow this with another thorough wash to get rid of these dissolved compounds.

After washing and drying, the print, which is now called a matrix, is soaked in water for anything from a few minutes to an hour or more. As the gelatin swells, water is absorbed by the untanned areas but not by those areas that have been tanned. With most papers it is possible at this stage to see an image in slight relief if you look at the surface of the paper at an angle.

Many bromoilists continue straight to the bleaching and tanning stage from washing the print after the first fixing. Others think that the print should be dried before bleaching and tanning, because they believe that the more drying and resoaking stages there are before inking, the more easily will the matrix ink up. I have tried both procedures and can find little difference in ease of inking with non-supercoated papers. However, I have found that prints on supercoated papers do ink up more easily if there are several drying and resoaking cycles, so I have standardized on this method for all my bromoils. And I prefer to keep the various stages of the process separate anyway, making a batch of prints one evening, bleaching and tanning them another evening, and inking them up yet another. But, as with so much in bromoiling, use the method that suits you best.

Now, after blotting all surface water from the matrix, you are ready to ink the print using oily pigments, either in black or various colours, to restore the original picture by hand. The ink is easily accepted by the tanned areas of the image but it is repelled by the swollen untanned areas holding water.

There have been several different theories advanced for why this happens. Perhaps the most popular is that, because oil and water do not mix, the water held by the untanned areas of the print repels the oily ink while the tanned areas, which do not hold water, accept the ink. This, incidentally, is the principle on which lithographic printing works. Another theory is that the surface texture of the image varies according to the degree of tanning and that it is the smooth texture of the swollen highlights that repels the ink while the rougher texture of the unswollen shadows accepts it.

Whichever theory is right matters little from a practical viewpoint. The most important thing is that the phenomenon allows the bromoil process to work, creating possibilities for producing beautiful and unusual images.

The inking procedure is where the real skill in making bromoils lies. It is possible to emphasize parts of the picture or subdue them, or even eliminate them altogether. In the hands of an experienced bromoilist, clouds and mountains can be added, television aerials and telephone wires can be removed, figures can be added to a landscape, and a great deal more besides. The amount of control possible is almost unlimited.

When inking is finished, the print needs to be put aside for a few days to allow the ink to dry completely and harden. If you are not satisfied with the result then, you can resoak it and apply more ink of the same or a different colour to enhance it. There is also a wide variety of other afterwork you can perform on your print. You can apply ink to the dry print to darken edges and corners uniformly. You can etch detail into highlights with a scalpel or razor blade. You can add colour with powdered pigments or coloured oil pencils. You can tint the paper base to produce a warmer or cooler effect. Indeed, the possibilities are enormous.

That, in essence, is all that there is to the bromoil process. The following chapters expand the various stages outlined here to provide full details. The main thing is not to be daunted by the process. It really is simpler than it sounds, as the diagram on the next page shows.

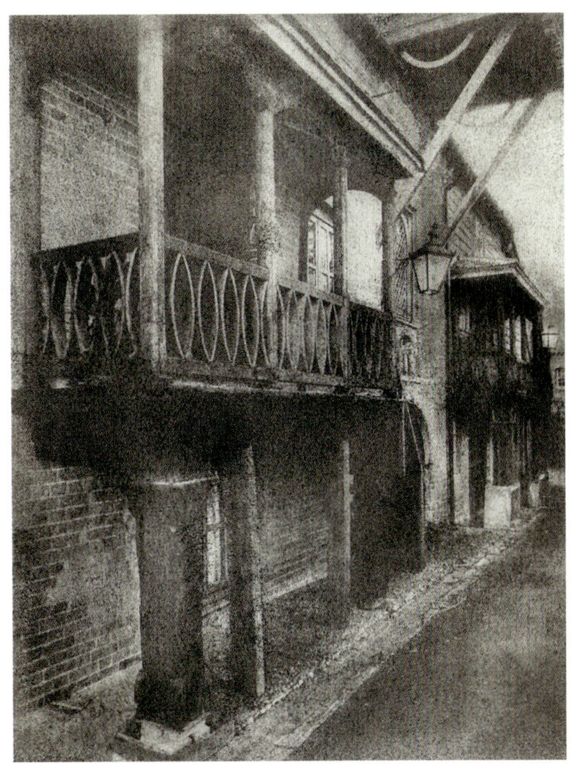

***Blackdown Mill* by Colin Ivison**

MAKING THE PRINT

Determine the required exposure by making a test strip. *See page 38.*

↓

Develop the print for two to three minutes in a 1:3 solution of D163 developer at a temperature of 68°F (20°C). *See page 51.*

↓

Place the print in a stop bath for approximately 30 seconds at 68°F (20°C). *See page 53.*

↓

Fix the print for one minute using a rapid non-hardening fixer (1:4 solution) at 68°F (20°C). *See page 53.*

↓

Wash the print for 30 minutes at 68°F (20°C) – although this time can be reduced with a washing aid. *See page 55.*

↓

Dry the print overnight at room temperature. *See page 55.*

Because the total quantities being made up are arbitrary, metric measurements have been used as they more clearly illustrate the relations of the weights and measures in terms of a percentage of the final quantity. A metric–imperial conversion table is provided on page 168.

MAKING THE MATRIX

Super-dry the print for one minute using a hair dryer 12in (30cm) from the print. *See page 55.*

↓

Soak the print for three minutes at 68°F (20°C). *See page 62.*

↓

Bleach-tan the print for 10 minutes at 68°F (20°C) using Gilbert Hooper's formula in a 1:10 solution under subdued lighting. *See page 63.*

↓

Wash for five minutes under running water at 68°F (20°C) or use five or six changes of water. *See page 63.*

↓

Fix the image for three to five minutes at 68°F (20°C) in a fresh 10% sodium thiosulphate solution. *See page 63.*

↓

Wash the matrix for 30 minutes (this can be reduced with a washing aid). *See page 64.*

↓

Dry the matrix overnight at room temperature. *See page 64.*

INKING THE MATRIX

Super-dry the matrix by using a hair dryer 12in (30cm) from the print for one minute. *See page 55.*

↓

Soak the matrix face up in water, soaking times and temperatures vary. Keep the matrix completely submerged, using cotton-wool buds to hold down the corners if necessary. *See page 73.*

↓

Prepare the ink by spreading it on a palette until it is smooth. *See page 73.*

↓

Dry the matrix between sheets of blotting paper, then remove all remaining water with a sponge. Tape it down onto a sheet of glass if preferred. *See page 74.*

↓

Apply the ink following the procedures laid out in Chapters 7 and 8.

↓

Dry the print at room temperature. *See page 115.*

↓

Finish the print by retouching, cleaning and reinforcing ink if necessary. *See page 116.*

Love Lane

St. Ives in Cornwall, England, is a mass of narrow streets and alleys packed with tiny cottages. Love Lane is one of these alleys, little more than a short-cut between two narrow streets.

Original taken on 6x6cm Rolleicord camera using Ilford FP4 Plus film and Pyro PMK developer. Inked with GC&I 1796 ink on Kentmere Art Document paper.

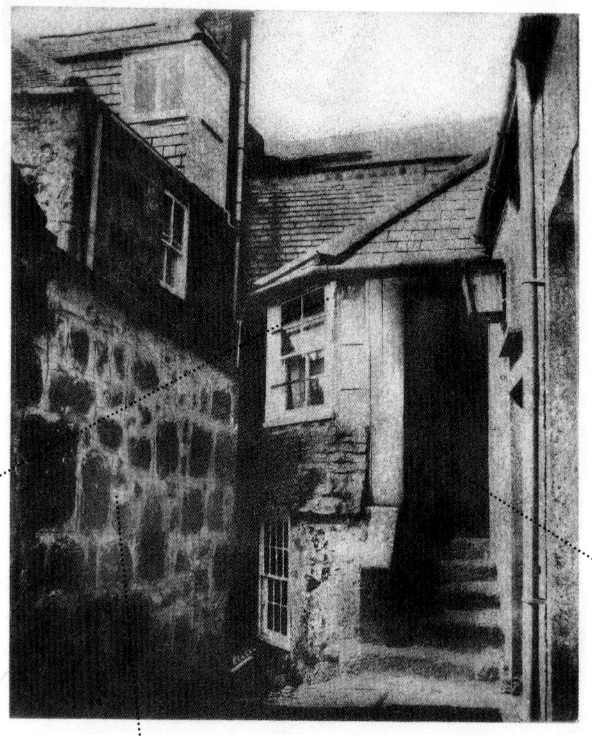

Highlights can be cleaned after inking by carefully wiping with wet cotton wool or a wet foam brush. For small areas, use wet cotton-wool buds

Remove excess ink from the mid-tone and highlight areas using a hopping action with a clean brush or with a specially made hopper

Inking the shadow areas of an image demands a careful balance between applying enough ink to produce a black and not so much that it will mask detail

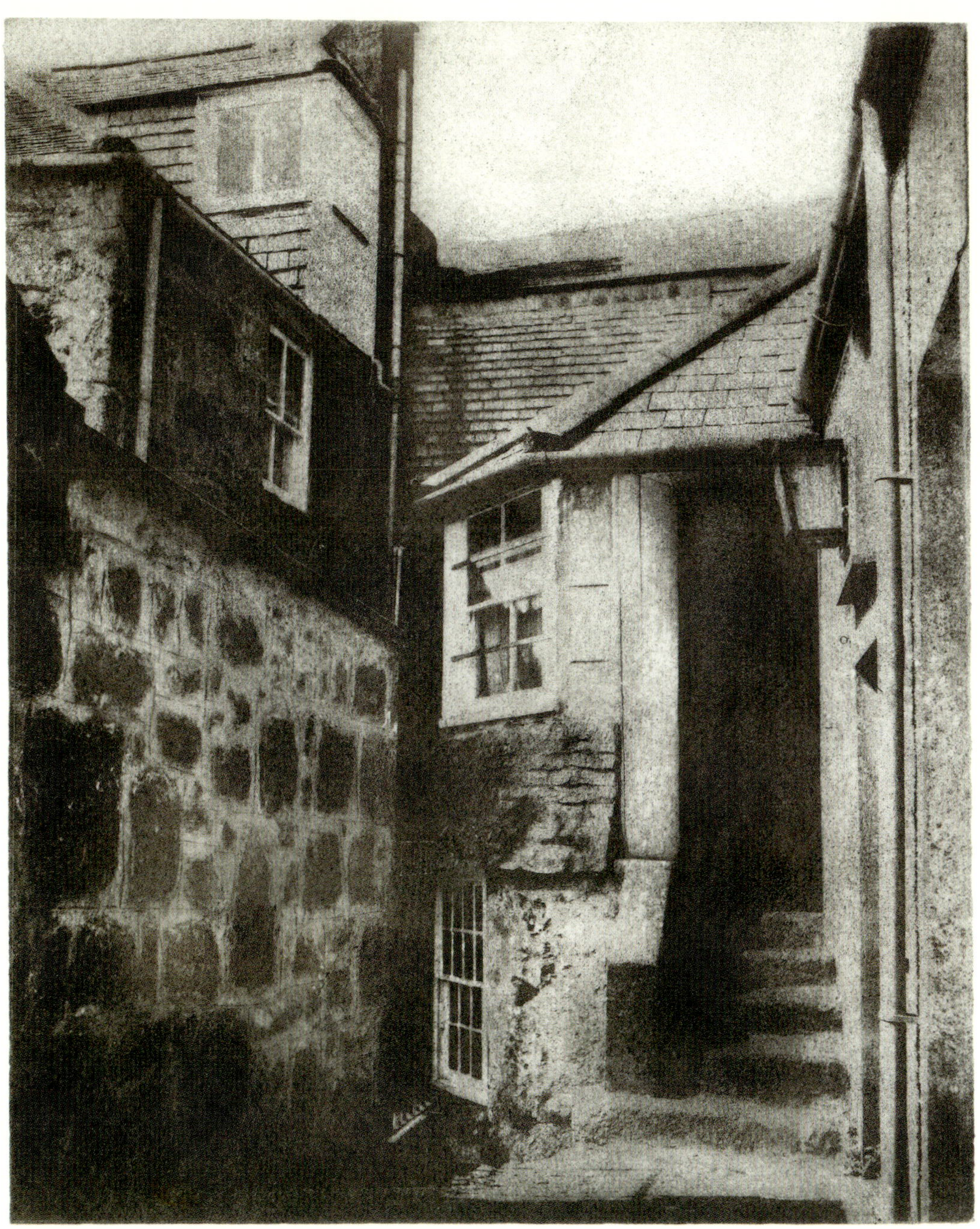

2 What you need

Like that required for many photographic processes the equipment needed for creating bromoils is simply a means to an end, and the real creativity lies with the artist.

The materials and equipment you need to make bromoil prints are very simple and, for the most part, inexpensive. As you probably make black & white prints already, you will have most of the equipment you need for the darkroom side of the process but here are a few notes on individual items.

Enlarger and lens – any enlarger will be fine for producing prints for bromoils. The golden rule is to buy the best lens you can afford, even if it means spending rather less on the enlarger itself.

Safelight – a standard amber/brown safelight is suitable.

Enlarging easel – if possible, use one that has four adjustable blades, although just two will be adequate.

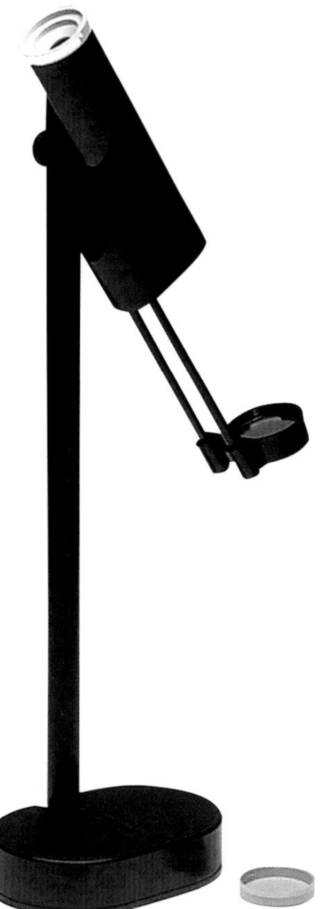

LEFT To ensure that your prints are really sharp you must focus your enlarger accurately. A focus finder, such as this one by Paterson, will make the task much easier.

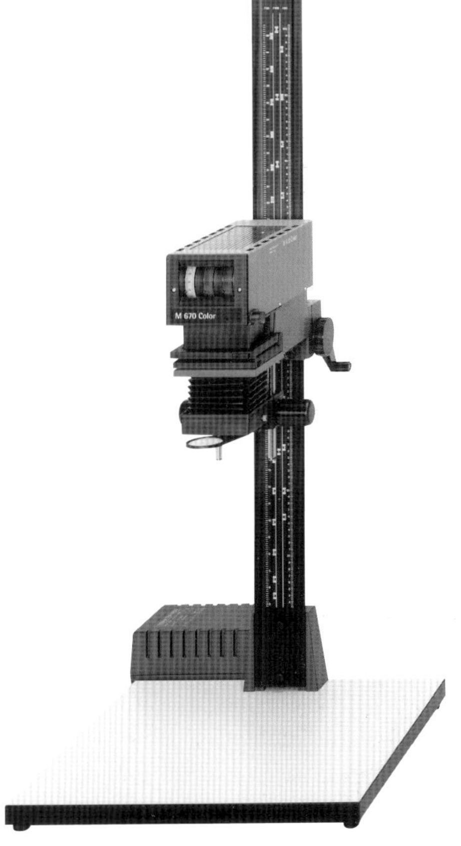

RIGHT A good enlarger is vital whatever type of printing you are doing, and the Durst M670 is a good solid model that will do everything you need. *Photograph by kind permission of Durst AG, manufacturer.*

Exposure timer – although not strictly necessary, a simple mechanical or electronic time switch will enable you to repeat exposures accurately.

Clock – essential for timing the various processing stages. A watch with a sweep seconds hand will be adequate.

Processing dishes – you need three developing dishes in order to make the initial prints, one is required each for developer, stop bath and fixer. As an alternative, I use a Nova deep-slot processor, simply because it takes up so little wet bench space. Added to this, because the Nova has a floating lid system, the developer, stop bath and fixer will stay in good condition and be fully active for several weeks. Of course this is as long as they are replenished regularly. You will need to get an extra dish for bleaching and tanning and, because many of the problems associated with failures in bromoiling can be traced back to contamination of the bleach, it is a good idea to buy a new dish and keep it set aside exclusively for this purpose.

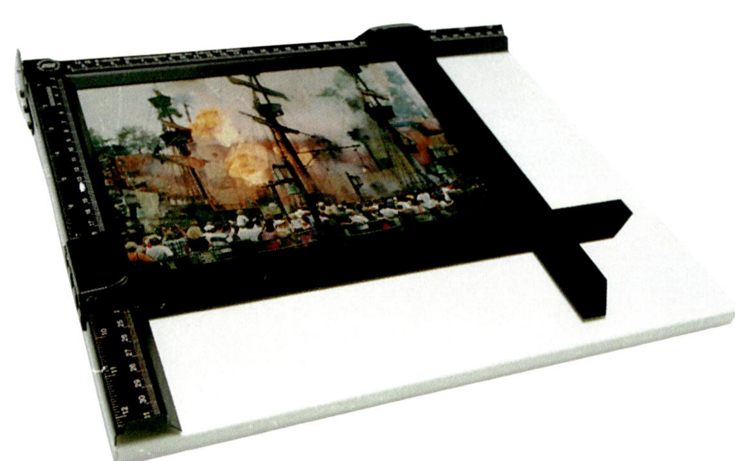

A good paper easel is useful to hold the enlarging paper flat and accurately aligned on the enlarger baseboard. This one by LPL is quite inexpensive but perfectly adequate.

Measures – do not buy glass measures, they break too easily. Clear plastic ones are just as good and far less expensive.

Thermometer – buy at least one and make sure it is accurate.

Print washer – making efficient washing arrangements is essential. Because prints for bromoils are nearly always made on fibre-based papers, thorough washing is a crucially important part of the process. An archival washer, such as the Nova or Paterson, is ideal. The use of a hypo clearing agent such as Ilford Galerie Wash Aid is also a good idea, as it reduces the amount of time spent washing the print considerably.

Dish heater – this is an entirely optional piece of kit, but it can be useful. It provides an even source of heat for precise temperature control of your solutions.

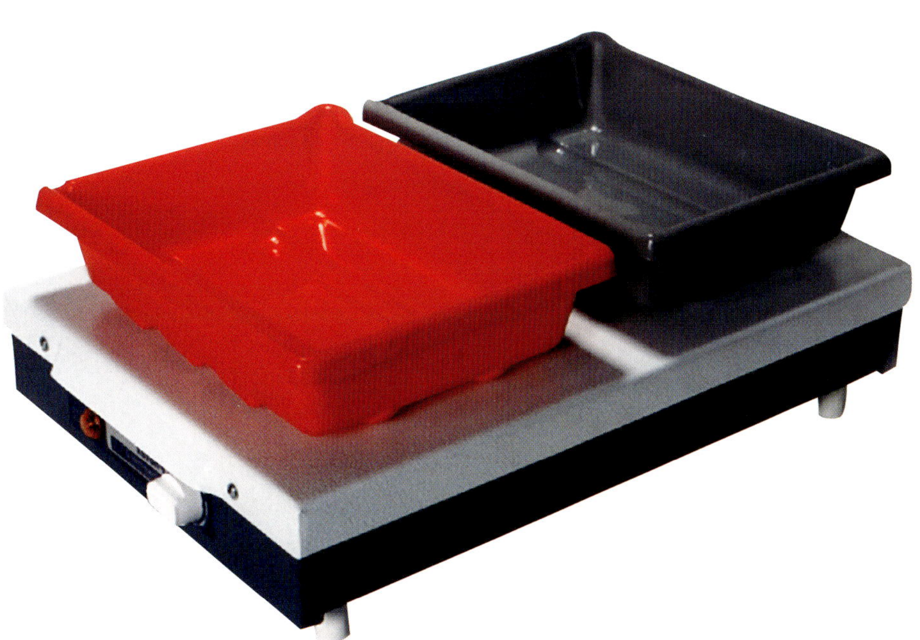

A set of three dishes is necessary for for making prints, two of which are shown above, along with a dish heater for regulating the temperature of solutions.

EQUIPMENT FOR INKING-UP

The inking-up stage is where the bromoil process really departs from conventional photographic processes, and a certain amount of special equipment becomes necessary. However, the first few items are ordinary enough and readily available.

Soaking dish

First you will need a dish in which to soak the matrix before you begin working on it. If you can find one, a dish with a flat bottom is best. It allows you to work on the bromoil under water with a ball of cotton wool or a foam brush to clear highlights.

If you cannot get a flat-bottomed dish, buy a piece of acrylic sheet a little smaller than the dish and rest it on the ridges at the bottom. This will provide you with a flat surface in the dish.

Choose a dish the next size up from the size of the print that you will be working with to make handling easy and reduce the risk of scratching the surface of the matrix.

Blotting paper

A pad of blotting paper is useful to remove the bulk of surface water from the matrix after soaking. Although photographic quality blotting paper is preferable, it is by no means an essential.

If you buy half a dozen full-size sheets you can fold them in half to form a book. Then place each matrix between two dry pages so that the surplus water is removed from the front and back simultaneously.

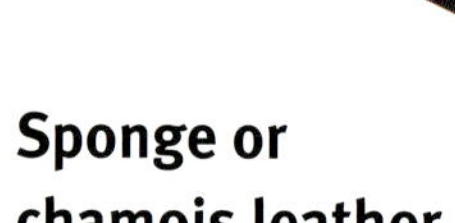

Sponge or chamois leather

Once you have removed most of the surplus water from the matrix using blotting paper, a sponge or chamois leather will remove what remains. Personally, I prefer the sponge to the chamois leather, but other workers like the chamois best. A fairly large sponge, either natural or synthetic, is best and if you choose a chamois leather, again both would be equally suitable.

Some bromoilists keep their chamois leather in a plastic container of water to which a teaspoon of sodium bicarbonate has been added. This prevents the leather becoming smelly. However, you must rinse the leather thoroughly and squeeze it out as dry as possible before using it. For this reason, when I do use a chamois, I let it dry out and dampen it before use.

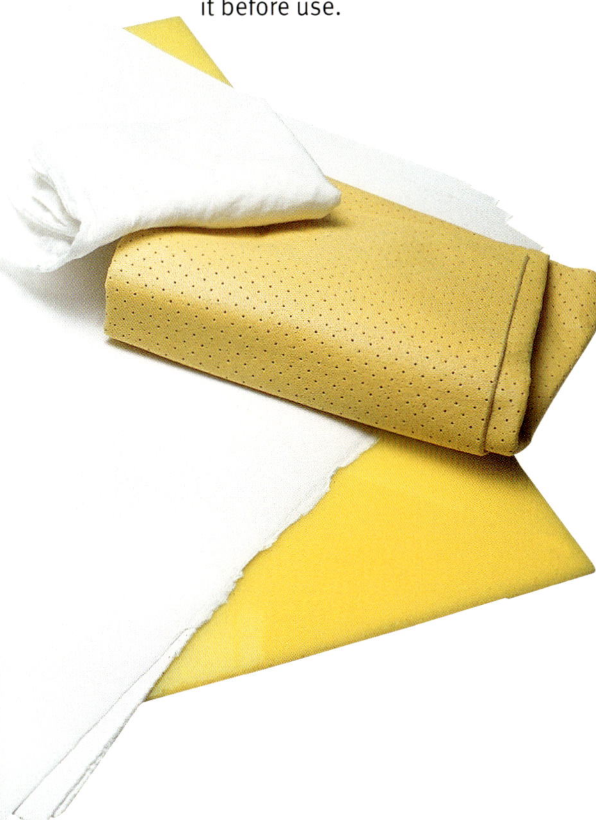

Old handkerchief

To make sure every trace of moisture is removed from the surface of the matrix, use an old handkerchief or other piece of soft cloth to give the matrix a final light wipe.

tip

Removal of surface moisture really is vital to the success of a bromoil. If even a tiny drop is left on the matrix it will repel the ink and leave a white spot which can be very difficult to remove.

Matrix support

It is important that the matrix is placed on a smooth, hard surface for inking to avoid uneven application of ink. By far the best surface is a sheet of ¼in (6mm) thick plate glass that is larger all round than the matrix on which you will be working, although a good alternative is a sheet of Perspex. If you buy a new piece of plate glass for this purpose, be sure to have the edges ground to make them safer.

Ink

The single most vital material in bromoil printing is a suitable ink, which must be very stiff and thick. If the ink is too soft it will simply adhere to the whole surface of the matrix, resulting in a very flat, grey print.

When bromoil printing was in its heyday, several companies produced inks especially formulated for the process. Many people still believe that these inks are the only ones that can produce successful bromoils. Indeed, there are companies perpetuating this myth by selling inks allegedly made especially for bromoil.

Let me state categorically that specialized bromoil inks are not strictly necessary. Virtually every bromoilist I know, as well as those with whom I correspond, use inks that are designed primarily for lithography. And most use inks manufactured by the Graphic Chemical & Ink Co in America. *See Useful Contacts page 173*. The two most popular GC&I inks are Senefelder's Crayon Black no. 1803 and Lithographic Black no. 1796. The latter is suitable for most conditions and I recommend starting with this one. Inks in a variety of other colours are also available from GC&I suppliers, and you can add these to your collection as you find necessary.

tip

Many bromoilists like to work on a matrix held at an angle of 30° or so to the horizontal. If you find you prefer to work this way, simply slip a block of wood under the rear edge of the glass to raise it.

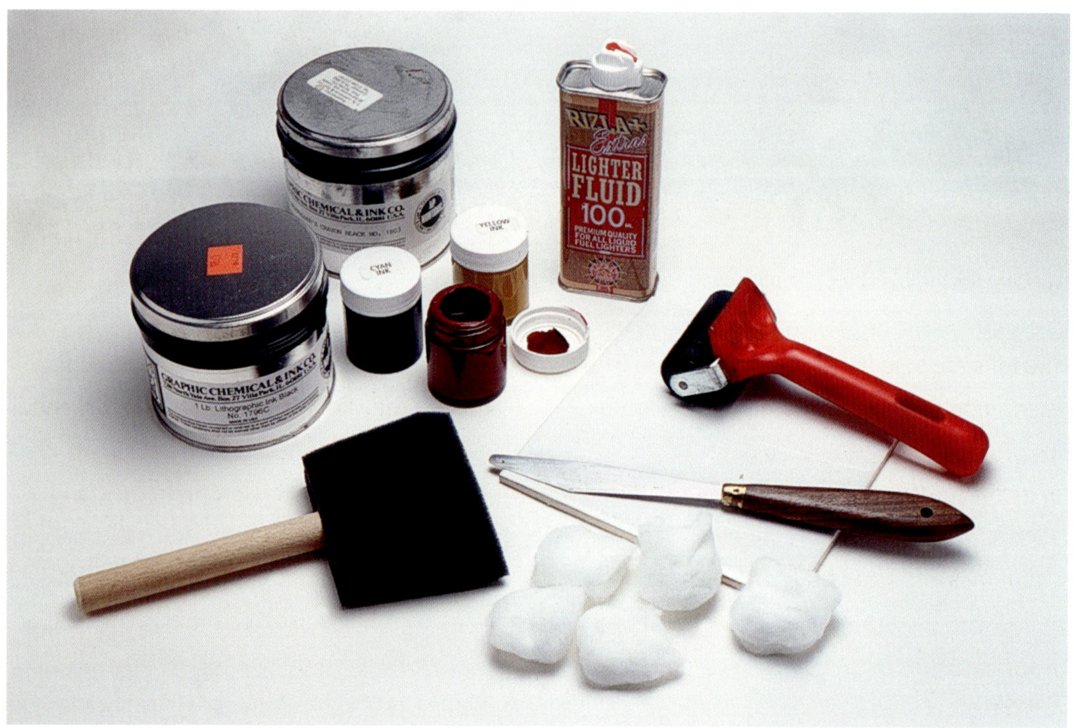

Stiff litho inks are suitable for inking bromoil prints. Tiles are suitable for palettes, and a palette knife or small, hard roller is used to spread the ink thinly on the tile. Cotton wool balls and a foam brush are used for cleaning the print, and lighter fluid for cleaning brushes.

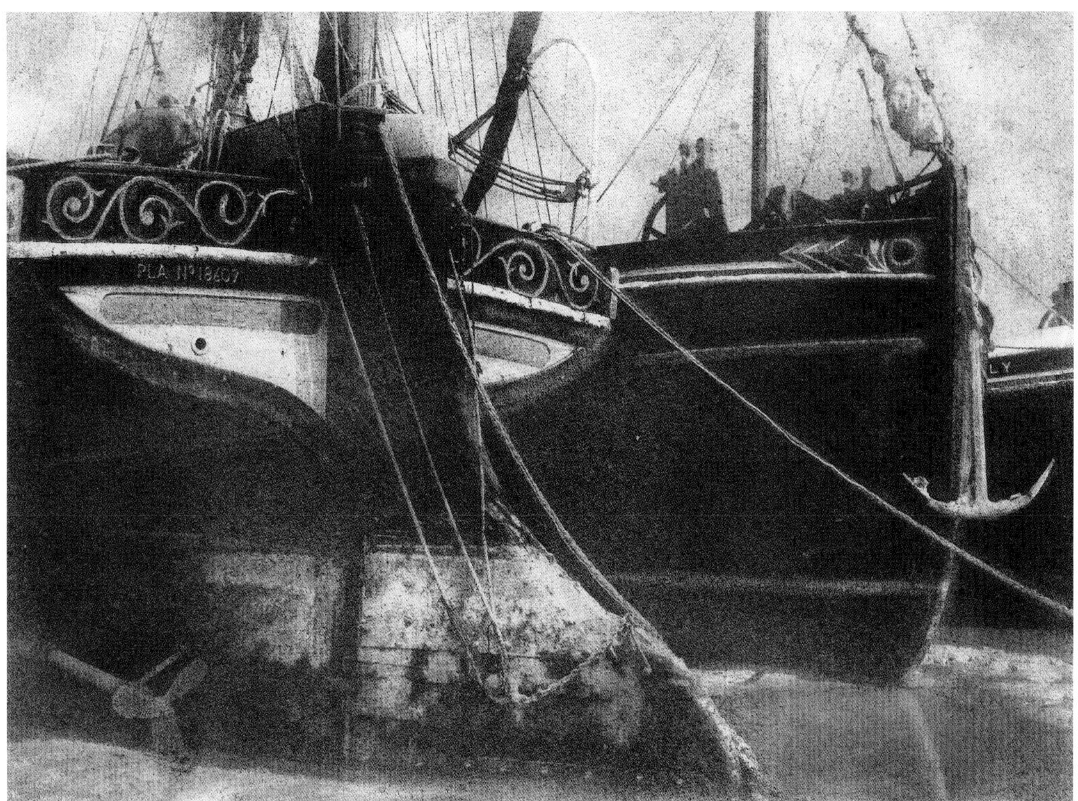

Waiting for the Tide by Colin Ivison

The inks are sold in 1lb (500 gram) tins, which is enough to last most bromoilists a lifetime, as long as you remember to cover the surface of the ink and seal the tin well after you have used it. You will find more detailed information about inks and ways that you can modify them in Chapter 8: Inking.

Brushes

To apply the ink to the matrix you will need a suitable brush, which should have strong but springy bristles. Special bromoil brushes have recently become available once more and, although they do a good job, it is not essential that you use them.

There are those who believe that the only brushes you can use to ink a bromoil print successfully are specially shaped 'stag-foot' brushes. These are so called because the top of the brush is cut at an angle.

Again, this is just a myth. Some of the finest bromoilists working today use shaving brushes, pastry brushes, stencil brushes and sash brushes among many other kinds.

In fact, I saw a demonstration by Ken Hill FRPS, one of the leading British bromoilists, who used an ordinary 2in (50mm) house-painter's paintbrush in order to ink a beautifully delicate bromoil.

But you do not even need to use a brush at all. Some workers apply the ink with a foam roller designed for applying gloss paint. These rollers are extremely cheap and are can be easily obtained at any hardware or home-decorating store.

To start with I suggest an inexpensive shaving brush. They are cheap, and the bristles have about the right degree of spring. You can either leave the bristles as they are or trim them to the stag-foot shape if you prefer. To do this, first cut the top of the bristles off at an angle of about 20° with scissors, then smooth them with an electric shaver or clipper. *See page 81.*

Large stencil brushes or pastry brushes can be treated in the same manner and will give equally good results.

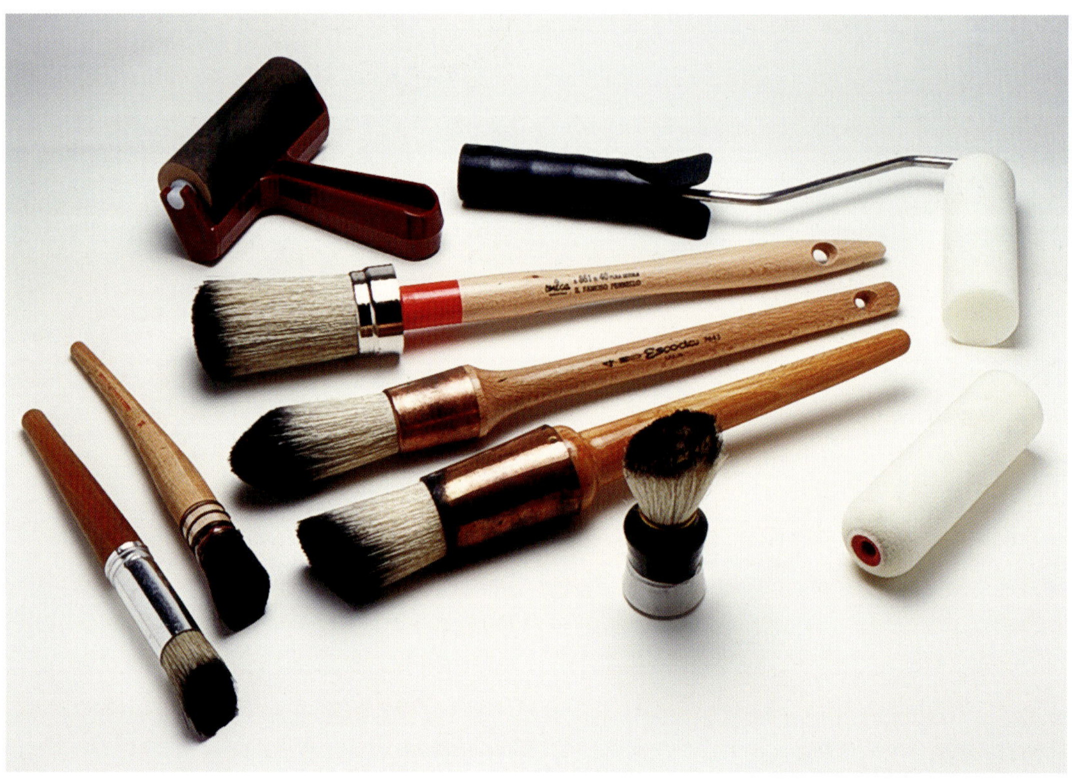

Just a few of the many brushes that can be used for inking a bromoil. They range from a traditional Sinclair stag-foot 'Mortimer' brush to modern dome-shaped artists' paintbrushes, stencil brushes and even a shaving brush. Foam gloss paint rollers can also be used for inking.

White tile

This forms the palette on which you will mix and spread the ink. An ordinary 6in (15cm) square wall tile is ideal for the job. In fact, it is a good idea to buy several of these tiles, then if you mix inks of different colours or consistencies you can keep each on a separate tile.

Palette knife or small roller

The ink must be spread very thinly on the tile to avoid too much being picked up by the brush. An artists' palette knife or old kitchen knife is ideal for this job. Alternatively, a small roller, such as those sold for inking lino-cuts, will do the job perfectly.

Cotton wool

A pack of cotton-wool balls is useful for a wide variety of jobs in bromoiling. You can use them for cleaning highlights, for cleaning the borders of the print, for applying colour, and for many other tasks. Equally useful is a pack of cotton-wool buds. They are ideal for working on small areas of the bromoil to remove excess ink and to lighten highlights.

Cleaning fluids

Many bromoilists do not bother to clean their brushes and palette tiles after use. The late Norman Gryspeerdt FRPS, a very fine bromoilist, claimed never to clean either his brushes or his inking tile, and his prints did not suffer as a result.

However, I prefer to clean my brushes and tiles and have found lighter fluid perfect for the job. Barbecue-lighter fuel and white spirit are also very good for cleaning tiles, but I find they tend to dry out too slowly for cleaning brushes, especially if you want to use them the next day. The problem is that if the spirit has not dried out completely it thins the ink down, making it difficult or impossible to achieve good results.

caution

The liquids mentioned here are all highly flammable and should be treated with due caution. They represent a serious hazard to both your health and safety and you should always follow the instructions on the container. As a rule they should be stored in a cool, dark place away from sources of ignition and be secured against tampering from children.

This basic equipment is all that you need to make a start in bromoiling. As you progress you will inevitably add more to your collection of tools and materials, especially brushes. I shall mention some of these additional items later in the book. Do not be tempted to buy too much too soon. Master the technique using the basic equipment and add to it only when necessary. Above all, enjoy your bromoiling.

Haworth Parsonage

This house in Yorkshire, England, is where the three Brontë sisters lived with their brother and father. On the day I took this photograph the weather was overcast, creating an atmosphere that I felt would be best captured in bromoil.

Original taken on 6x6cm Rolleicord camera using Ilford FP4 film and Microphen developer. Inked with GC&I 1796 ink on Kentmere Art Document paper.

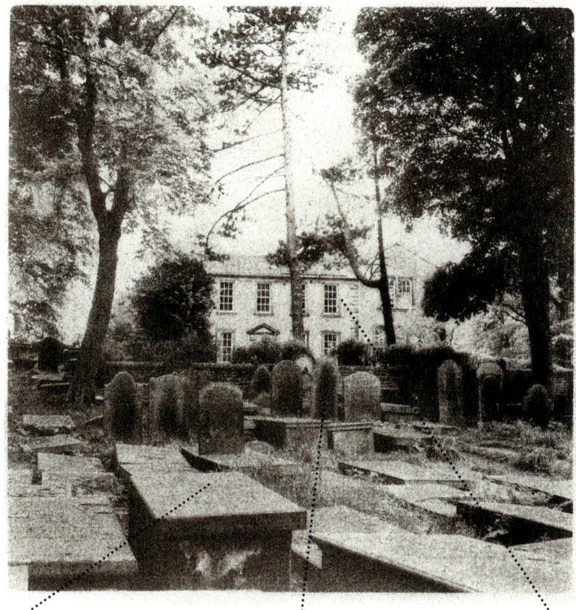

Use a large brush or even a foam roller to apply an initial thin layer of ink to all areas of the print

Use a large or medium brush to add depth to the inking, especially in the shadow and mid-tone areas

A small, softer brush is useful for working up fine detail in the print's lighter areas

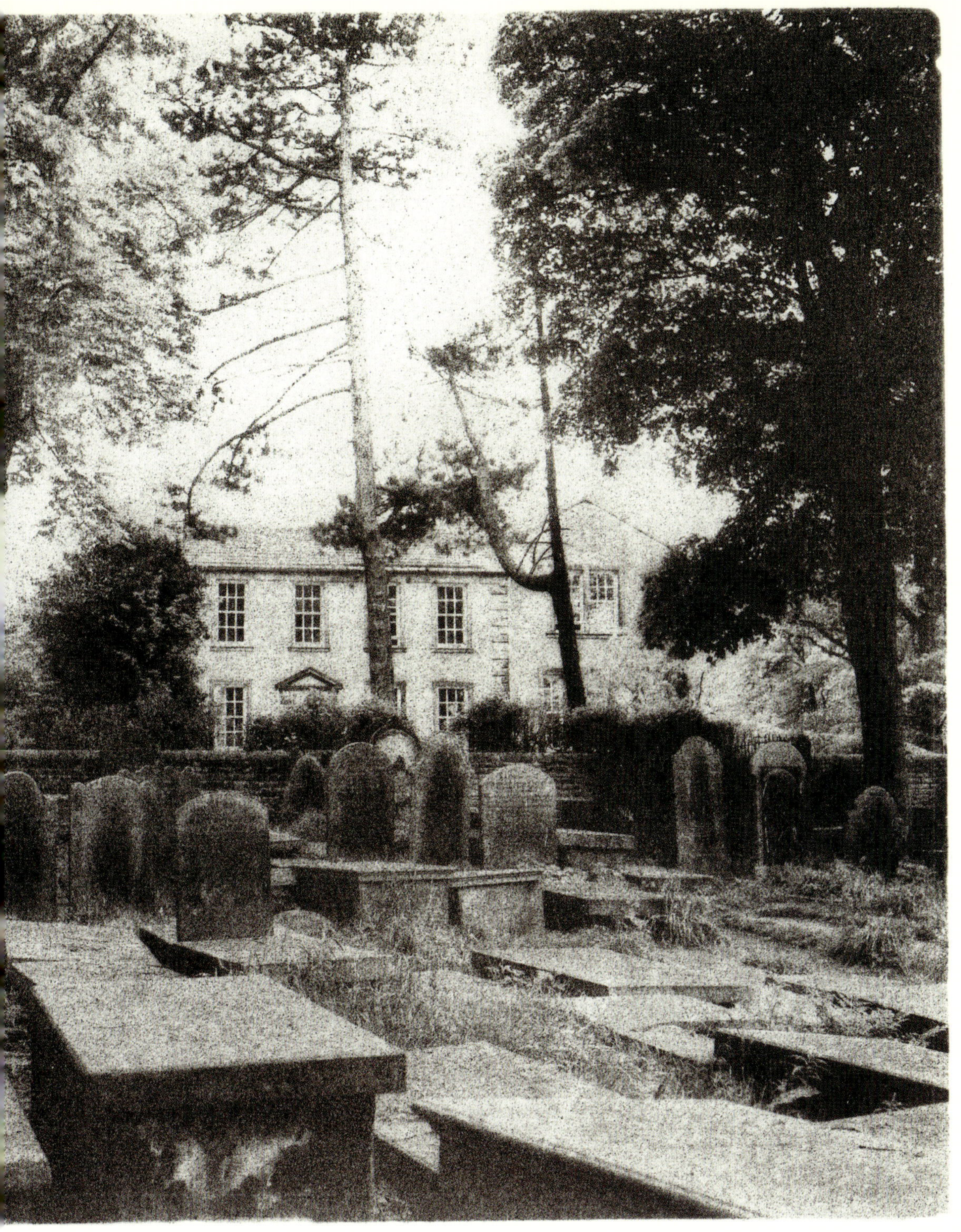

3 The right kind of negative

While the bromoil process is unique, its early stages do rely on creating a suitable negative and photographic print. If you produce a suitable print you will create a solid foundation.

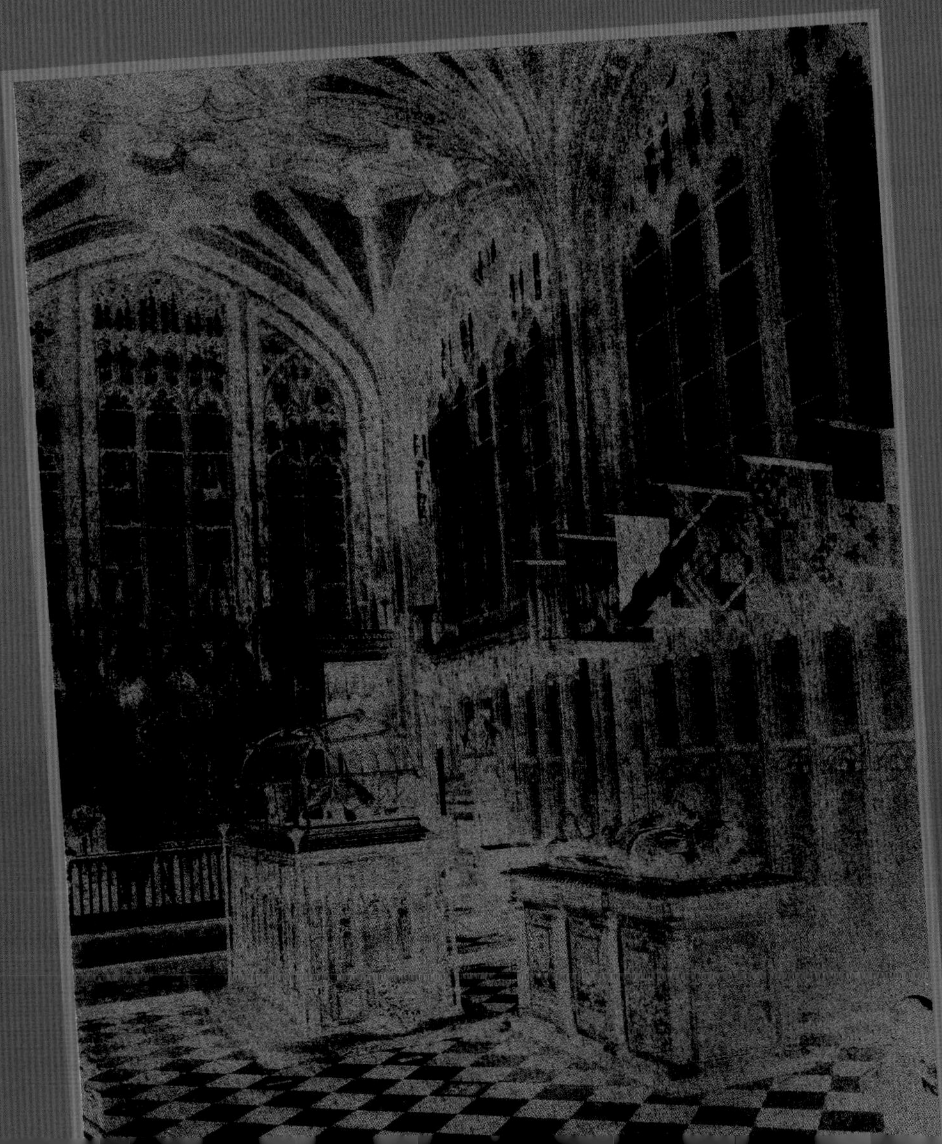

As with any photographic process, you cannot hope to produce a good bromoil print unless you start with a good negative. The first step is to choose a suitable subject.

THE RIGHT SUBJECT

Although you can make a satisfactory bromoil print from any kind of subject, some subjects are more suitable than others, especially for newcomers to the process. Landscapes make good bromoils, as do architectural subjects and street scenes. Much more difficult, although very rewarding, are portraits and figure studies.

Landscapes, especially those with broad areas of tone and, perhaps, receding hills, lend themselves particularly well to the bromoil process. You can easily vary the inking to emphasize depth in the print, darkening the foreground and lightening the distance. And with practice you can create cloud effects even if none exist in the original photograph.

For architectural subjects, the characteristics of the process enable you to suggest texture in brickwork and stone. And by using a soft brush you can bring out fine detail in window frames and tiled roofs.

Portraits and figure studies are tricky subjects for the beginner because of the difficulty in achieving delicate, smooth skin tones in the bromoil process. But it is far from impossible, and when you get it right the effect can be stunning.

So having chosen and photographed your subject, how do you ensure the resulting negative is suitable for making bromoils?

THE RIGHT NEGATIVE

It is often said by those who should know better that only a soft negative is any good for making prints that will be turned into bromoils. This is quite untrue. Any negative that will make a good black & white silver print is suitable, although it should have plenty of shadow and highlight detail. A contrasty negative is not ideal, but then neither is it ideal for straightforward black & white printing. Contrasty negatives often have clear film where there should be shadow detail and almost solid blacks where the highlight detail should be. Faced with a negative like this it would be almost impossible to produce a satisfactory silver-gelatin print never mind a good bromoil.

What you need to aim for is a full range of tones from the deepest shadow in which you want detail to the brightest highlight in which you want to hold detail. And the best way to achieve that is a combination of avoiding underexposure and overdevelopment, the two greatest enemies of high-quality prints.

A simple test

To find out if your exposure and development combination is correct, try the simple test on the following page:

TERMINOLOGY / Chromogenic film

A chromogenic film is essentially a black & white film that can be developed using the colour-chemistry process of C-41 processing. This means that it is very convenient if you wish to use a local laboratory to process your films for you.

Expose a roll of your usual film at the speed at which you normally rate it, but part way through the roll make an exposure with the lens cap on your camera. This will give you an unexposed frame. Develop the film in your usual developer for the time you normally give, then fix, wash and dry it.

Set up your enlarger for a 10x8in (25x20cm) print, focusing carefully on one of the negatives. Replace the negative on which you focused with the unexposed frame and close the enlarging lens by two stops. Make a test strip in the usual way, giving exposures in two-second increments. Develop the test strip for a full two minutes, fix, wash and dry it. Ensure you have a good light and find the first step that is completely black – the step before is a very dark grey and the step after is also black. The exposure that produced this first fully black step is your basic exposure.

Now, without changing the position of the enlarger head or the lens aperture, make prints from a selection of the negatives on the same roll of negatives as your unexposed frame. Make sure you develop them for two minutes, fix, wash and dry them. You do not have to make these prints a full 10x8in (25x20cm), instead cut a sheet of 10x8in (25x20cm) paper into four and print a representative section of each negative. When the prints are dry, take them into a good light and examine them carefully. If they all show a full range of tones with plenty of detail in both shadows and highlights, you have nothing to worry about; the film speed and development time are fine.

However, if the prints are consistently too dark, you are underexposing the photos and you should set the film speed on your camera or exposure meter to a lower value. Try setting it at half the recommended speed. On the other hand, if the prints are consistently too light, you are overexposing the film and you should set the film speed higher. Try doubling the recommended film speed. If the shadows are showing plenty of detail but the highlights are burned out, you are overdeveloping. Try cutting the development time by 25 per cent. And if the shadows are good but the highlights are too dark you are underdeveloping, so increase the development time by 25 per cent.

This simple test should put you well on the road to producing consistently good negatives that will not only be suitable for making bromoils, but will also help you to make better straight prints.

SUITABLE FILMS

You can use just about any type of film for bromoil negatives. Because of the nature of the bromoil process, which produces prints with a painterly or etching-like quality, high resolution and very fine grain are not normally essential. You can also use colour-negative films; I have seen some quite superb bromoils made from colour negatives. Chromogenic films, such as Ilford XP2 Plus and Kodak T400CN, are very suitable. They also have the crucial advantage that you can rate them at speeds from ISO 50 to ISO 800 depending on the conditions that you face, and all on the same roll of film. They are processed in normal C-41 colour negative chemicals, either at home or by your local colour lab.

SUITABLE DEVELOPERS

Bearing in mind the need for detail right through the tonal range of the negative, a developer of the compensating type is ideal.

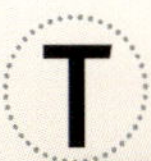

TERMINOLOGY / Compensating developer

Essentially, a compensating developer is a weak developer, one with a low concentration of developing agent. The classic is the Windisch. It was formulated in Germany in the 1930s by Hans Windisch. It contains just 2.5 grams of metol and 25 grams of sodium sulphite per litre of water, and for most films needs development times of around 18 to 20 minutes at 68°F (20°C).

The metol is the developing agent and the sodium sulphite does dual service, first as a preservative that prevents the metol from oxidizing and second as a mild alkali that accelerates the action of the metol.

Inherently a soft-working developing agent, metol tends to act fairly quickly on lightly exposed silver halides that make up the shadow areas of the negative, but very slowly on the more heavily exposed areas where it quickly becomes exhausted. In practical terms, this means that shadow detail builds rapidly while highlights evolve more slowly. The result is a negative with punchy shadows and soft, gentle highlights.

A compensating developer is a soft-working solution that enables the build-up of shadow detail without allowing the highlights to block up, giving a full range of tones. Developers containing just metol or phenidone as the developing agent fall into this category and include formulas such as Windisch, Kodak D-23 and Pota.

Dilute developers

The easiest way to make a compensating developer is simply to dilute your normal fine-grain developer and extend the development time. To be honest, this will normally produce a semi-compensating developer because there is usually a second developing agent in the form of hydroquinone in most commercial fine-grain developers. This is a much more vigorous agent than metol and tends to give a more contrasty negative in normal use. However, if you take, say, Kodak D-76 or Ilford ID-11 and use it diluted with one, two, three or even four parts of water you will produce negatives that are, in most cases, vastly superior to those that are produced by the undiluted developer.

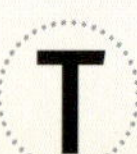

TERMINOLOGY / Characteristic curve

The characteristic curve for a film – or paper – is a graphical illustration of how light acts on the emulsion to produce a density during development. When exposed in the camera, areas of light of different intensities fall on the film for a constant length of time. This produces, in effect, a wide range of exposures of a uniform time but varying brightness.

When the film is developed, a wide range of silver densities is produced. These densities are plotted on a graph against the logarithms of the exposures that produced them, and this forms the characteristic curve.

For practical photography, you do not need to understand fully the characteristic curve of the material. However, it can provide useful information about the combination of film and developer you are using. For example, if the lower part of the curve is steep, this means the shadow areas will give plenty of well-separated detail. And a slight flattening of the curve at the top will give highlights that do not burn out to pure white. If the overall slope of the curve is steep it indicates that the negatives will be quite contrasty, but if it is shallow, the contrast of the negatives will be softer.

They also give much better results than by simply reducing the development time. This lowers the density of the highlights in the negative, but does so from a point midway up the characteristic curve. Using the developer diluted, however, lowers just the upper part of the curve, leaving the mid-tones well separated. As a starting point, I suggest using the development times in the following table.

Developer dilution	Increase in development time
Undiluted	0%
1:1	25%
1:2	50%
1:3	75%
1:4	100%

For most situations I have found that the diluted developer works very well and I have standardized on dilutions according to the speed of the film I am using. For example, if I am using an ISO 400 film like Kodak T-Max 400 I dilute my developer to the ratio of 1:2, for a medium-speed film such as Ilford FP4 Plus I dilute 1:3, and if I am shooting on a higher-contrast film like Ilford Pan F Plus or Agfa APX 25 I use a dilution of 1:4.

The technique works well with most standard fine-grain developers. I have tried it with D-76, ID-11, Ilford Microphen and the excellent Kodak D-23, which I mix up myself. The formula just could not be simpler.

But before giving formulas for developers, a few words of warning are in order:

- When weighing, handling and mixing chemicals always wear rubber gloves, a dust mask and eye protection.
- Do not use domestic spoons for handling chemicals; use either a plastic or metal spoon or spatula kept exclusively for the purpose.
- Keep all chemicals out of the reach of children and pets.
- Keep all chemicals in clearly labelled jars and bottles. And never use old soft drinks bottles to store liquid chemicals.
- Never eat, drink or smoke anywhere near where you are handling or using chemicals, and that includes your darkroom.
- Clean up spillages immediately.
- Always use print forceps to handle prints in solutions.
- If you get chemical splashes on your skin, wash the affected area in plenty of clean, warm water immediately.
- If you splash chemicals into your eye, wash immediately with an eye bath and seek medical advice.
- Follow the instructions and warnings on the containers of the chemicals that you are using, paying particular attention to any hazard warnings.

Kodak D-23 developer	
Metol	7.5 grams
Sodium sulphite, anhydrous	100 grams
Water to	1 litre

Development times are broadly similar to those for D-76 and ID-11, which you can use as starting points. When diluted 1:3, this developer is almost identical to the classic Windisch formula, which is:

Windisch compensating developer	
Metol	2.5 grams
Sodium sulphite, anhydrous	25 grams
Water to	1 litre

This developer needs fairly long development times of around 18 to 20 minutes at 68°F (20°C).

Concentrates

You can also achieve a compensating effect with concentrated one-shot developers such as Paterson Acutol, Tetenal Ultrafin and that old favourite Agfa Rodinal. The instruction leaflets usually give you two dilutions that you can choose from, one giving a higher contrast than the other. Just use the dilution that is recommended for lower contrast to gain the compensation effect.

With Rodinal in particular it is possible to achieve remarkable results in this way. Agfa generally recommends a dilution of 1:25 or 1:50 for most films. By increasing this to 1:75 for medium-speed and fast films or 1:100 for slow films and for medium-speed films if you want extra highlight control, the negatives hold highlight detail really well. Naturally, you will need to increase the development times to compensate for the greater dilution.

I have even found that Rodinal can tame that notoriously difficult film Kodak Technical Pan. Diluted 1:200 and given a development time of 10 minutes at 68°F (20°C) it produces beautiful negatives without losing effective film speed.

Two-bath developers

If you really want the maximum control and compensation in your negatives, there is little doubt that a two-bath developer will give them to you. It is almost impossible to get blocked highlights using this technique, and it has the advantage that the development times for all but fast films are the same. Fast films need a little extra time, but even they can all be developed for the same times.

There are several two-bath developers available commercially, and they seem to be enjoying something of a revival. Tetenal has Emofin in both liquid concentrate and powder form, Speedibrews has Resofin 2-B, and Williams of Hove have Stöckler, perhaps the original two-bath developer. *See Useful Contacts page 173.*

However, if you would rather mix your own processing chemicals, a simple two-bath developer should consist of Kodak D-23

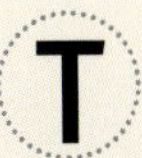

TERMINOLOGY / Two-bath developers

The principle of the two-bath developer is very simple; development is split into two stages instead of just one, with each stage taking place in a separate bath. The first bath contains only the developing agent and a large amount of preservative, and the second contains just alkali.

In the first bath the film absorbs developer solution, the actual amount depending on the thickness and absorbency of the emulsion. But in this first solution only a very small degree of development takes place. After a few minutes in the first bath the film is transferred, without rinsing, into the second solution which is absorbed into the emulsion very quickly and activates the developing agent already there from the first bath.

In effect, the emulsion now contains a complete developer with a limited amount of developing agent and a large amount of alkali. Development begins and continues until the developing agent has become exhausted or diffused from the emulsion.

This results in two characteristics. First, in areas that have been heavily exposed – highlight areas – the developing agent becomes quickly exhausted. Development therefore halts fairly quickly after the film has been transferred to the second bath. This produces highlights with excellent gradation and lots of delicate detail.

Second, in shadow areas, which have received only a small amount of exposure, the developing agent carries on working for much longer before becoming exhausted. In areas of deep shadow the development will continue throughout the whole of the time that the film is in the second bath. As a result the shadow areas of the negative become well developed, building up detail.

(*see facing page*) for the first bath and a two per cent solution of borax for the second bath.

Development times are four and a half minutes in the first bath and three minutes in the second for all slow- and medium-speed films, and six minutes in the first bath, four minutes in the second for all fast films. It is important not to rinse the film between the first and second baths. The operation of the developer depends on the alkali in the second bath reacting with the developing agent retained by the film from the first bath.

It is also important to keep agitation to the minimum, especially in the second bath. My preferred method of agitation is to pour in the developer, tap the tank on the table to dislodge any air bubbles and invert it once. Then invert very gently just once each minute. This allows the developer to work in the way it is designed to. The second bath activates the developer retained in the emulsion. That in the highlights quickly becomes exhausted while that in the areas of shadow keeps working, building up shadow detail while limiting highlight density.

A new version of an old favourite

One of the most popular developers in the late nineteenth and early twentieth centuries was pyro, and this developer is currently enjoying a revival thanks largely to American photographer Gordon Hutchings. He has taken a fresh look at it and evolved a developer that he calls Pyro PMK. The PMK stands for Pyrogallol Metol Kodalk, the three main constituents of the developer.

The most significant characteristic of pyro developers is that they produce a yellowish stain in direct proportion to the amount of silver in the negative. Because of its colour this stain is seen by the enlarging paper as density in the same way as silver. This means that the negative can be developed to have a lower density of silver and therefore less grain, while the stain still builds up the rest of the density. Therefore, the total printing density is the combined silver density plus the stain density.

Other characteristics of PMK are superb edge effects, which make the negative appear sharper, and also beautifully graduated highlights. These are due to the compensating effect, which is, of course, exactly what you need for bromoil negatives.

The formula for Pyro PMK is very simple. It consists of two concentrated solutions, which you mix together with water immediately before use. Because you need so little of the two concentrates, it is a very economical developer to use.

Pyro PMK developer

Solution A

Distilled or de-ionized water	400 ml
Metol	5 grams
Sodium bisulphite	10 grams
Pyrogallol	50 grams
Water to	500 ml

Solution B

Distilled or de-ionized water	700 ml
Kodalk (sodium metaborate)	300 grams
Water to	1 litre

For use take 1 part solution A and add to 100 parts of water, stirring, then add 2 parts solution B. As you add solution B the colour of the solution will change from clear to pale amber. This is normal and is, in fact, a good way to check that all is well.

Development times at 70°F (21°C) are:

Ilford FP4 Plus	12 mins
Ilford HP5 Plus	13 mins
Ilford 100 Delta	9 mins
Ilford 400 Delta	11 mins
Kodak Tri-X	14 mins
Kodak T-Max 100	12 mins
Kodak T-Max 400	15 mins
Agfa APX 25	11 mins
Agfa APX 100	13 mins
Agfa APX 400	16 mins

After development, retain the developer. Stop and fix the film in the usual way, then pour the

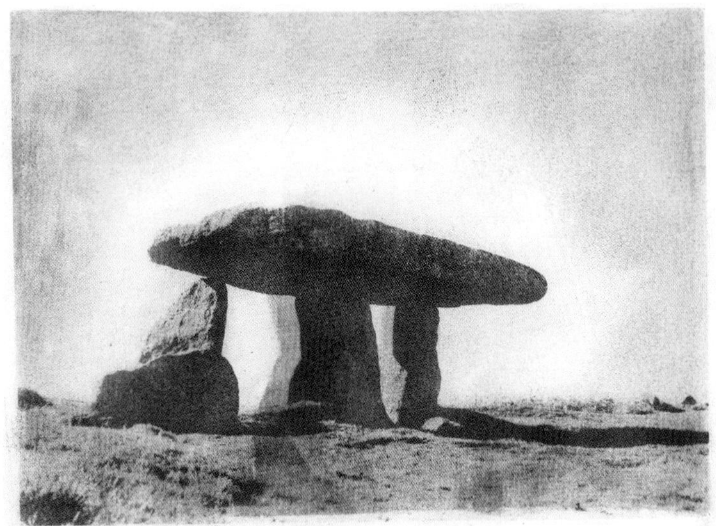

Lanyon Quoit, Cornwall, England. Original taken on 6x6cm Rolleicord camera using Ilford XP-2 film developed in C-41 colour chemicals. Inked with GC&I 1803 on Kentmere Bromoil paper.

developer back into the tank for 2½ minutes, agitating every half a minute. This builds up the maximum stain. Finally, wash the film thoroughly and dry.

If you want to know more about the theory and technique of using this remarkable developer, I can do no better than recommend that you read Gordon Hutchings's book *The Book of Pyro,* for full details *see page 172*.

Pyro PMK is available commercially from Silverprint, Film Plus and Bostick & Sullivan, among others, if you do not want to mix it up yourself. *See page 173*. I have been really impressed with this developer and it has now become the standard for the majority of my work, both bromoil and conventional.

CHROMOGENIC FILMS

Finally, you can achieve the compensating effect without special developers or techniques by using a film that has compensation effectively built in. I use two films in this category: Ilford XP2 Plus and Kodak T400CN. These films use colour-film technology and seem never to produce blocked highlights no matter how you treat them. This is because after processing there is no silver left in the negative at all, as the image is made up of dye – rather like the stain produced by pyro. It is the high density of silver in a film that produces blocked highlights, so its complete absence largely solves the problem. Added to this is the convenience of being able to hand the film over to your local lab for processing in C-41 chemicals. Combined with an almost unbelievable latitude – you can expose the films at anything from ISO 50 to ISO 800 or even higher and still get very printable negatives – it is little wonder that these films are becoming increasingly popular.

The techniques I have outlined in this chapter will produce negatives that are suitable for making bromoil prints. But to reiterate the two golden rules: do not underexpose and do not over-develop. With this in mind you should have few problems.

Beauchamp Chapel, St. Mary's Church, Warwick

In this small chapel are the tombs of Richard Beauchamp, Earl of Warwick from 1401 to 1439, and Ambrose Dudley, Earl from 1561 to 1590. Dudley's tomb is the one in the foreground.

This interior had a very wide tonal range, so a two-bath developer was used to control the highlights while building shadow detail. Taken on Mamiya 645 camera with 55mm lens. Inked with GC&I 1796 ink on Kentmere Art Document paper.

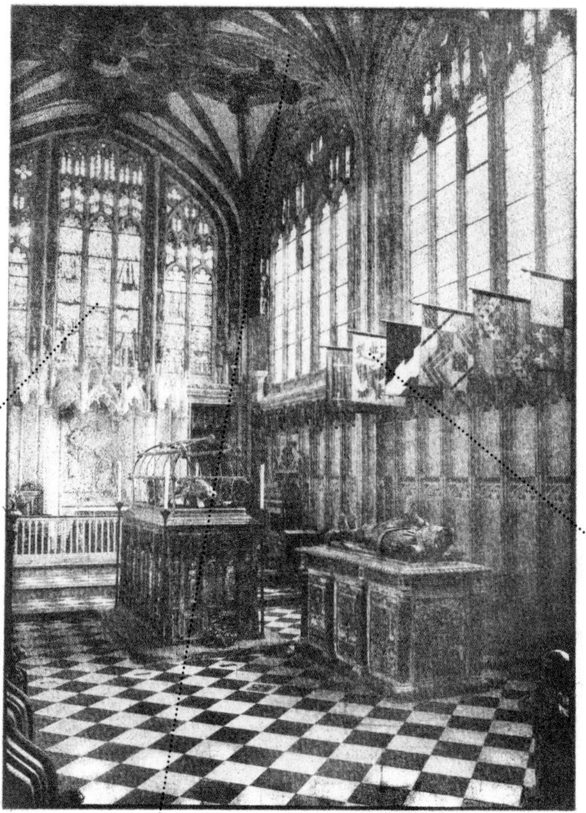

The two-bath developer quickly halts action in the bright highlight areas to prevent loss of detail

The combination of a fine-grain film – Ilford FP4 Plus – and medium-format camera captured maximum detail throughout

Shadow detail continues to build throughout the development period

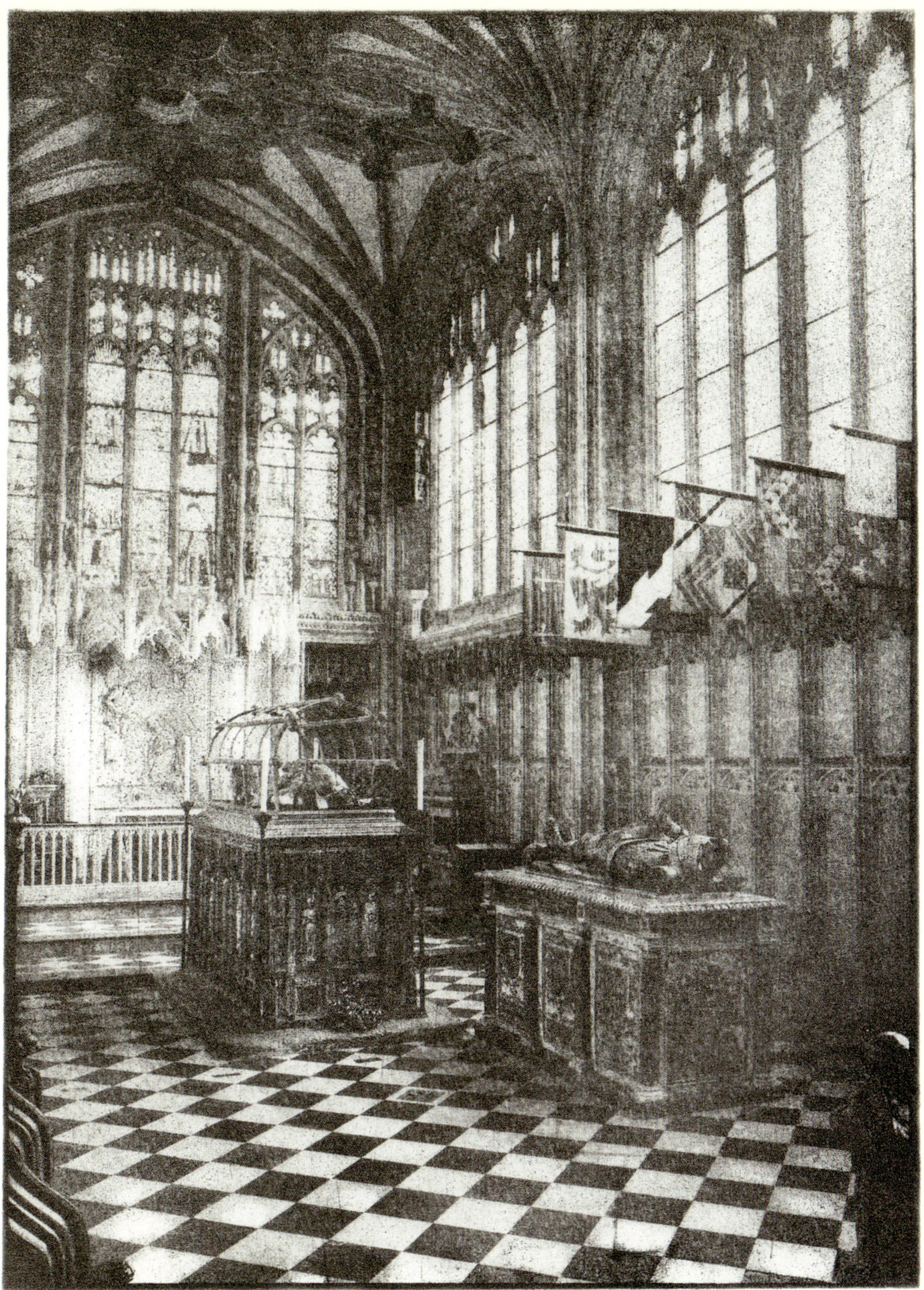

4 Making the bromide print

The success of every bromoil is based on a good-quality bromide that is printed on suitable paper, and it should contain a full range of tones and detail throughout.

The ideal starting point for making a bromoil is a bromide print that has plenty of both shadow and highlight detail. But the shadows should be rather lighter than would be normal for a silver print, and the highlights should be rather veiled. In other words, the print should appear flatter in contrast than is normal for a silver print. This is because the bromoil process, by its very nature, tends to give an increase in contrast. So the deep shadows you would normally have in a fine silver print will tend to block, and the delicate highlights in a normal silver print would lose all detail.

PAPERS

Traditionally, fibre-based papers without a gelatin supercoat on top of the emulsion were used for making bromoils. During the heyday of the process most manufacturers had a non-supercoated paper or two in their catalogues. Sadly, this is no longer the case, and there are few papers of this type currently available. The most readily available are Kentmere Art Document, a lightweight paper with a rather artificial surface texture; Kentmere Bromoil, a new paper produced under the persuasion of the Bromoil Circle of Great Britain; and Bergger Brom 240, a high-quality French paper.

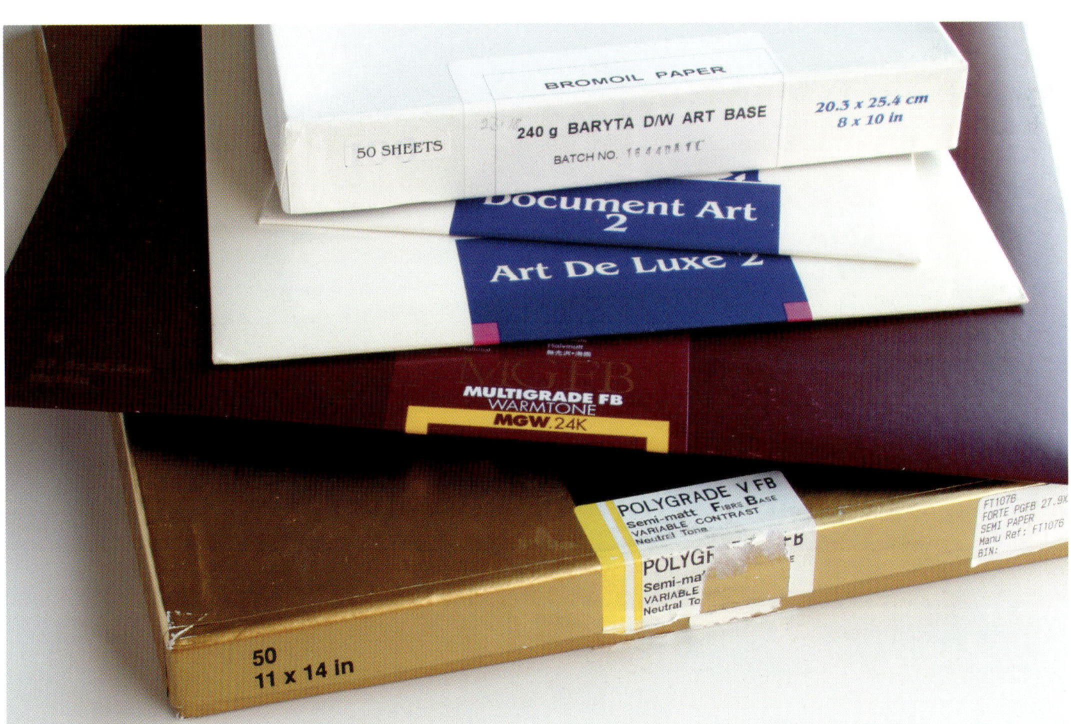

Just a few of the many currently available papers that are suitable for making bromoil prints.

TERMINOLOGY / Variable contrast papers

Ordinary bromide papers are made in a range of five or six separate grades, typically from 0 to 5, each with a single emulsion and with progressively greater contrast. Variable-contrast papers such as Ilford Multigrade, on the other hand, have two sensitized layers, one that is sensitive to blue light and one that is sensitive to green. The blue-sensitive layer produces a relatively high-contrast image and the green-sensitive layer produces a low-contrast image.

If the paper is subjected to blue light, both emulsions are exposed to more or less the same degree and the silver images they produce add to each other to give a full range of densities resulting in a contrasty print. Now, if increasing amounts of green light are added, the green-sensitive layer becomes effectively more sensitive while the blue-sensitive layer becomes less so. This results in the green-sensitive layer becoming more predominant resulting in a progressively less contrasty image.

The amounts of blue and green light are controlled by yellow and magenta filters, which are placed in the enlarger light path. These are usually supplied in sets giving grades 00 to 5 in half-grade steps, allowing fine control over print contrast. Alternatively, an enlarger with a colour-mixing head can be used to adjust the filtration. This has the advantage of giving continuously variable contrast, but often over a somewhat reduced grade scale.

It is still believed by many that you can only use non-supercoated papers for making bromoil prints. This is in fact untrue. Many modern supercoated papers are quite suitable, and indeed offer certain advantages. Among the fibre-based supercoated papers that have been found to produce good results with the bromoil process are Agfa Multicontrast Classic 118, Ilford Multigrade IV, Forte Polygrade and Kentmere Super Art. The Agfa, Ilford and Forte papers are variable contrast, which is a real bonus as it allows you to adjust the paper grade to suit your negative.

One of the leading bromoilists in the United States, Gene Laughter, has standardized on Agfa MCC 118 and produces beautiful bromoils in large numbers. Even some resin-coated papers will ink up fairly easily, but they are very delicate and not really to be recommended, especially for the beginner. They are, however, ideal for making bromoil transfer prints because the ink leaves the print so easily.

A recommendation

My advice to anyone making a start in bromoil printing is to begin with Kentmere Art Document paper. Not only is it less expensive than some of the other papers, it inks up extremely easily. For this reason alone, it gives encouragement to the beginner. Kentmere Art Document was, in fact, the only non-supercoated paper available at all for some years and it has been used by members of the Bromoil Circle to produce some really delightful prints.

EXPOSURE

When exposing non-supercoated papers for bromoil prints no special precautions are necessary. But because the absence of a supercoat makes the surface rather delicate, you should avoid touching the surface of the paper as far as possible to minimize marking.

Prints on supercoated paper require more density throughout the image to make successful bromoils. Gene Laughter's rule of thumb for Agfa MCC 118 is 'one stop more, one grade less'. In other words, find the exposure and paper grade filtration that will give you a good silver print, then double the exposure time and use the filtration for the next lower grade. It is advisable with both supercoated and non-supercoated papers to leave a margin of about 1in (25mm) – called the safe edge – all around the image to enable handling and allow the print to be taped down while it is being inked, without damaging the image.

DEVELOPMENT

The developer traditionally used for making bromoils was amidol. This is a very fine developer, but it has a couple of major drawbacks. First, the developing agent,

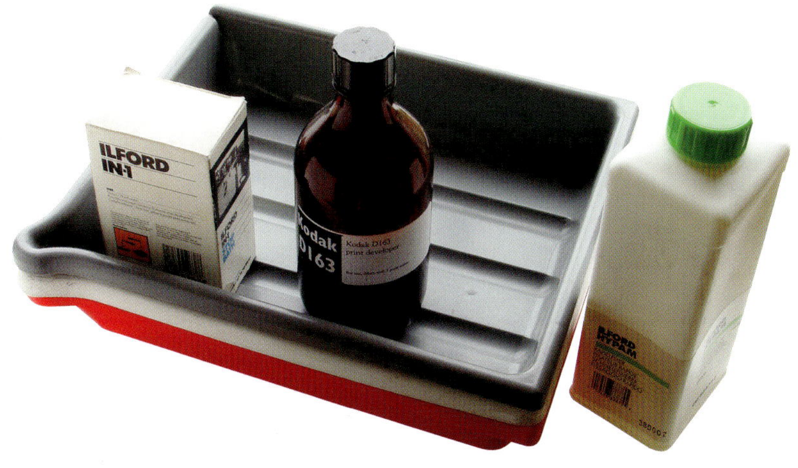

You need developer, stop bath and fixer to make black & white prints. Also, keep a special dish for each chemical. Buying a set of three different coloured dishes is a good idea.

amidol, stains fingers and clothes very easily, and the stains are difficult to remove. Secondly, the mixed developer oxidizes very rapidly. Once poured into the developing dish it will keep for only about one hour. Having said all this, amidol is capable of producing extremely good results. It is rather soft-working and gives prints with a long tonal range and neutral colour, not that this is of any consequence for bromoil printing. A typical amidol developer is:

Amidol developer	
Sodium sulphite, anhydrous	25 grams
Potassium bromide	0.25 gram
Amidol	6 grams
Water to	1 litre

Many photographers believe that amidol is the only developer suitable for making bromoil prints. Once again, this is completely false. Very few bromoilists use amidol these days, largely because it doesn't keep very well.

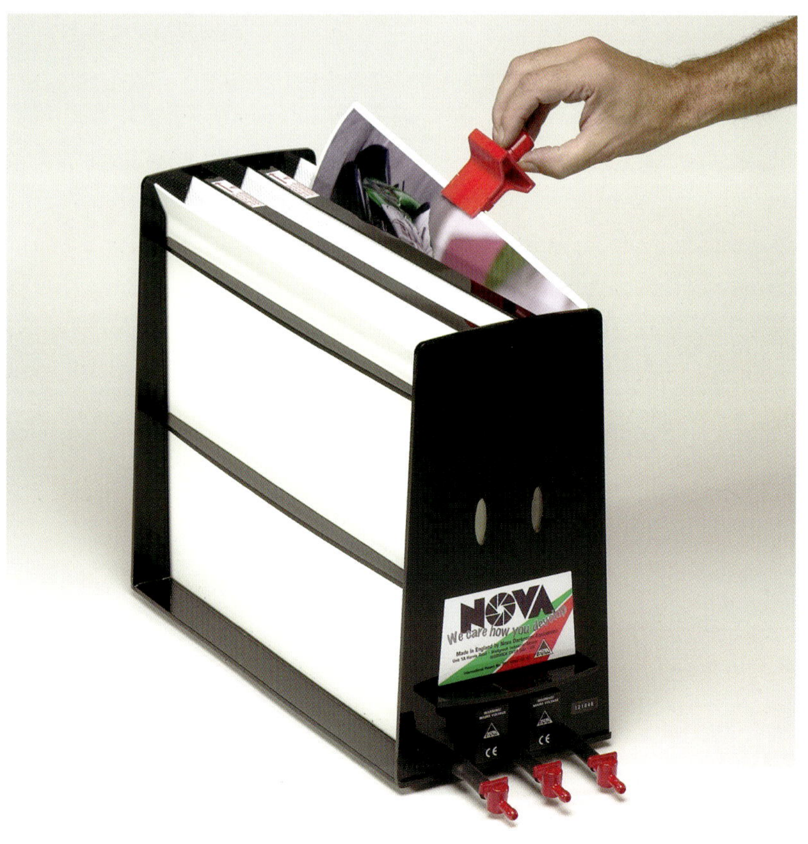

The innovative Nova deep slot print processor takes up very little bench space yet enables large prints to be processed. The developer and other chemicals can be left in the processor and, with proper replenishment, will last for many weeks.
Photograph by kind permission of Nova Darkroom Limited, manufacturer.

Today, you can use any standard print developer. I tend to use whatever happens to be in my Nova deep-slot processor, though this is usually my old favourite Kodak D-163. After being unavailable commercially for some years, it is now being made once again by Speedibrews. However, if you wish to mix your own, the formula is simple enough:

Kodak D-163 developer	
Metol	2.3 grams
Sodium sulphite, anhydrous	75 grams
Hydroquinone	17 grams
Sodium carbonate, anhydrous	65 grams
Potassium bromide	2.8 grams
Water to	1 litre

For use dilute 1:3 and develop fully. The usual recommended development time for D-163 is 1½ minutes at 68°F (20°C), but because it is important that bromoil prints are developed, I increase this to 2 or even 3 minutes. Some bromoilists I know dilute D-163 up to 1:9 for softer results and increase the development time accordingly. At a 1:9 dilution the development time should be about 7 or 8 minutes at 68°F (20°C).

Other suitable developers include Kodak Dektol, Ilford Multigrade and Bromophen, Agfa Neutol and Fotospeed PD5. Kodak D-165, a soft-working developer preferred by several bromoilists, is also very good but it is not available commercially. The formula is:

Kodak D-165 soft gradation developer	
Metol	6 grams
Sodium sulphite, anhydrous	25 grams
Sodium carbonate, anhydrous	37 grams
Potassium bromide	1 gram
Water to	1 litre

For use dilute 1:3 and develop for 2 minutes at 68°F (20°C).

POST-DEVELOPMENT

After development, some bromoilists simply rinse the print in water for 30 seconds or so before transferring it to the fixer. On the other hand, many prefer to use an acid stop bath in the usual way. Not only does it halt the action of the developer immediately, it also prolongs the life of the fixer.

The reason why some bromoilists use only a plain-water rinse is that they believe that the acid makes subsequent inking-up more difficult. But as the bleach and tanning solution usually has sulphuric acid in it, this argument does not seem to me to hold true. Anyway, I have found no significant difference in ease of inking whether I use either water or a stop bath.

Fixing

There is one golden rule about suitable fixers: you must use a non-hardening fixer. This is because the principle of the bromoil process depends on the gelatin in the print being tanned or hardened proportionately to the amount of silver in the original print. If you fix the print in a hardening fixer, this differential tanning will not be possible and the ink will simply adhere evenly to the whole of the image.

Any standard non-hardening fixer is suitable, or you can use a simple 10 per cent solution of plain sodium thiosulphate (hypo). My own preference is for a standard rapid fixer such as Ilford Hypam, which I use at its 1:4 dilution.

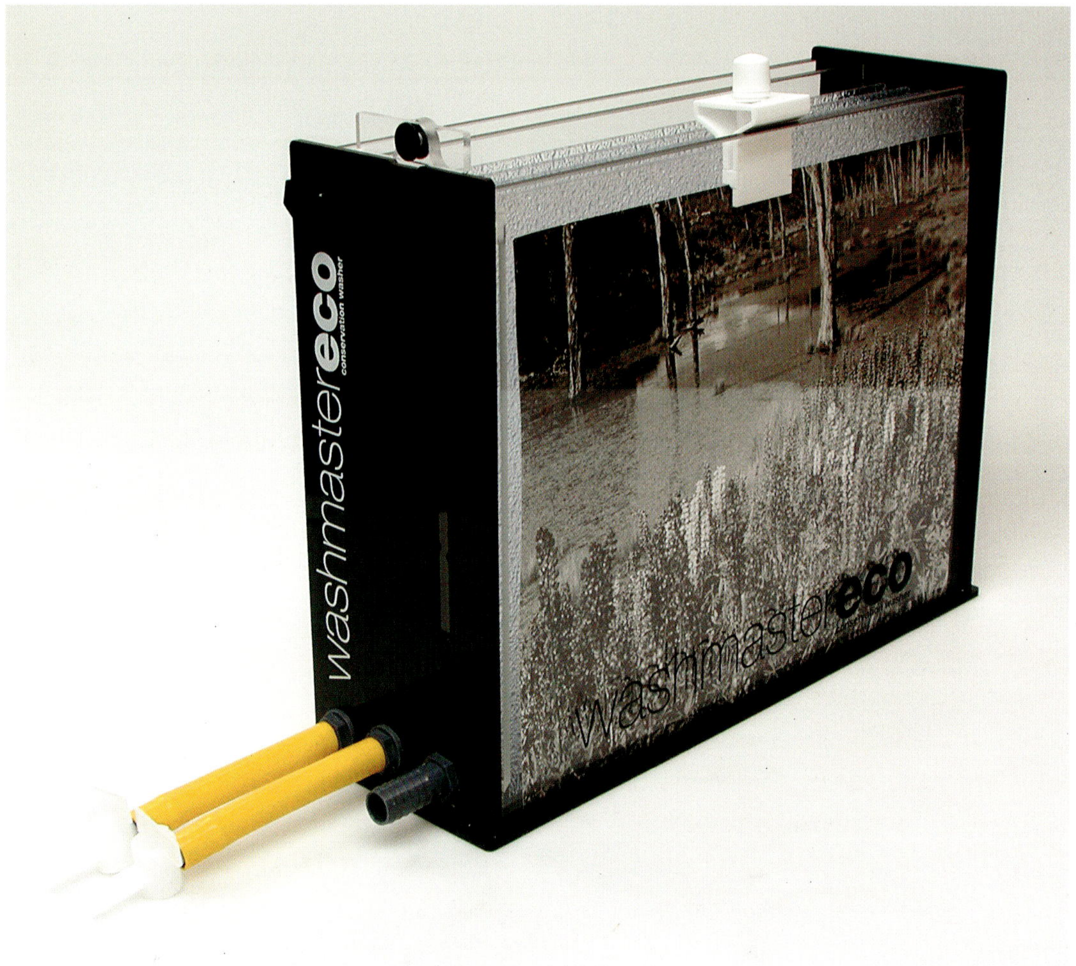

An archival washer such as this one by Nova will ensure that your prints are always thoroughly washed and free from residual fixer, especially if you use it in conjunction with a washing aid such as Ilford Galerie Wash Aid.

Photograph by kind permission of Nova Darkroom Limited, manufacturer.

Because you will be using fibre-based paper, it is important to fix your prints adequately, but not to over-fix them as this makes it more difficult to wash the fixer out of the paper. Based on extensive research, Ilford now recommends fixing for no more than 60 seconds in fresh rapid fixer at the 1:4 dilution. A hypo-based fixer will need longer because it works more slowly; no more than three to five minutes should be necessary.

Washing

It is most important to wash your prints thoroughly at this stage. If you do not want to use a washing aid such as Kodak Hypo Clearing Agent or Ilford Galerie Washaid, you need to wash the prints for at least half an hour in running water. However, the use of a washing aid enables you to reduce this time considerably, saving a great deal of water. Taking Ilford's recommendation as a basis again, wash the prints in running water for five minutes, then transfer them to a bath of Galerie Washaid diluted 1:4 for 10 minutes with intermittent agitation. Finally, wash them in running water for another five minutes. According to Ilford, this fixing and washing procedure will result in archival permanence.

Drying

When you remove your prints from the wash, make sure that you blot the front and back gently to remove surface water, then hang them up with plastic or wooden spring pegs to dry naturally for several hours; I usually dry my prints overnight. To prevent them from curling as they dry, you can hang two prints back to back using a single pair of pegs at the top and another pair at the bottom. As the prints tend to curl so that the emulsion is on the inside, in this way they will cancel each other out and dry virtually flat.

> **tip**
>
> *A good alternative to Galerie Washaid or Kodak Hypo Clearing Agent is a simple 20 per cent solution of anhydrous sodium sulphite.*

Super-drying There is also a school of thought among bromoilists that believes the more times a matrix is soaked and dried the more easily it will accept the ink, because the gelatin becomes softer. This is an argument against using the short process, these bromoilists preferring to dry the print after the first fix and wash and then again after the bleach-tan and subsequent fixing and washing stages. Indeed, some apply a considerable amount of heat to the already dry print before the bleach-tan and again before inking. This so-called super-drying was advocated in the early 1950s by G. E. Whalley ARPS, especially

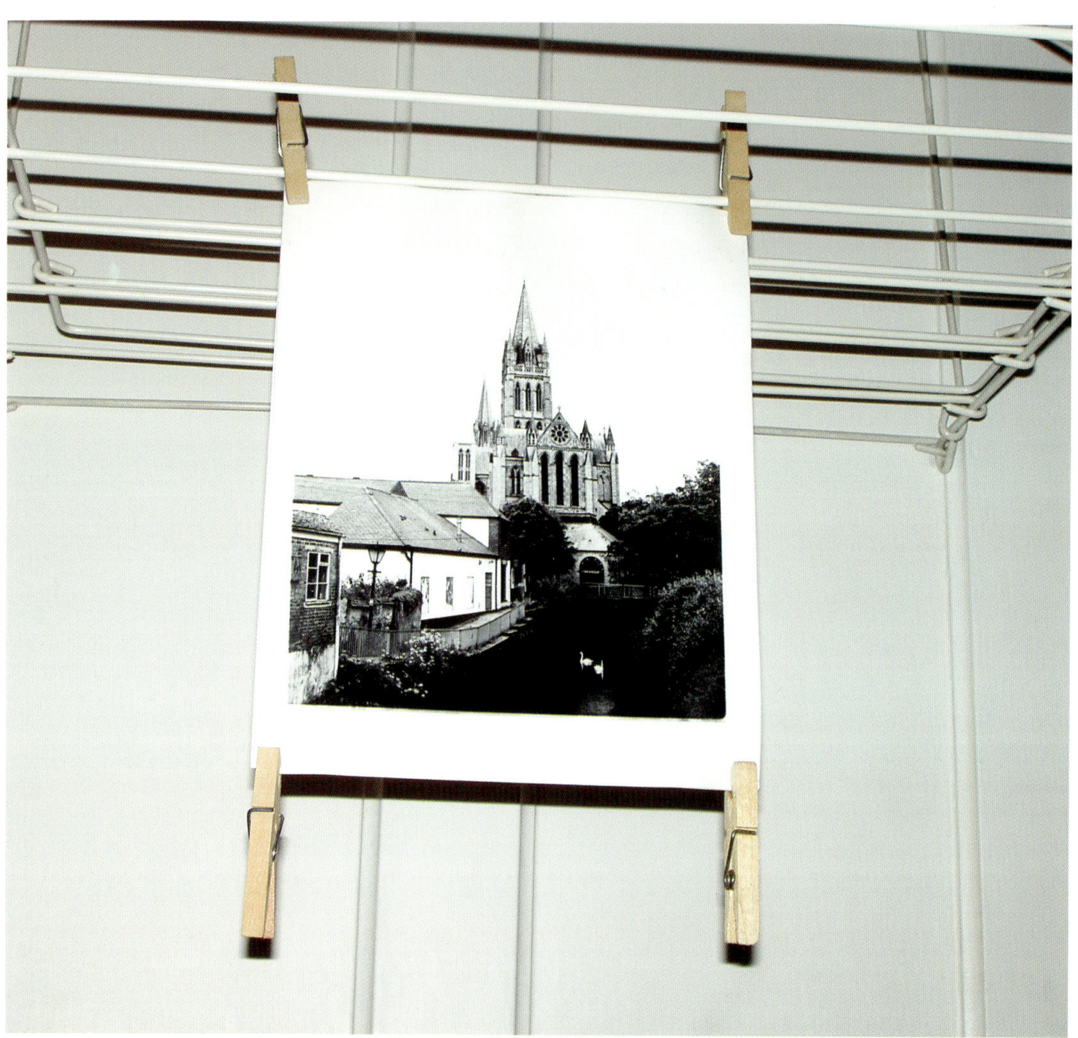

Dry prints that are subsequently to be made into bromoils naturally. Heat drying will tend to harden the emulsion so that it will not take the ink easily. I use a clothes dryer that hangs on the back of a door, hanging two prints back to back with wooden clothes pegs.

when using supercoated papers. The idea was to remove every last trace of moisture from the paper and emulsion, presumably so that the paper will become uniformly soaked when subsequently immersed in water. I have tried using the technique and doing without it and found that super-drying does seem to help in the subsequent inking, so I normally use it. There are several ways to do this. You can use a hair dryer on high heat and held about 12in (30cm) from the emulsion side of the print, or you can hold the print emulsion side down about 18in (45cm) above a gas burner for approximately 30 seconds. You can even put the print in a microwave oven for half a minute on full power. Most bromoilists who use this method super-dry the print again after it has been bleached, tanned and dried ready for inking.

Once the prints are dry they are then ready to be treated with the next stage, which is bleaching and tanning. You do not have to do this immediately or even within a day or two. In fact, the prints will keep indefinitely and can be bleached at any time in the future. Just ensure that you keep their surfaces protected from damage by storing them face to face in a large envelope.

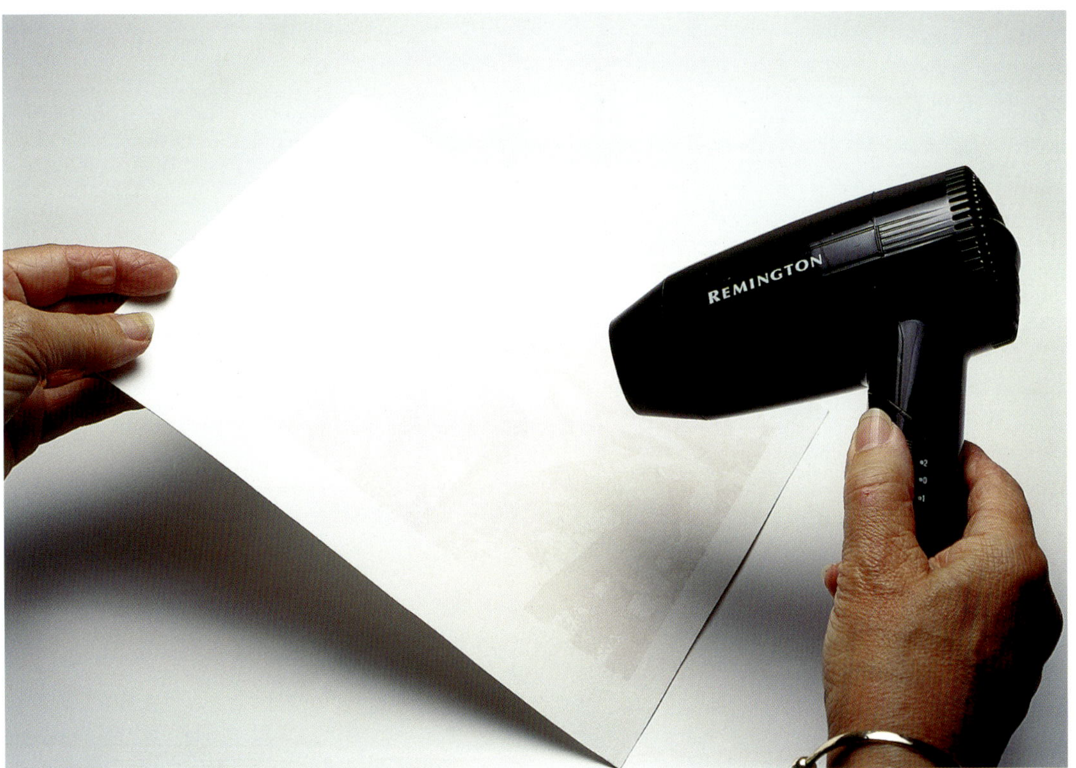

Many bromoilists super-dry the print after processing and before soaking. This is said to make inking easier. The simplest method for super-drying is with a hair dryer, although you can also hold the matrix about 18in (45cm) above a lit gas burner.

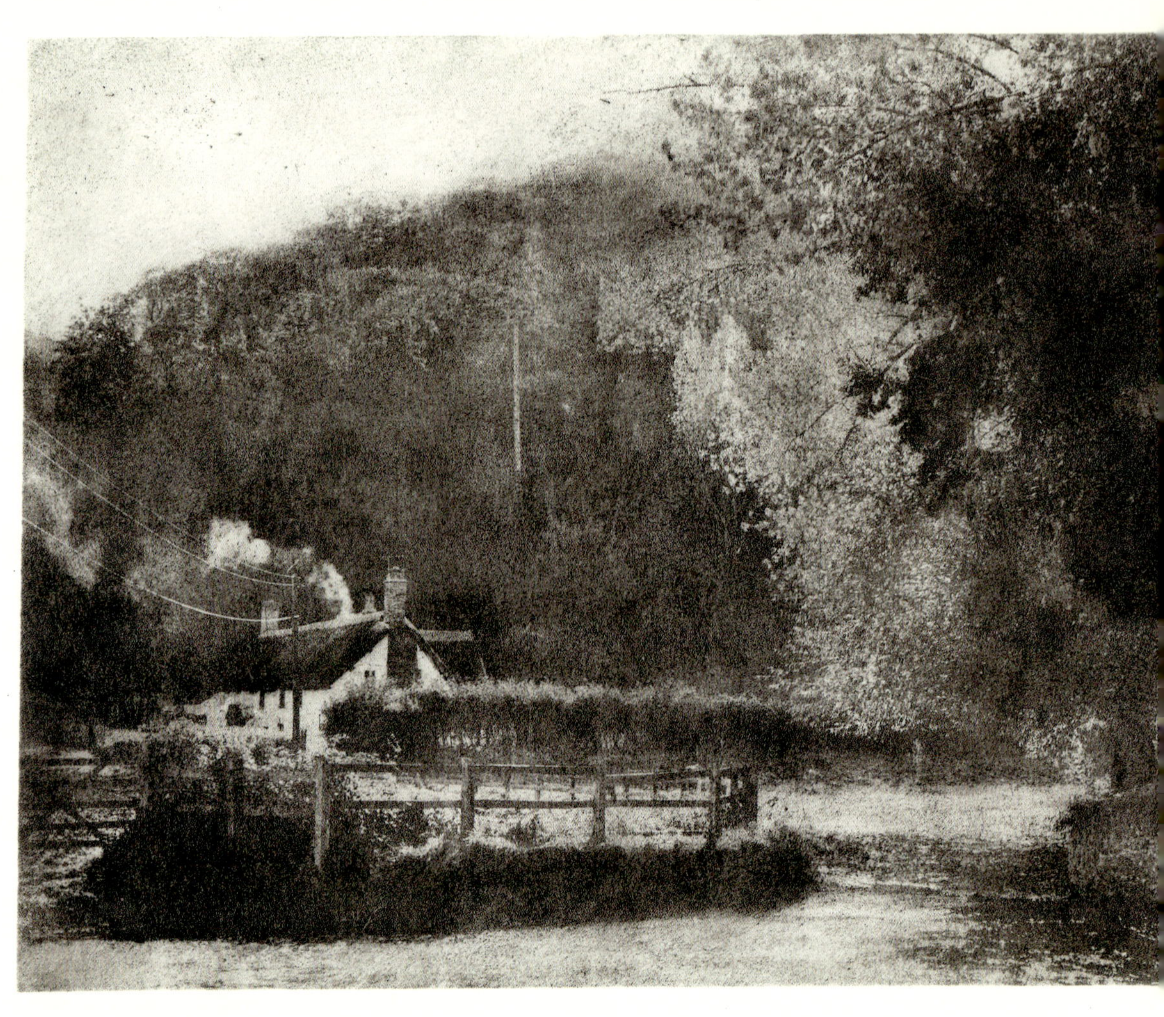

Gallox Bridge, Cornwall

This country scene was taken one October morning just outside Dunster in Exmoor National Park, Cornwall, England. The pack horse bridge, known as Gallox Bridge, on the right-hand side is many hundreds of years old.

Original taken on 35mm Olympus OM-1 camera with 50mm lens using Ilford FP4 film and Microphen developer. Inked with GC&I 1796 ink on Kentmere Bromoil paper.

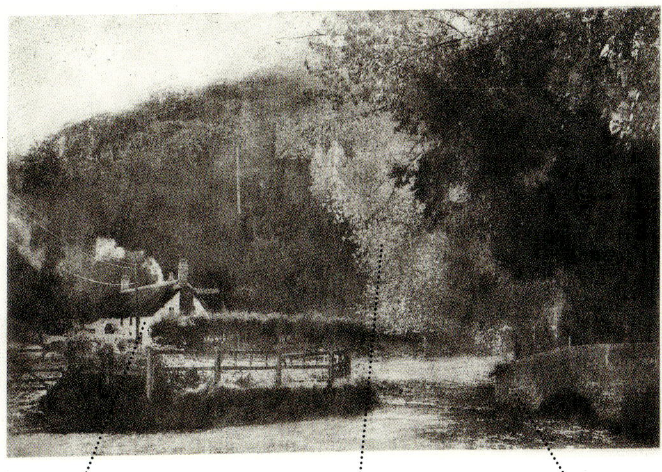

The smoke and cottage walls were cleaned with a wet cotton-wool bud after inking to remove any muddiness

Plenty of detail in the original print ensures that the brickwork on the bridge is not lost in the final bromoil

Inking the backlit leaves required delicate work with a small brush and the use of a hopper to retain the sparkle

5 Bleaching and tanning

Before you can use your bromide print to make a bromoil you must prepare it to accept the ink. After the print has been treated, and it is ready to accept the ink, it becomes known as a matrix.

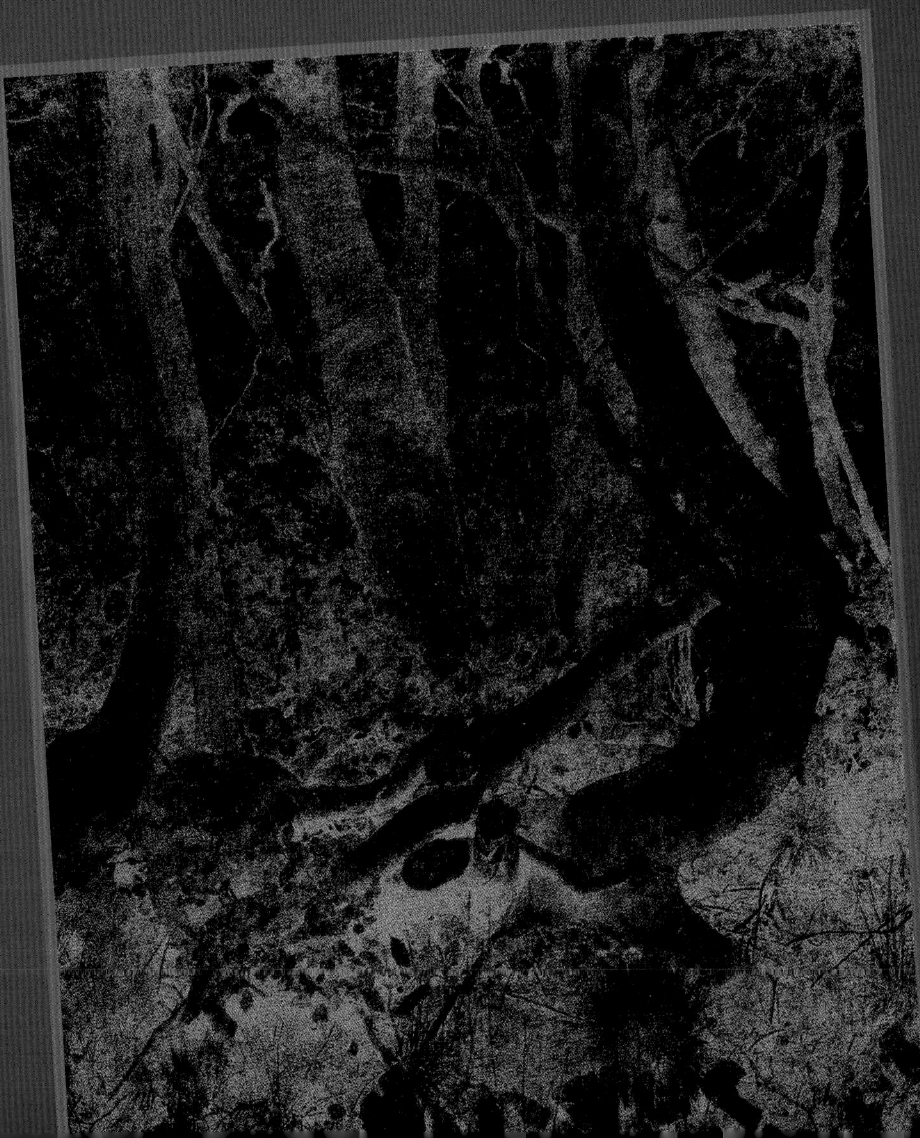

To prepare the matrix, two chemical reactions must take place. First, you must bleach the black developed silver image so that it becomes almost invisible. And secondly, you must tan or harden the bleached image to allow it to absorb water in inverse proportion to the density of the original image. The chemicals making up the bleaching agent react with the silver in the image to form a compound that, in turn, is converted to chromium trioxide by the tanning agent.

WHICH BLEACH?

Most bromoil workers use a single bleach-tanning solution to achieve these two chemical reactions simultaneously, although some use separate bleach and tanning solutions. I started with a combined bleach-tanning solution, which works well so I have seen no reason to change and add another step to the process.

There are countless formulas for bleach-tanning solutions that have appeared over the years. In *Photographic Facts and Formulas* by E. J. Wall and F. I. Jordan, there are no fewer than 37 solutions listed. They all do a good job and, in truth, there are only minor differences between many of them, so it really is a matter of personal choice.

The formula that I now use was given to me by Gilbert Hooper FRPS, past president of the Bromoil Circle of Great Britain and a master bromoilist.

Gilbert Hooper's bleach-tan solution	
Copper sulphate	25 grams
Potassium bromide	25 grams
Potassium dichromate	1.25 grams
Sulphuric acid, 10% solution	10 ml
Water to	400 ml

Add the sulphuric acid to the water first, then dissolve the rest of the chemicals. For use, dilute 1:10 and treat the print for 10 minutes at 68°F (20°C).

Maija McDougal FRPS, now president of the BCGB and another master of the art, uses a two-bath formula first published in the *British Journal of Photography* in 1926.

Venn two-bath bleach-tan	
Solution A – Bleach	
Copper sulphate, 10% solution	250 ml
Potassium bromide, 10% solution	13 ml
Solution B – Tan	
Potassium bromide, 10% solution	70 ml
Potassium dichromate, 1% solution	30 ml
Water to	250 ml

Bleach the print in Bath A for 30 seconds at 68°F (20°C) or until only a yellow image remains. Drain and transfer, without rinsing, to Bath B for four minutes at 68°F (20°C).

caution

Potassium dichromate is a very toxic chemical and a suspected carcinogen. Therefore, when mixing or using any bromoil bleach always wear rubber gloves. In fact, because potassium dichromate is a very fine powder, it is advisable to wear a dust mask as well when mixing the solutions.

THE PROCEDURE

First, mix up your bleach-tan solution and pour it into a dish that you keep exclusively for the purpose. This is to avoid contamination, which is one of the main causes of failure in bromoil printing.

Soak the print in clean water at about 68°F (20°C) for five minutes then remove it and blot any surplus water from the surface before placing it in the bleach-tan solution. Slide it

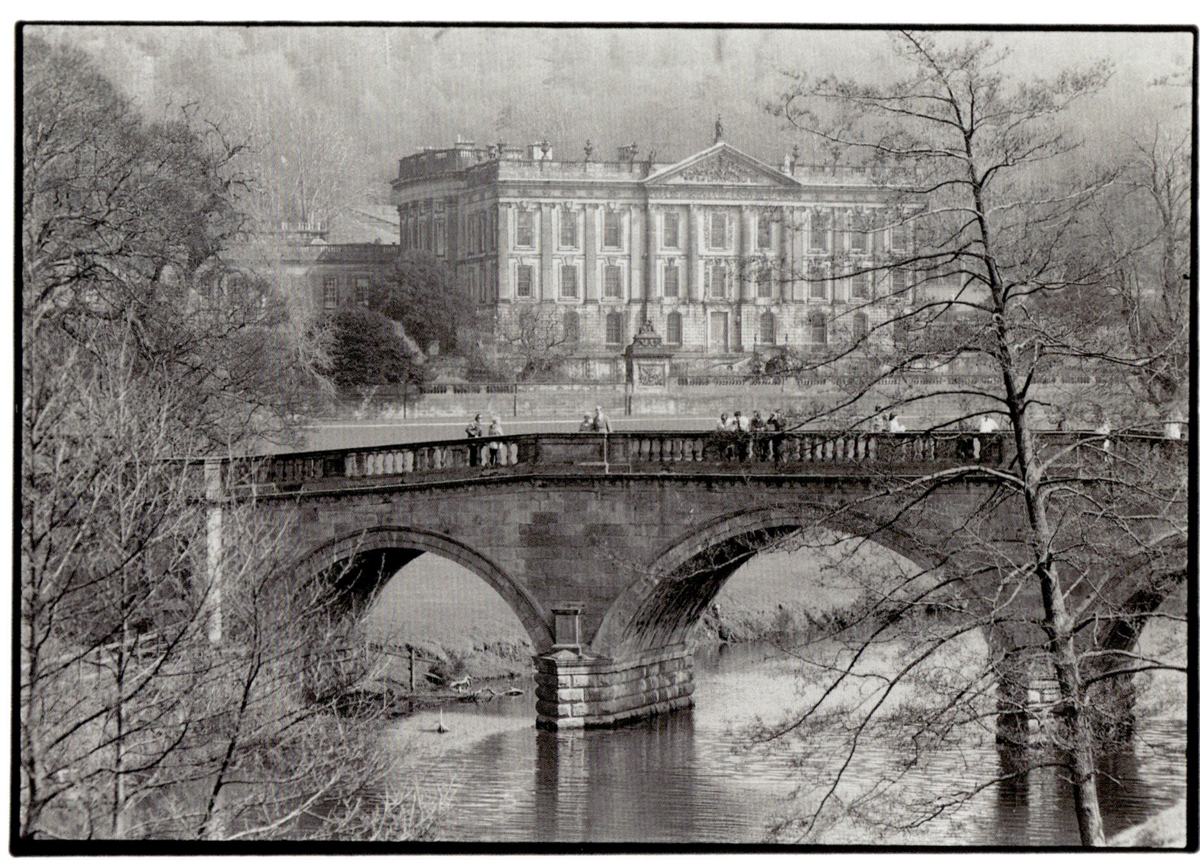

After processing the original print looks exactly like any other straightforward bromide print.

carefully into the solution face down then turn it over and ensure that there are no bubbles.

Agitate the print gently for 10 minutes at about 68°F (20°C). The image will start to disappear after about three minutes and will have bleached completely after about five or six minutes. It is, however, important to leave the print in the solution for the full 10 minutes in order to allow the tanning action to be completed. If you prefer to use separate bleach and tanning solutions, follow the times given on *page 61*.

A useful tip passed on to me by Gilbert Hooper is to bleach-tan two prints at a time, back to back. This is a good idea because bleach-tanning is by far the least interesting stage of the whole bromoil process. Although Gilbert uses fresh bleach-tan solution for every print, or pair of prints, I have found that I can satisfactorily treat up to ten prints sized 10x8in (25x20cm) in a litre of solution.

When the bleaching and tanning operations are complete, the print will have a light yellow stain. Wash briefly to remove all traces of this stain, leaving a light greenish-grey image. You can use either running water or five or six changes of fresh water to achieve this.

Now place the matrix in fixer in order to remove the bleached silver from the emulsion. You can use either a standard non-hardening rapid fixer or a fresh 10 per cent solution of sodium thiosulphate – 100 grams of sodium thiosulphate in one litre of water. Fix for 60 seconds in the rapid fixer at 1:4 dilution or three to five minutes in the plain fixer. After completing the fixing, the image should

The bleaching and tanning stage prepares the print, now called a matrix, for inking. This stage removes the silver image and hardens the gelatin in direct proportion to the depth of tone in the original image.

have virtually disappeared, leaving just a faint trace of a grey image. You must now wash the matrix thoroughly once more to remove all traces of the fixer. Follow the same procedure outlined in the previous chapter, using a wash aid if you prefer. Finally, hang the matrix up so that it dries naturally.

The short process

Many bromoil workers prefer to get all the processing stages out of the way in one session. To do this they use what has become known as the short process, which eliminates the first fixing stage and its subsequent wash and drying stages.

After developing the print, transfer it to an acid stop bath for 10 seconds, then into the bleach-tanning solution for 10 minutes at 68°F (20°C). Do not rinse after the stop bath. Agitate the print gently all the time it is in the bleach-tan. Then, at the end of the 10 minutes, wash it in running water or a few changes of fresh water to remove the yellow bleach stain.

Now transfer the print to rapid fixer diluted 1:4 for 60 seconds or a fresh 10 per cent plain sodium thiosulphate solution for five minutes, agitating constantly.

Finally, wash the matrix for at least 30 minutes or rinse for five minutes, transfer to hypo clearing agent for 10 minutes, then wash for a further five minutes in running water before hanging up to dry naturally. You can, if you wish, proceed directly to inking-up after washing the matrix, instead of drying it.

Personally, I prefer to make the prints in one darkroom session, bleach and tan them another day, and ink them at a later time. That way I can keep the three distinct stages

tip - A word of warning

It is best to carry out the bleach-tanning and subsequent wash in subdued lighting. This is because the potassium dichromate in the bleach-tan solution effectively re-sensitizes the silver in the emulsion and if exposed to bright light the image will darken again. Subsequent fixing does not remove this darkened image. Although it will not alter the way the gelatin accepts ink when you apply it, the darkened image can change the appearance of the finished bromoil. The only way to get rid of this darkened image is to pass the print through the bleach-tan a second time. But the problem with this is that there is a danger of tanning the gelatin too much with the result that the highlights will not reject the ink as efficiently, leaving a very flat and muddy bromoil.

This darkening problem is particularly troublesome if the prints have been stacked in the wash following bleach-tanning. If they only partly overlap you could find parts of the image have been darkened while other parts have not. In fact, this is how I first discovered the problem.

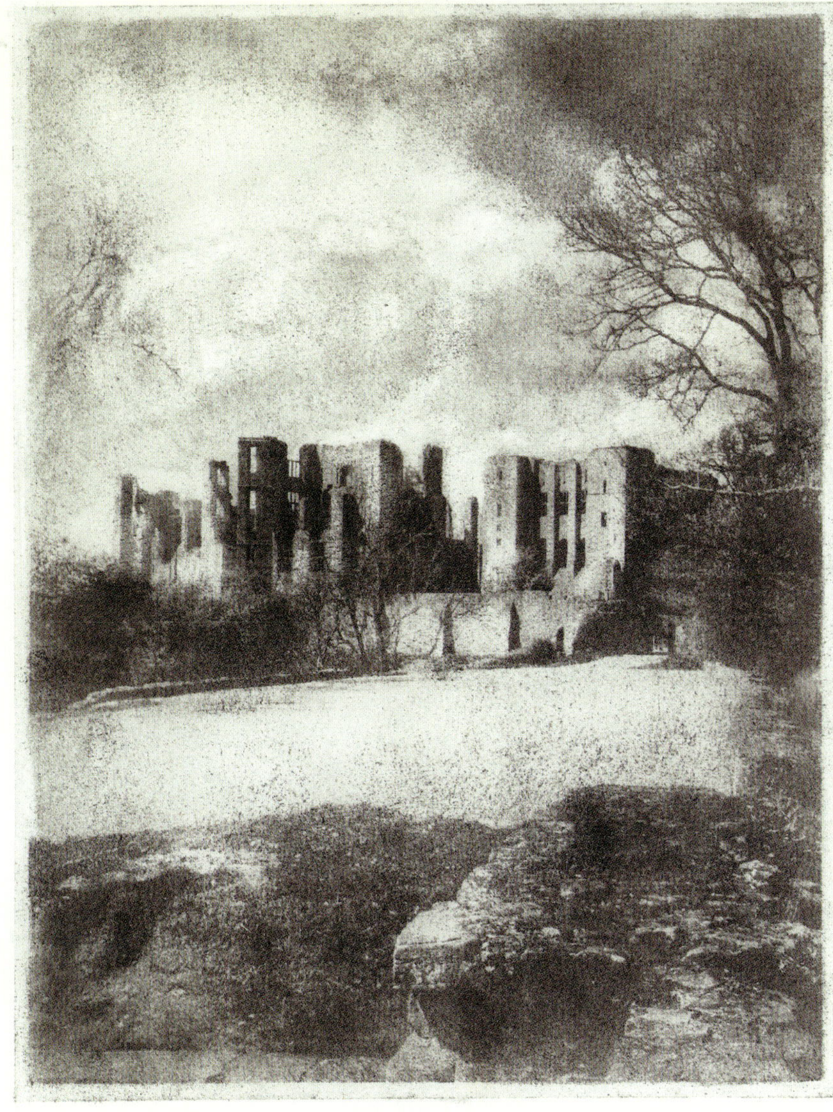

Kenilworth Castle
by Colin Ivison

of the process separate and concentrate better on each stage. It also means that I always have a few matrices waiting to be inked, so if the mood takes me I can ink a few without having to make prints first. That is just my preference though; I know several bromoilists who use the short process and whose prints are none the worse for it.

When the matrices have dried and, if you use the method, super-dried after bleaching and tanning you can ink them at any future time. Provided you have fixed them properly and washed them thoroughly, they will stay in good condition for months or even years. Protect the matrices by storing them face to face in a large envelope made from acid-free paper.

Twisted roots

I came across these fantastically twisted tree roots while out walking on Exmoor in Somerset, England. They seemed to me to be the perfect subject for the tremendous degree of control offered by the bromoil process.

Original taken on 35mm Olympus OM-1 camera with 50mm lens using Ilford FP4 film and Microphen developer. Inked with GC&I 1796 ink on Kentmere Art Document paper.

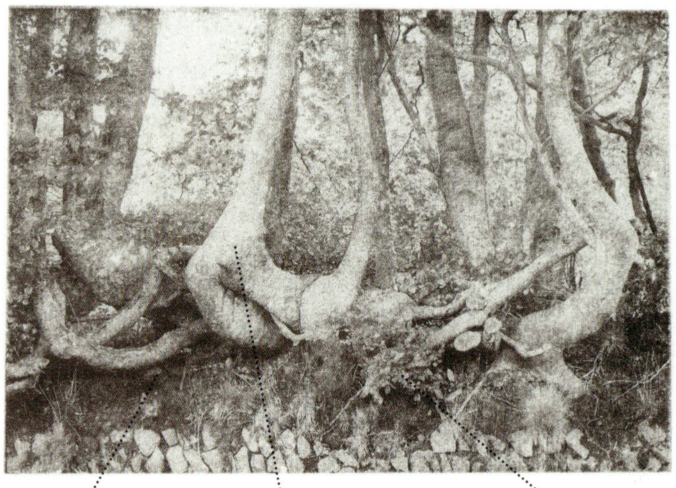

The shadow areas beneath the roots were dodged slightly during printing to prevent them blocking up when inked

Because there was a great deal of delicate detail in the tree trunks I burned them in a little so that they would not ink as flat grey areas

To bring out all the detail in the grasses and leaves in the foreground, I used a small stiff brush to remove ink from the lighter areas

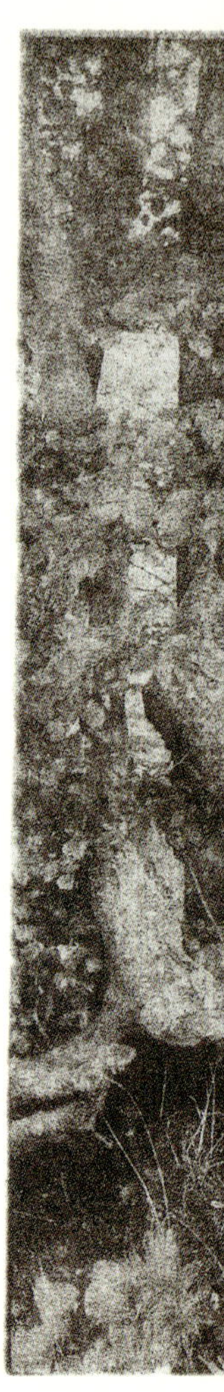

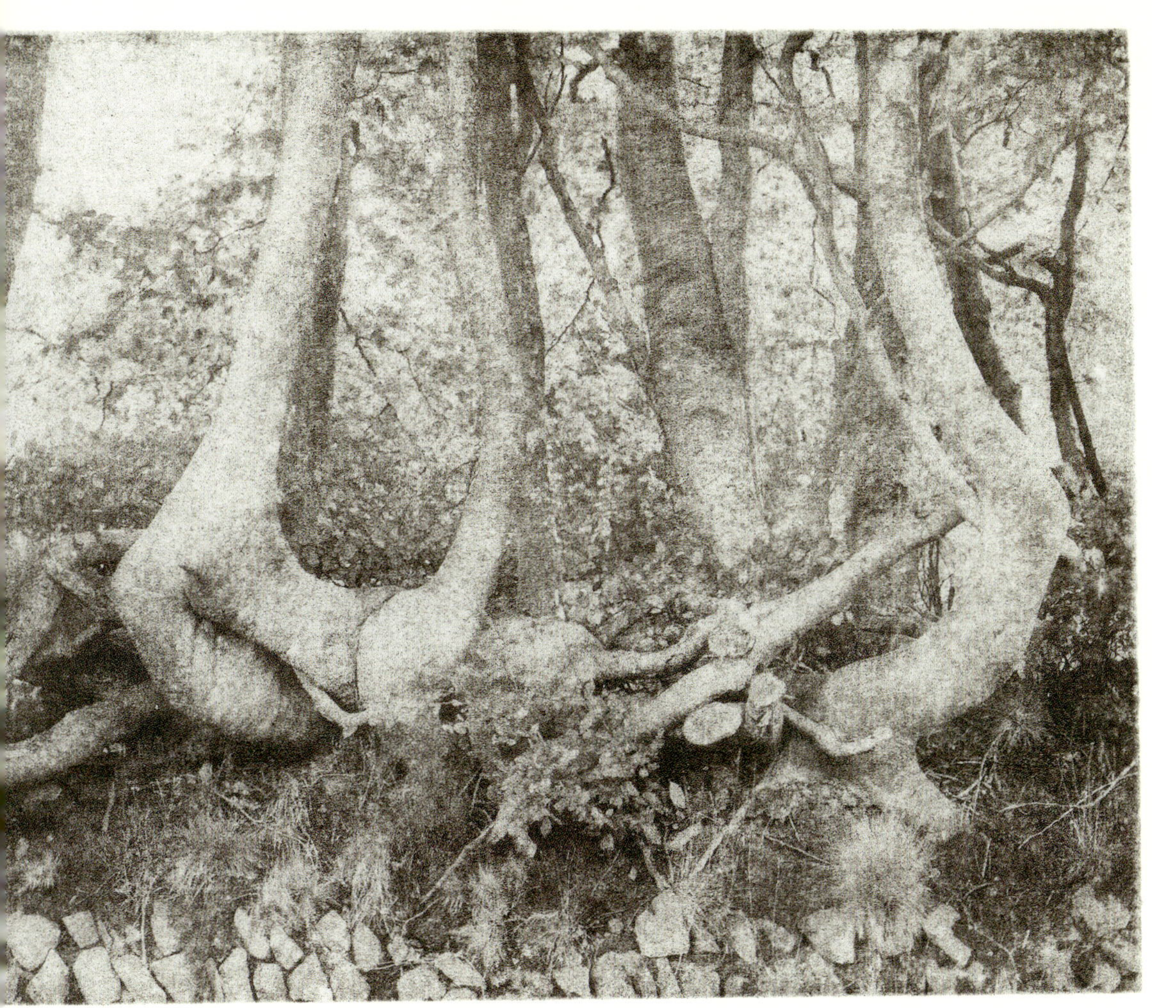

6 Preparation for inking

Trouble-free inking depends on careful preparation of the matrix to allow it to accept the ink easily, and that means giving it a correct soaking and removing the surplus water.

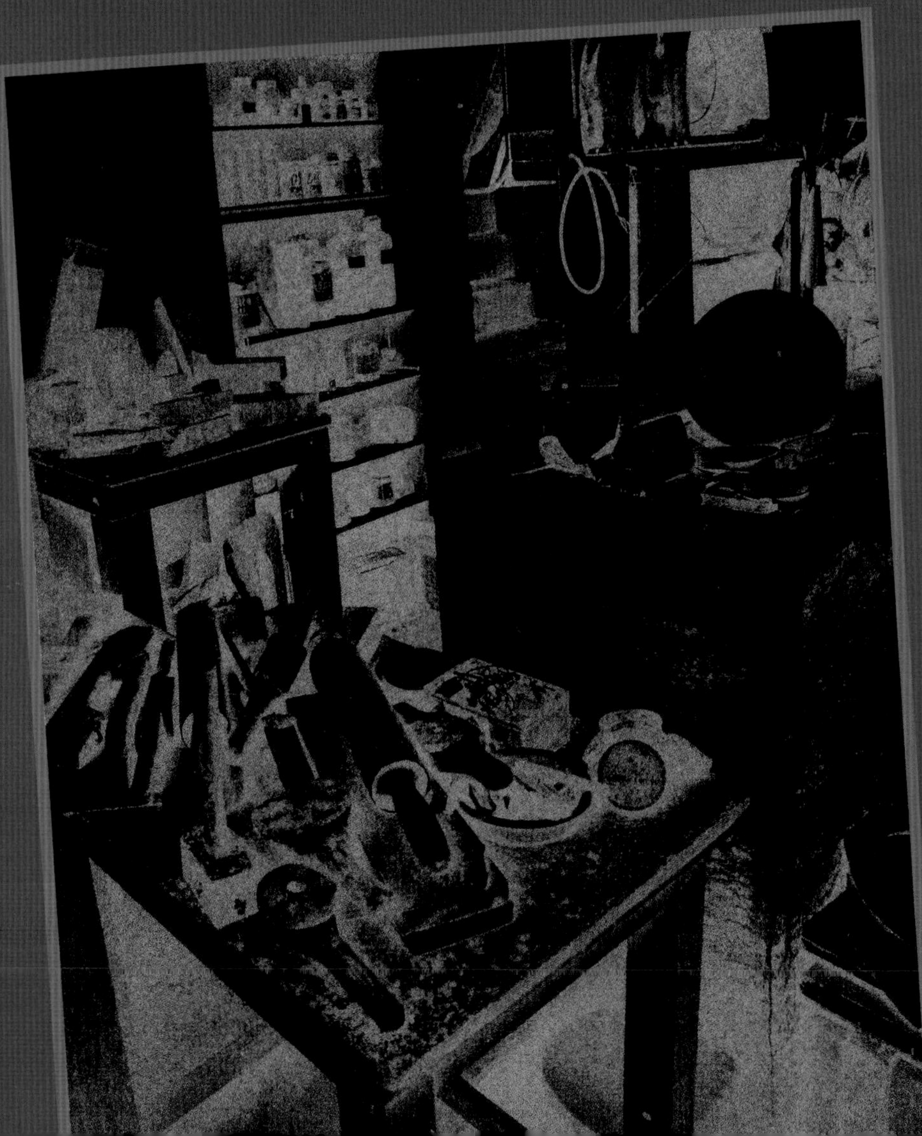

Before you can begin inking your bromoil print you will need to soak it in clean water to swell the gelatin in the light and mid-tone areas. This will enable the ink to be accepted or rejected in proportion to the density of the original silver image. However, there is a great deal more to this preparation than simply immersing the matrix in water. Several factors have an important bearing on just how long you need to soak the matrix.

First, the hardness or softness of the water in your area affects the soaking time. Generally speaking, the harder the water the longer the matrix needs to be soaked, and it can vary quite considerably – to the extent, in fact, that two members of the Bromoil Circle who regularly give demonstrations and run workshops always take a container of their own local water supply with them so that they know exactly how long to soak the matrix for. Indeed, some bromoilists go so far as to use distilled water for this soak, but this seems to me a little unnecessary and over the top.

The second factor is the type of paper on which you have made your original print. Broadly speaking, heavyweight papers need more soaking than lightweight materials to make sure the paper is fully saturated. A good rule of thumb is that once you have established the correct time for a lightweight paper, you should use double this time for a heavier paper.

Next, the temperature of the soak water has a profound effect on the soaking time. Higher temperatures enable shorter soaking times, but the temperature has much more of a part to play than simply this. Some regular types of paper, those not made specifically for the bromoil process, have a more substantial supercoat than others and you need to soak them at a higher temperature in order to get the gelatin to swell sufficiently.

From this it follows that the time of year when you are making your bromoils will have an effect on the soaking time. For example, during a very hot summer you will need to soak for a shorter length of time than during the winter, even with central heating. Unless, of course, you have air-conditioning in your darkroom to keep the temperature down during the summer.

The temperature of the soaking water can also be used as a useful control over the contrast of the finished bromoil. Generally, the higher the temperature the more the gelatin swells, and therefore the more the highlights repel the ink leading to a higher contrast in the final print. However, if the temperature is too high it will thin the ink and this will have the opposite effect, so it is all a question of getting the balance right. On the other hand, if you want to lower the contrast of the bromoil, soak the matrix at a lower temperature. Be careful though, if the temperature is too low it will thicken the ink and this will increase the contrast.

TEST PROCEDURE

With all these factors affecting the necessary soak time and the ultimate print quality, there is only one sure way to find out just how long you need to soak the matrix, and that is to carry out a test. Fortunately, this is a simple and inexpensive procedure and you only need to do it once for each combination of paper and ink.

First, make a matrix in the usual way. Do not be tempted to cut corners simply because you know that it is only going to be used for a test. If you do the test will be useless because it does not replicate your usual procedure. Next, cut the matrix into four strips, making sure that each strip contains both highlights and shadow areas. Then super-dry each strip as described in Chapter 4, *see page 55*.

Pour water at 68°F (20°C) or 77°F (25°C) – according to paper – into a developing dish, immerse one of the matrix strips in the water and begin timing. If you have a process timer it is a good idea to use it for the sake of accuracy. Slide the strip into the water face down, agitate for a few seconds, then turn it face up. Leave the matrix strip soaking for five minutes held down with small pieces of cotton wool to keep it completely immersed. Finally, remove the strip and ink it up as described in the next chapter.

When you have finished inking this first strip, soak the second strip in the same way but for 10 minutes then ink that. Then repeat this with the third and fourth strips, soaking for 15 and 20 minutes respectively.

Now allow all four strips to dry and place them side by side in a good light. It should be quite obvious which strip has given the best results in terms of depth of ink and contrast. You should also have found that the chosen strip accepted the ink more easily than the others. However, before carrying out this test, please read the next chapter on inking technique carefully.

Starting points

To help you reduce the amount of time spent on testing you may find the soaking times in the following table helpful. But I must stress that these are only starting points; there is no substitute for testing to establish the correct time for your particular working conditions and the paper you are using.

Paper	Soaking time	Soak temperature
Kentmere Art Document (known as Luminos SW Art in US)	8 mins	77°F (25°C)
Kentmere Bromoil	10 mins	77°F (25°C)
Kentmere Art Deluxe	20 mins	77°F (25°C)
Kentmere Classic	20 mins	77°F (25°C)
Agfa PRN118	10 mins	77°F (25°C)
Ilford Galerie DW Matt	15 mins	77°F (25°C)
Ilford Multigrade DW Matt	12 mins	68°F (20°C)
Forte Polygrade	10 mins	68°F (20°C)
Bergger Brom 240	12 mins	77°F (25°C)
Resin-coated papers	5 mins	68°F (20°C)

All these times assume that the matrix has been super-dried and that the temperature remains within a degree or so of the recommended figure. If the room in which you are working is very cool, start with the water at a slightly higher temperature than that given in the table and allow it to cool during the soaking period.

Additives

Some workers add various chemicals to the soak water in order to achieve more thorough and more even soaking. Among these additives are isopropyl alcohol and sodium hexametaphosphate (commonly available as the anti-limescale agent Calgon).

I have never found the need to add anything to the water except a few drops of wetting agent, but I can understand why others do. In areas of particularly hard water, for example, adding 10 grams or so of Calgon to two litres of soaking water will soften the water and reduce the necessary soaking time.

Wetting agent lowers the surface tension of the water, effectively making it wetter, and this can aid the uniform swelling of the emulsion.

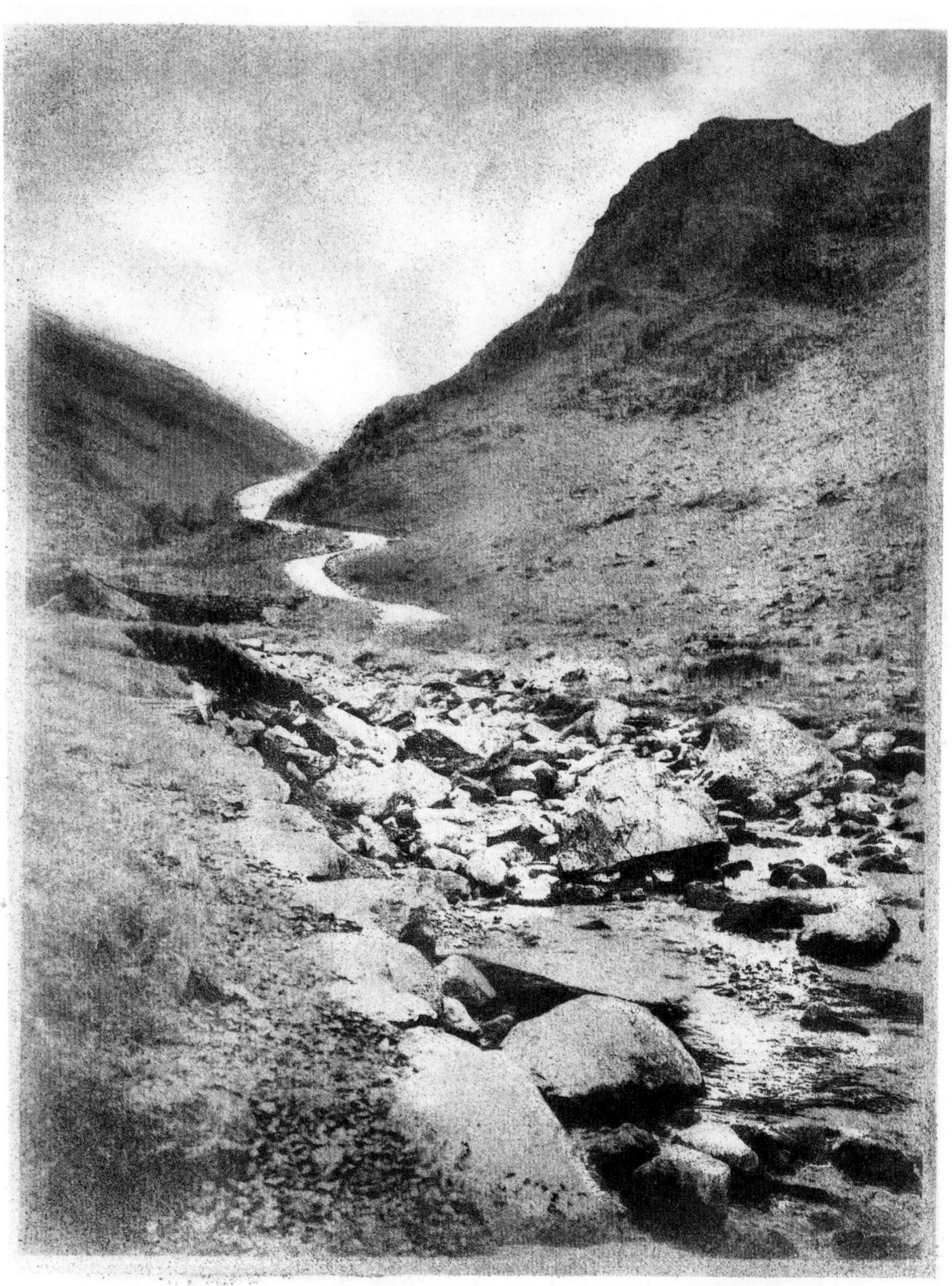

Honister Pass by Colin Ivison

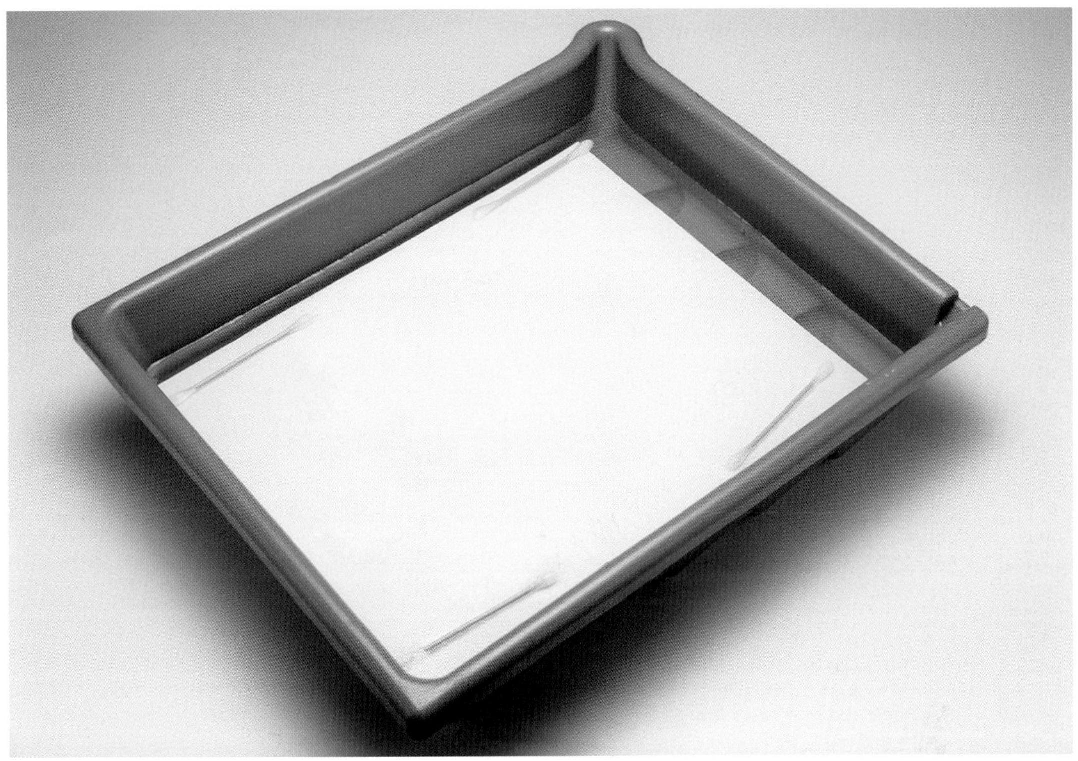

After super-drying, the matrix is soaked in plain water. In this picture the print is held below the surface of the water with a cotton-wool bud at each corner.

SOAKING THE MATRIX

The soaking procedure for a final matrix is exactly the same as that for the soaking test. The most important things to remember are:

1. Super-dry the matrix after bleaching and tanning. If you are unsure whether or not you have done so it will do no harm to super-dry it again immediately before you soak it.
2. Make sure that the matrix remains immersed in the soak water for the entire soaking period. Small pieces of cotton wool or cotton-wool buds to hold the corners down will help.
3. If your workroom is very cool, start with the water a few degrees warmer than recommended and allow it to cool during the soaking period. Conversely, if the room is very warm, start with the water a few degrees cooler and allow it to warm up during soaking.

Drying the matrix

At the end of the soaking time remove the matrix from the water and place it between two sheets of blotting paper to remove most of the surface water. It is vitally important to remove all traces of surface moisture from the matrix before inking.

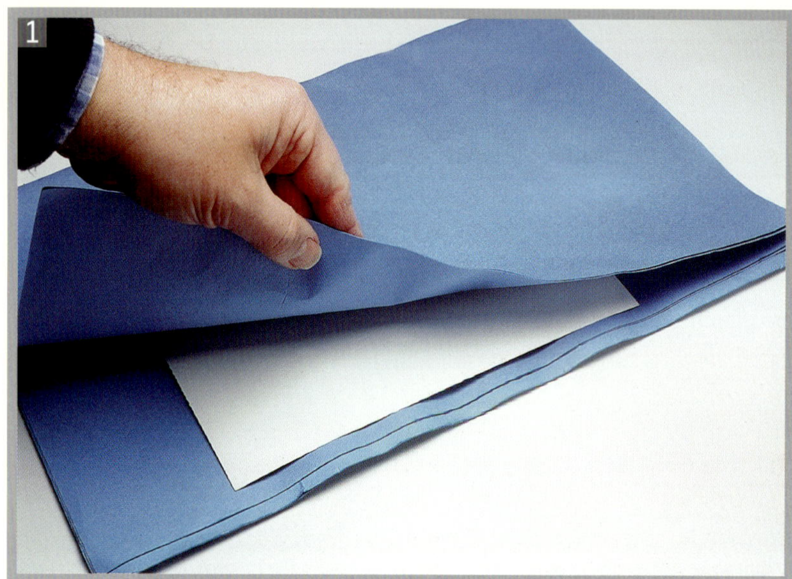

1 The first step is to place the print between sheets of blotting paper. Then place the print face down on the blotting paper and remove any remaining water from the back using a sponge.

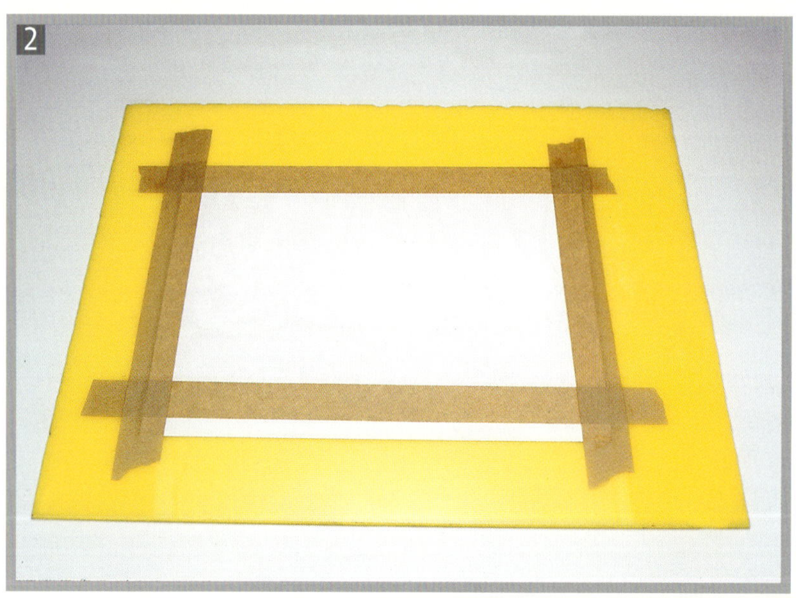

2 Fix the matrix face up on a sheet of glass or Perspex with adhesive tape. Take the tape right up to the image area so that when you remove it after inking, you are left with clean white borders.

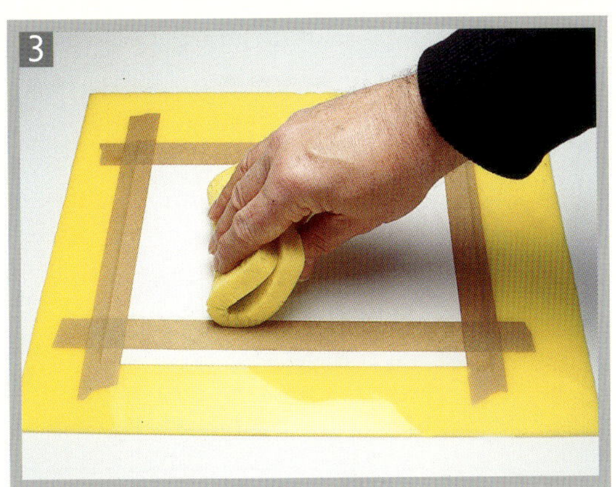

3 Now blot the print again and carefully remove any remaining surface moisture with a sponge or chamois leather.

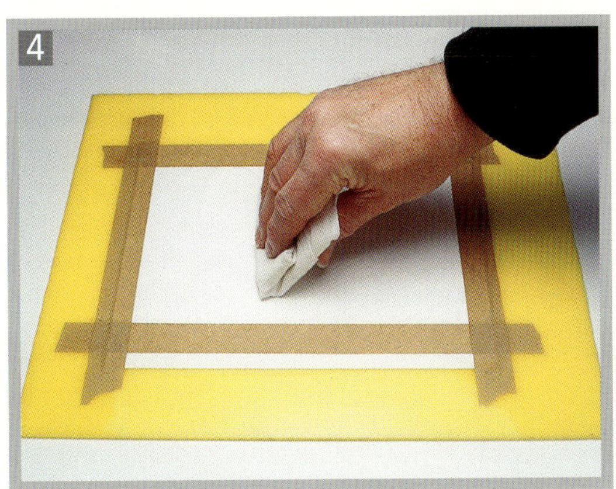

4 Finally, wipe the surface of the matrix with a folded handkerchief or soft, well-washed cotton cloth. It is vital that there are no signs of surface water anywhere on the matrix or the ink will not take and you will be left with white spots on your finished print.

tip

If you choose to use gummed tape you may prefer to wipe the matrix with your sponge and handkerchief before taping it down to prevent any chance of the gum spreading on to the surface of the print.

To make sure that the matrix is completely free of surface moisture before you start inking, hold it at eye level after fixing it to the glass or Perspex support and look across the surface. Any spots of moisture still remaining will show up easily and you can get rid of them with your sponge or chamois leather. You may also be able to see the image of your picture in slight relief or in varying textures as a result of the bleaching and tanning process. You are now ready to start inking your matrix.

Sculptor's studio

When the sculptor Barbara Hepworth died, her studio in St. Ives, Cornwall, England, was left exactly as it was when she finished work, as shown in this picture. The studio now forms part of the Barbara Hepworth Museum, which also includes her garden containing many of her large-scale sculptures.

Original taken on 35mm Olympus OM-1 camera with 28mm lens using Ilford HP5 Plus film and Pyro PMK developer. Initial inking with GC&I 1803 followed by finishing with GC&I 1796 on Kentmere Bromoil paper.

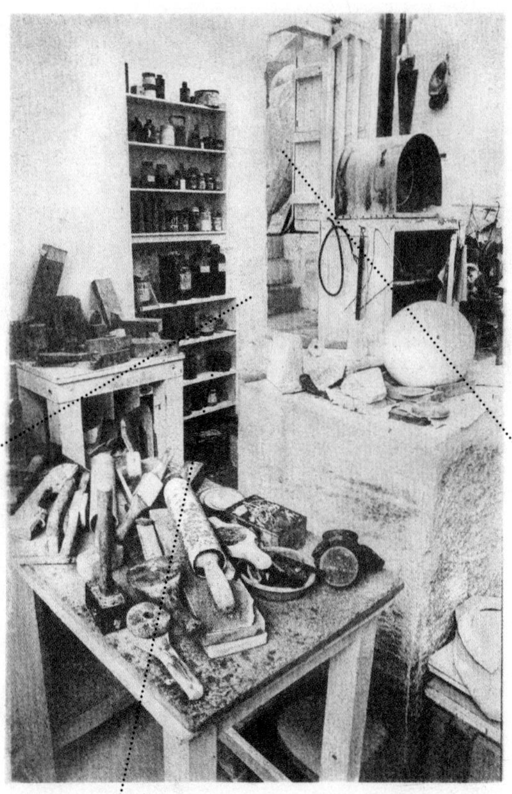

Because two different inks were used for this picture the soak temperature was an important factor. Before the first inking the matrix was soaked at a slightly lower temperature than usual, then before final inking it was soaked again at a higher temperature

Starting with a very hard ink (1803) applied by a foam roller established the basic image contrast and shadow detail

Changing to a softer ink (1792) and brushes reinforced the density in the shadows and built highlight detail in the doorway

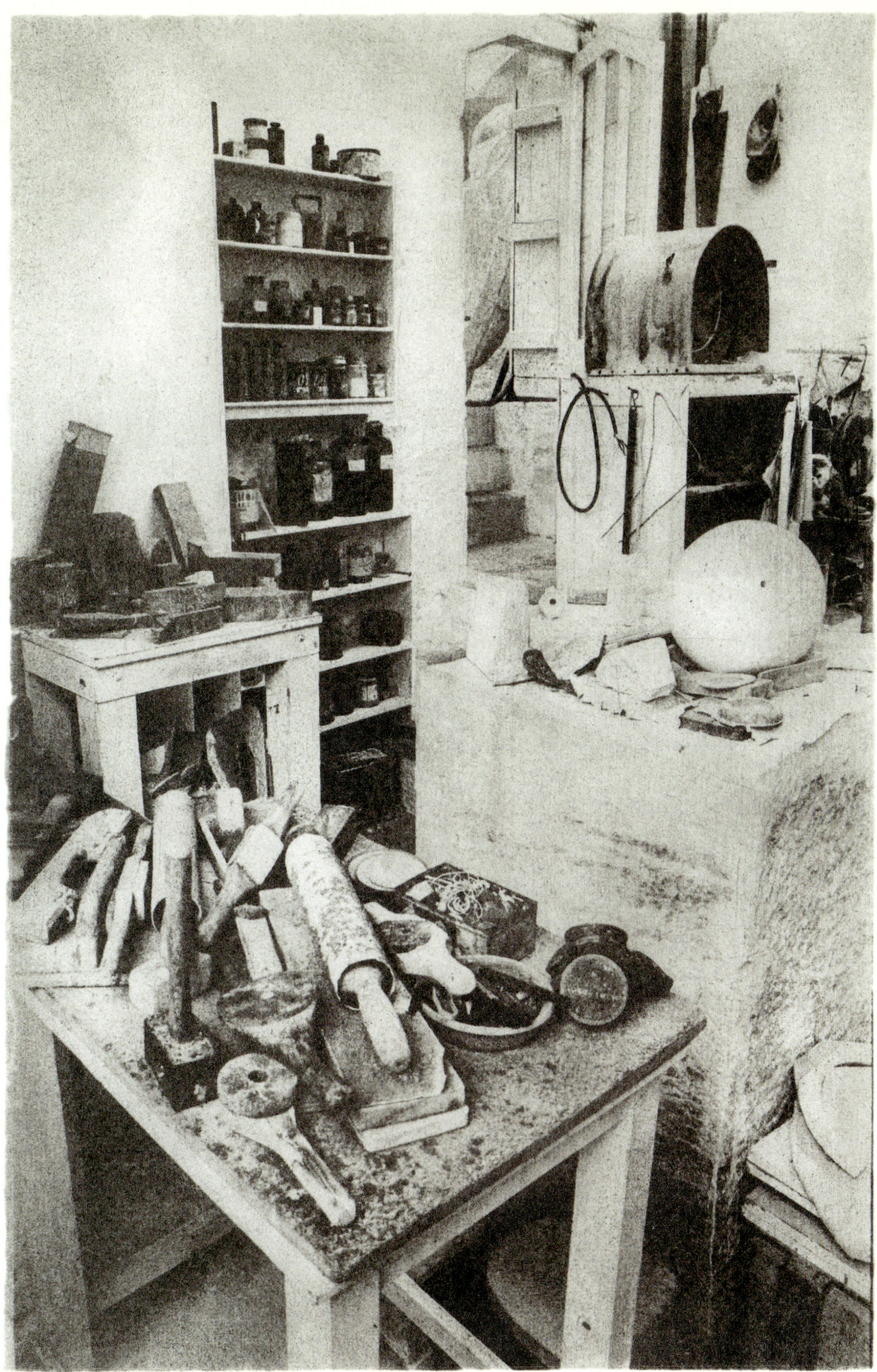

7 Inking the matrix

We now come to the heart of the bromoil process; applying ink to the soaked matrix. This is the point where art takes over from science, because the inking process gives you almost unlimited control over your final bromoil print.

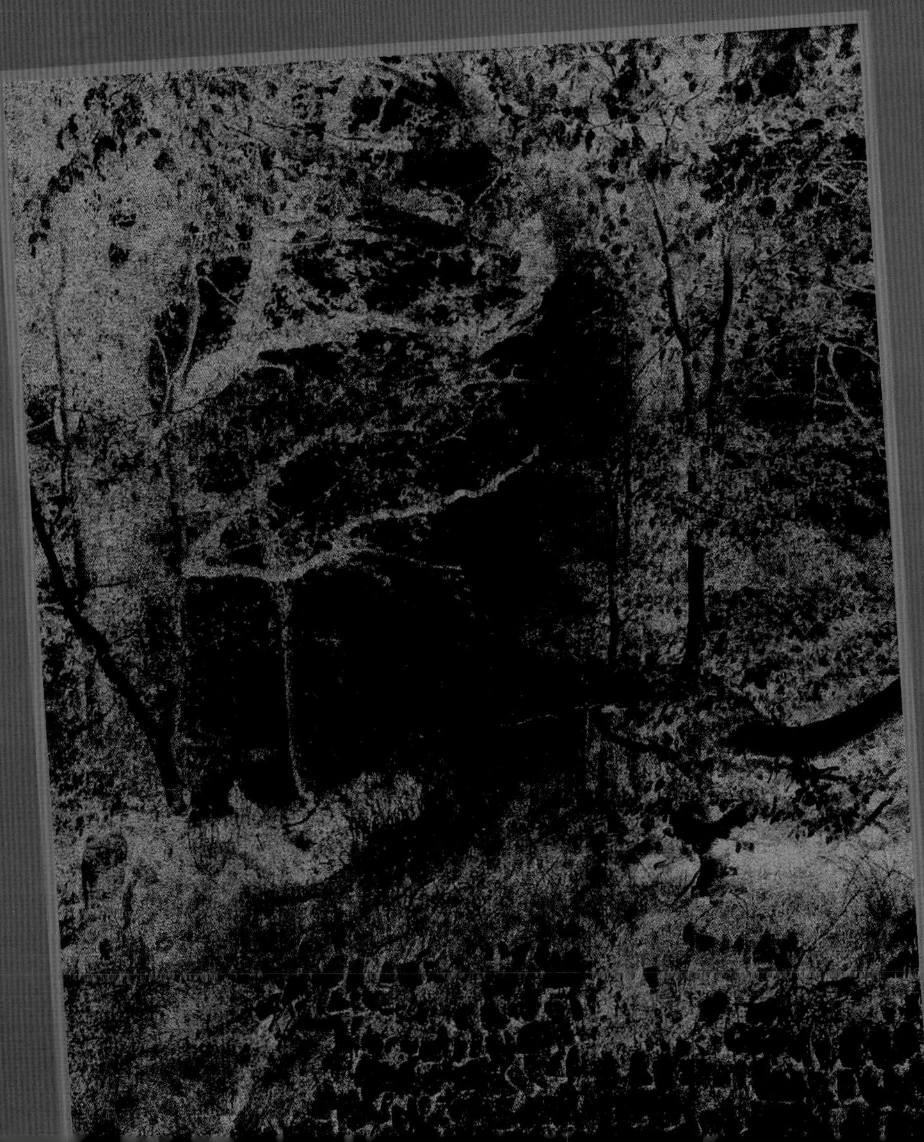

A lot of the skill involved in creating a bromoil is wrapped up in the techniques of the inking process, but before going into the techniques in detail, let us first have a look at the types of inks and brushes to use.

SUITABLE INKS

In the heyday of bromoiling, several companies, such as Sinclair of London, produced inks especially formulated for the process. Sadly, those days have long since gone and the specialist suppliers have gone with them. Today we have to make the best of what is available.

Inks for the bromoil process need to be extremely thick and stiff. The most suitable and popular for bromoiling are lithographic printing inks. The Graphic Chemical & Ink Co of America makes suitable inks in a wide range of colours and these inks are readily available all over the world.

The most suitable inks from the GC&I range are 1796 Black and 1803 Senefelder Crayon Black. You can use one or two of the coloured inks such as Burnt Umber, Litho Purple, and Process Red, Yellow and Blue to add a little warm or cool tone to the basic black ink, but these are not strictly necessary, at least to begin with.

Of the two black inks, 1803 is stiffer than 1796 and is therefore more suitable for use when the soaking has taken place at a lower temperature. To begin with though, I would recommend using 1796, which is fine for most conditions. All the GC&I inks can be used straight from the can and will rarely need to be stiffened or thinned.

Other ink manufacturers include Charbonnel, and other types of ink that can be used include relief-printing inks, although these often need to be stiffened with resin or wax. For this reason I suggest that you start by using a stiff lithographic printing ink. Once you have mastered the basic techniques you can then experiment with other inks.

BROMOIL BRUSHES

In the early days of the bromoil process, at the beginning of the twentieth century, F. J. Mortimer FRPS, at that time editor of *Amateur Photographer* magazine, advocated the use of brushes with a 'stag-foot' shape. The bristles on one side of such a brush are slightly longer than those on the other side. The reason for this was so that you could work on small areas of a print without having to change from a large brush to a small one.

At that time the brushes were made of polecat fitch hair, which was very springy and made the application of ink remarkably easy. The brushes were made commercially and became known as 'Mortimer' brushes.

It is unfortunate that these superb brushes are no longer made and good substitute brushes made by Sinclair from bear hair have also disappeared.

However, there are plenty of alternatives available, although few of them are trimmed to the stag-foot shape. Among those that are is a range available from Silverprint in London and another from David Lewis in Canada.

The truth is, though, that the stag-foot shape is not really necessary. You can ink a bromoil just as easily with a large dome-shaped artists' paintbrush, a shaving brush or a pastry brush. I have even seen an ordinary 2in (50mm) house painters' brush used to ink a bromoil and the result was quite superb. Among the artists' paintbrushes I have used I like the Whistler series, available from good art shops everywhere. These brushes have a really good dome shape and work just as well as the traditional stag-foot shape. The ones I have found particularly good are Series 203, which have a more pointed rather than domed shape; Series S861, a large domed brush with long bristles and a lovely springy action; and Series 71, another dome-shaped brush but rather less expensive. Of all these I like to use the S861 for getting the ink on quickly, and the Series 203 for finer, more delicate work. House painters' sash brushes are a good alternative to the more pointed shape of the Series 203.

Stencil brushes, too, make good bromoil brushes. However, these usually have a flat-ended shape so you may need to trim them. They are available in a wide range of sizes and are relatively inexpensive. You can buy them at art shops, hobby craft shops and at some painting and decorating stores. If you would prefer to use a brush with the traditional shape, it is not difficult to trim one yourself. Inexpensive shaving brushes are particularly suited to home trimming.

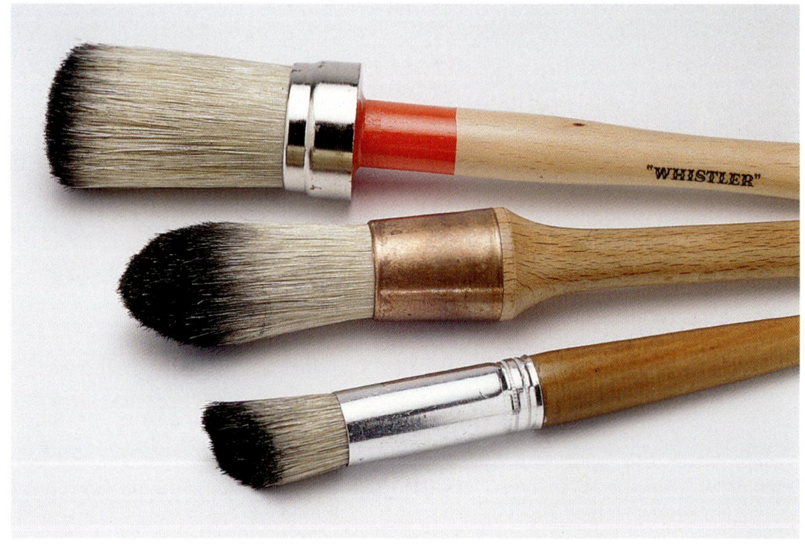

No more than three brushes are necessary to start bromoil inking. A good set is, from top to bottom, a large domed 'Whistler' brush, a rather more pointed brush, and a smaller stencil brush, trimmed to the stag-foot shape if you prefer.

Trimming a shaving brush

The only tool you need to trim a shaving brush to the stag-foot shape is a small pair of sharp scissors. Some workers use electric hairdressers' clippers, but I have never found the need for these except, perhaps, to give a smooth finish.

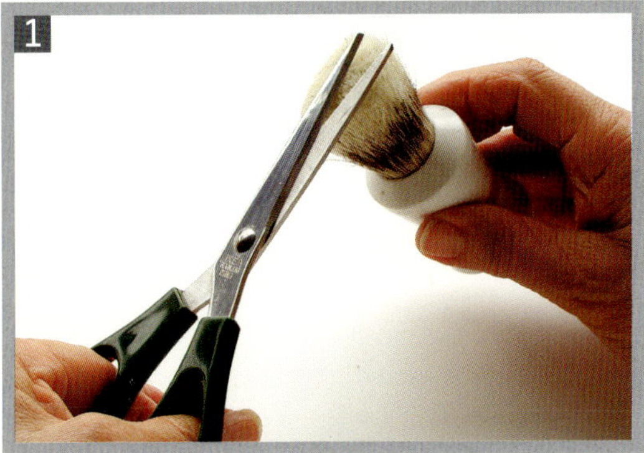

1 A shaving brush makes a good bromoil brush. You can trim it to the traditional stag's-foot shape if you prefer. The first step is to trim the ends of the bristles with a small pair of scissors. Simply take the scissors and carefully start to trim one side of the brush to an angle of about 20 degrees. Cut only a few bristles at a time and take care to get the cut absolutely level. When you have a small angled area on the end of the brush, slowly increase the size of the cut area until you have trimmed the full width of the brush.

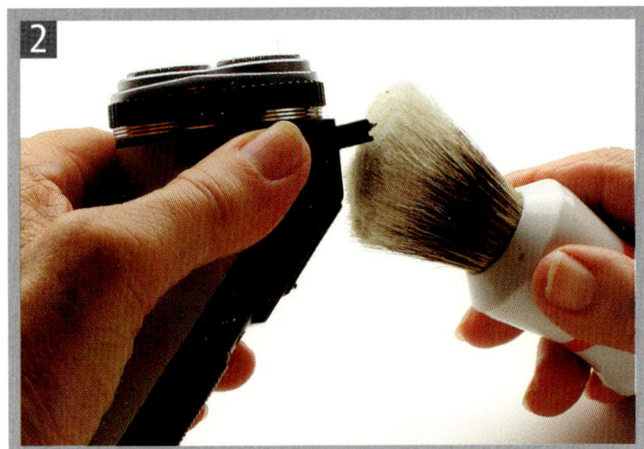

2 Finish the brush by trimming the cut bristles using hair clippers or the beard trimmer on an electric shaver. You may find it easier to use a larger pair of scissors or an electric shaver or clipper for this so that you are able to trim the entire area at once rather than in smaller sections.

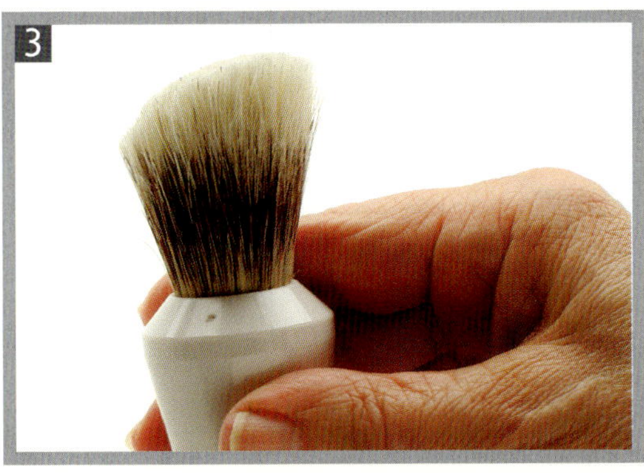

3 Finally, comb the bristles with a fine comb to remove any bristle debris that may have worked its way down to the base of the bristles. If you do not do this, you can be sure that the debris will find its way on to your print when you start inking. You can trim a pastry brush or a large artists' paintbrush in exactly the same way. But as I mentioned earlier, if you buy a dome-shaped paintbrush there is really no need to trim. The finished brush will give good service for many years.

Making a hopper

Back in the 1920s and 30s, Sinclair of London produced an ingenious tool that they called the Sinclair Adjustable Hopper. Its purpose was to make contrast control easier in a bromoil print by enabling the bromoilist to use a very light touch when applying ink in the later stages of the inking process.

The hopper was simply a metal rod about 12in (30cm) long with an adjustable clamp at one end and a wooden handle at the other. The bromoilist slipped the handle of an ordinary bromoil brush into the clamp and tightened the screw. Then, holding the handle of the hopper, he or she could apply the brush very gently to the print with a delicate springy action, or hop – hence the name.

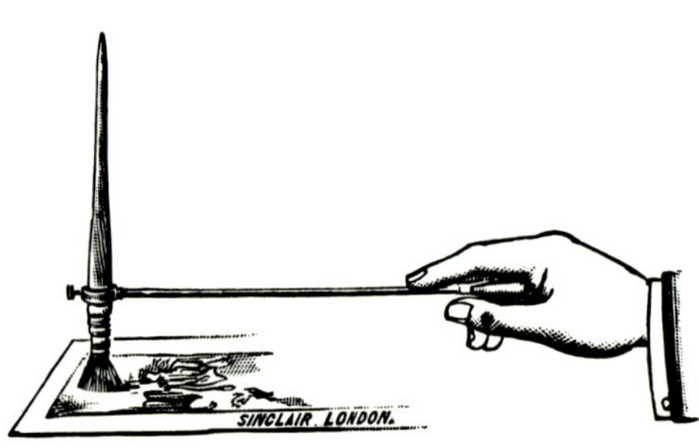

In the heyday of bromoil, Sinclair produced this ingenious device to attach to a bromoil brush to make cleaning up the print easier. Sadly, this is no longer available.

To find out just how effective this tool was, I made one from a shaving brush and a long metal kebab skewer.

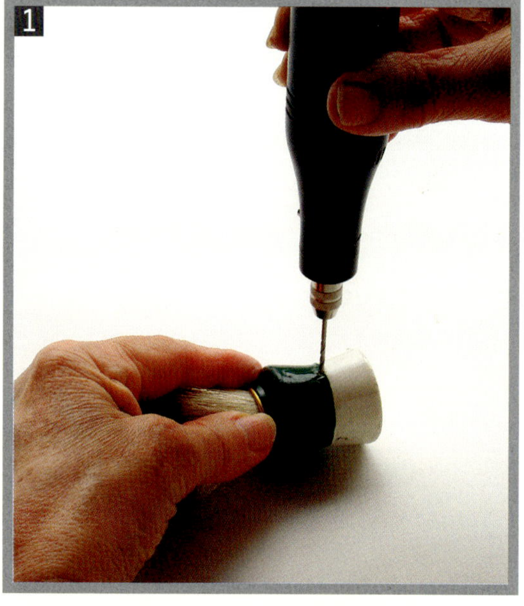

1 You can make a hopper similar to the one made by Sinclair many years ago by modifying a shaving brush. First, drill a hole in the side of the brush of a diameter to suit a kebab skewer.

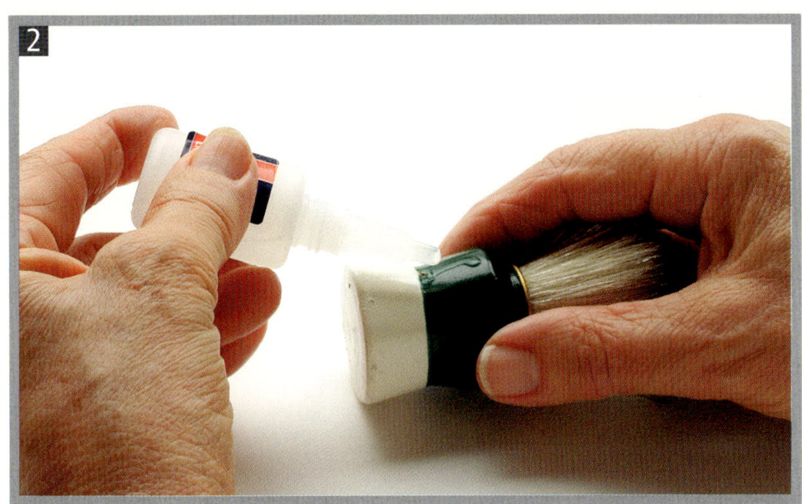

2 Next, put a couple of drops of superglue into the hole.

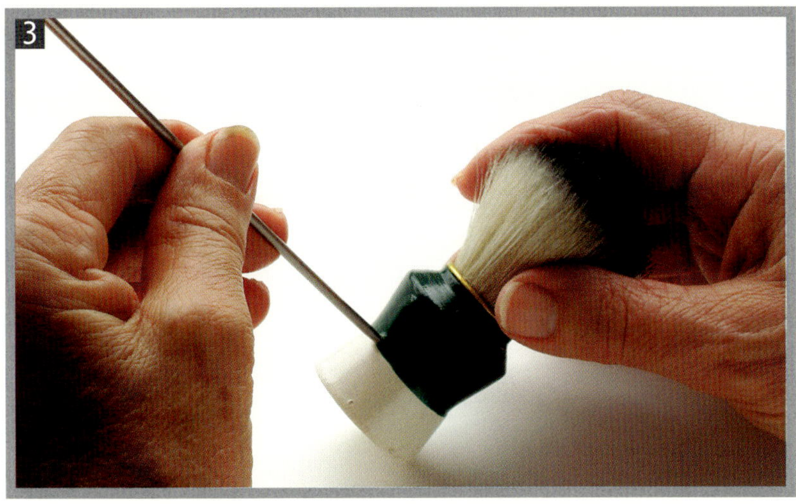

3 Finally, push the skewer into the hole and wait a few seconds for the superglue to set.

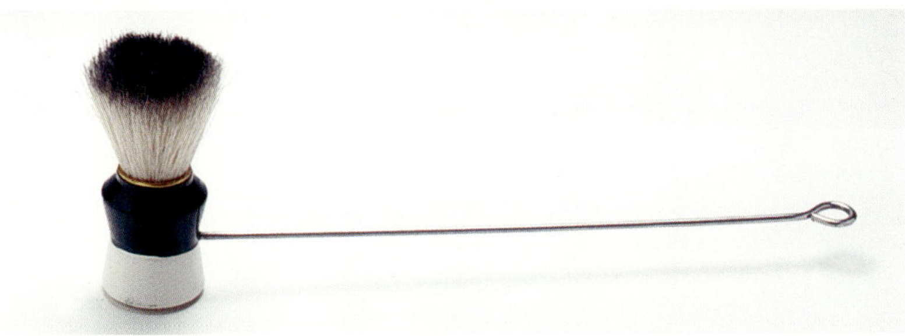

When I tried the finished brush I was amazed at just how easy it made contrast control, cleaning up highlights beautifully and strengthening shadows.

A working set of brushes

When starting out in bromoil printing the temptation is to buy brushes of all sizes by the dozen. But you very quickly find yourself using just one or two and the rest sit in your brush box hardly ever touched. I know, because I have done this myself.

Better by far is to start with just a couple of brushes and add to them as you find the need to. One of your starter brushes should be a large dome-shaped brush that will cover large areas of the matrix quickly and can be used at an angle to work on smaller areas. You can use a shaving brush – trimmed or untrimmed – for this. The other should be a smaller brush, possibly with somewhat softer bristles, for adding detail towards the end of the inking process. You can, if you like, add a second large brush with a more pointed shape, and perhaps a home-made hopper to make contrast control easier.

This will provide a good set of brushes to start with. Learn to use them properly and practise your inking technique on scrap matrices. You will probably find that you want to add other brushes later, but only do so if you really feel the need for a particular brush to make a certain task easier.

Looking after your brushes

Unless you intend to ink more matrices within a day or so, clean your brushes carefully when you have finished. Some bromoilists do not clean their brushes regularly and at least one, the late Norman Gryspeerdt FRPS, claimed never to clean his brushes or his inking tile at all. But personally I do not feel happy leaving my brushes in a dirty, inky state.

By far the best cleaning medium I have found is petroleum-based lighter fluid. It gets rid of the ink easily and evaporates quickly

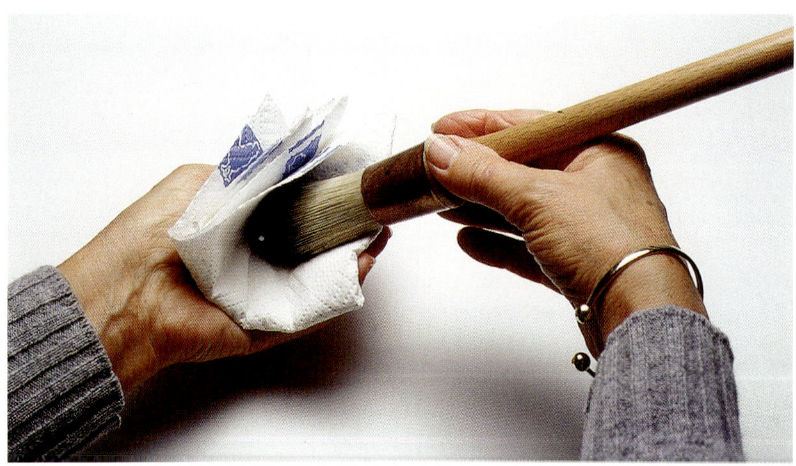

Clean brushes by sprinkling a little lighter fluid onto a paper kitchen towel and gently dabbing the bristles until no more ink comes off.

leaving the brushes dry and clean. You only need to sprinkle a very few drops on to a cloth or paper towel and work the bristles of the brush with the towel until no more ink will come off them.

White spirit is another good choice, but it does not evaporate as quickly. Even a day or two after cleaning brushes in this solvent, traces can be found and will thin the ink when you start work next time.

caution

Both lighter fluid and white (mineral) spirit are highly flammable and noxious substances. Take care not to expose them to sources of ignition and not to inhale their fumes or otherwise ingest them. Always ensure that they are stored safely.

To keep your brushes in shape, make a thin card hood that slides over the bristles from the handle end of the brush. Just cut a length of thin card, wrap it fairly tightly round the bristles and use a piece of sticky tape to hold the ends of the card together. This will prevent the bristles from spreading and keep the brush in shape for many years.

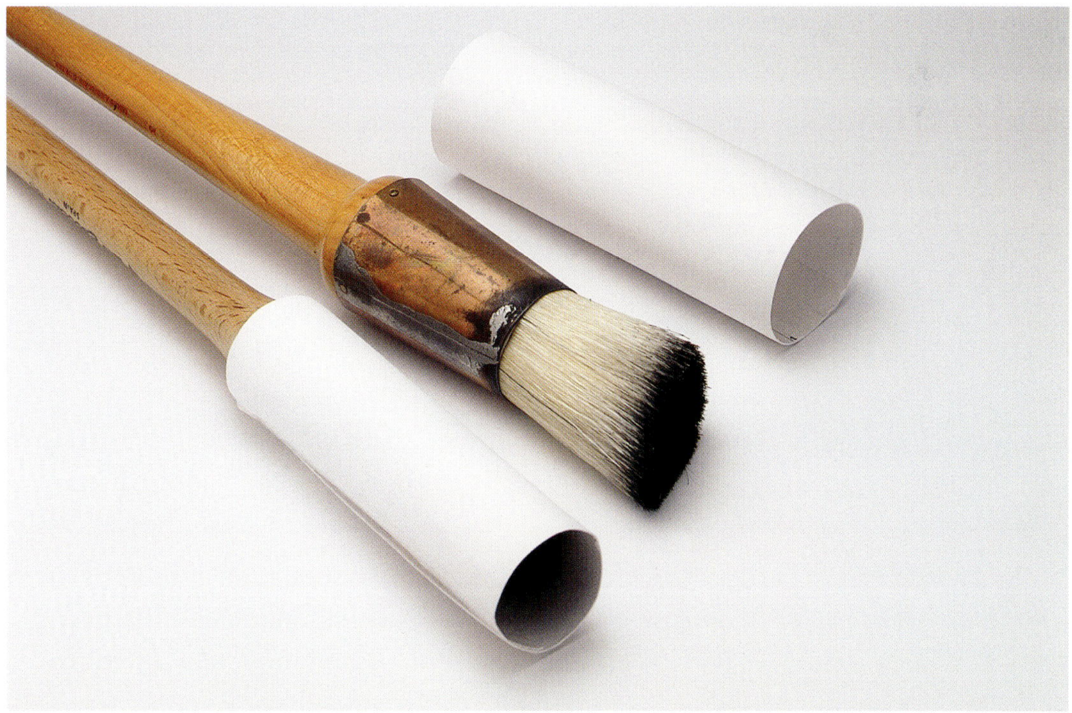

When you are not using your brushes, protect the bristles with a hood of thin card.

T TERMINOLOGY / Ferrule

This is the metal sleeve around the end of a brush handle, which holds the bristles in place. It is one of the most important features of a brush because a poorly fitting ferrule can cause the bristles to become loose and fall onto the bromoil print.

Day-to-day maintenance During any inking session a certain amount of debris, such as dried ink and pieces of broken bristle, will build up in your brushes. If you do not remove this rubbish it will inevitably find its way on to the surface of one of your prints. Although it is quite easy to remove this debris from the finished print it is far better to prevent it getting there in the first place. However gently you try to brush it off the print there is always the danger of smudging the ink.

The easiest way to remove debris from your bromoil brushes is to use a small brush with stiff bristles – like a brush you would use to clean suede shoes. Clean the bromoil brush by gently brushing down from the ferrule to the ends of the bristles. If you do this over a piece of white paper you will see just how much debris has collected in your brushes.

When you store your brushes, always make sure they have their protective hoods in place. Store them flat in a box, hang them up or stand them upright in a pot with the handles down. Never store them standing on their bristles or you will distort the shape of the brush. If you take these elementary precautions with your bromoil brushes they will give you a lifetime of reliable service.

Brushless bromoil

Although the practice makes many traditionalist bromoilists throw up their hands in horror, it is quite practical to ink up a bromoil without using brushes at all. Instead, you can simply use a foam roller.

The advantages of this method are that it is much quicker to ink a print and that less skill is required than when using brushes. On the downside, you do not have the same degree of control that is possible when using brushes.

The type of roller you need for inking in this way is that normally sold for applying gloss paint to doors. It is made of soft foam and should not be confused with the sheepskin type of roller used for applying emulsion paint. The soft foam type of roller is very cheap to buy and when it becomes too inky to use reliably it can be thrown away and replaced with a new one at minimal cost.

THE INKING PROCESS

While the matrix is soaking, take a small amount of ink – about the size of a pea – on the tip of your palette knife and spread it in a small patch on the inking tile. Mix the ink well by spreading and removing it with the knife until you have a patch about 1½in (3cm) square.

Now, holding the palette knife at an angle of about 45 degrees to the tile, gently scrape the ink off the tile until there is just a thin layer left. Leave the surplus ink on the knife to replenish the supply on the tile later. The ink should be very stiff and will be quite difficult to spread evenly at first. But do not be tempted to thin it with linseed oil or turpentine. You should always aim to use the ink at full strength, at least for the initial inking; if necessary you can thin it a little during the later stages of inking. Alternatively you can use a small hard-rubber roller to spread the ink on the tile. Spread and remove the ink as before, but instead of scraping it off the tile, use the roller finally to spread the ink in a very thin layer. This will provide a larger patch of ink than the spreading method but this does not really matter as you will use it eventually anyway.

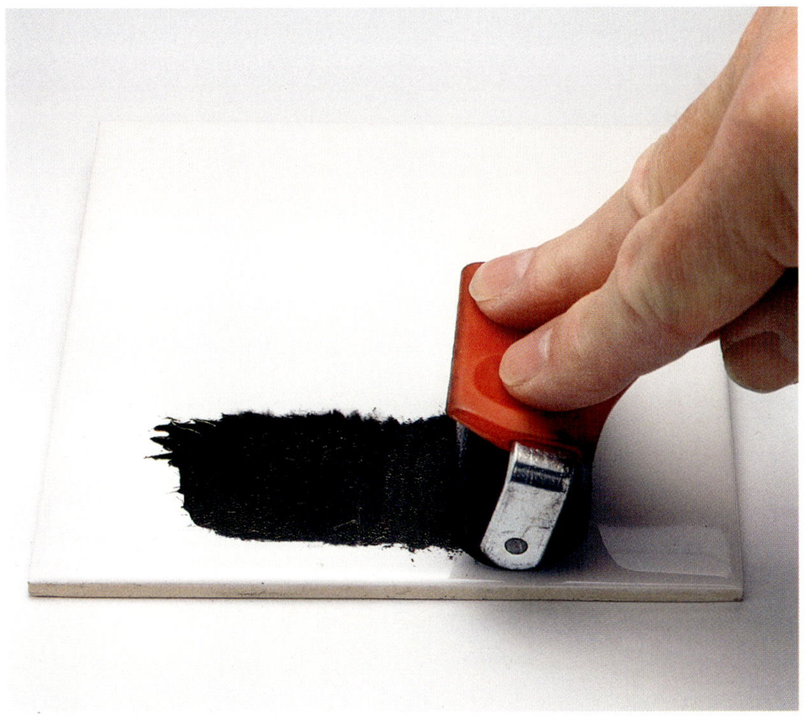

Spread a small amount of ink on the tile using either a palette knife or, as shown here, a small hard rubber roller.

Now take your large inking brush and dab it on the patch of ink so that only the tips of the bristles pick up ink. Dab the brush on a clean area of the tile to deposit the ink. Repeat this procedure until you have a second, very thin, patch of ink. When you begin applying ink to the matrix take it only from this second patch.

Initial inking

The purpose of the initial inking is to get an even, moderate layer of ink over the surface quickly while the matrix is still uniformly damp. Take your largest brush, preferably a stag-foot or slightly pointed shape, and charge it with ink. Tap the bristles lightly on the second, very thin, patch of ink on your palette. Make sure that only the tips of the bristles pick up the ink but ensure that all of the bristles are charged.

Now apply the ink using a pressing and dragging action – press-drag-lift, repeat – over the whole surface, at no stage should the brush be lifted completely from the surface. Hold the brush nearly vertically with a firm grip near the top of the handle. Dab it down firmly until the whole of the working area touches the matrix, spreading the bristles a little. Then drag it towards you slightly and relax your grip on the handle allowing the natural spring of the bristles to lift the brush as shown right. With practice you can 'walk' the brush.

When the ink has been spread thinly on the palette, use you brush to transfer as little as possible to a clean area of the tile, producing a very thin patch of ink. Take the ink only from this patch when inking the print.

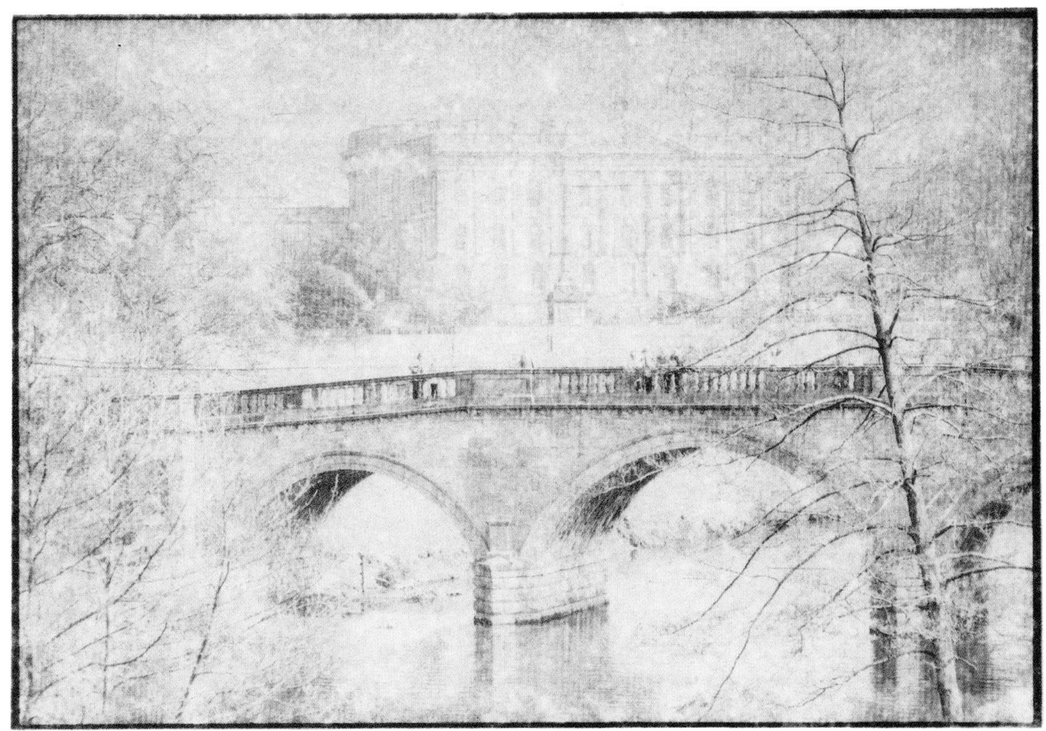

The purpose of the initial inking is to cover the whole matrix with a uniform thin layer of ink.

Start at the top left and work in strips to the bottom right-hand corner, recharging your brush as necessary. If you are left-handed you can reverse this process if it is easier.

When you have finished applying the ink to the whole matrix, turn it through 90 degrees and repeat the process. Then turn it through a further 90 degrees and repeat the inking again, and finally turn it through yet another 90 degrees and apply the ink once more. By the time you have finished you will have applied four thin layers of ink, and the matrix, will have been rotated completely.

The matrix is now covered by a thin, even layer of ink. It looks grey, muddy and grainy, but the image should show through.

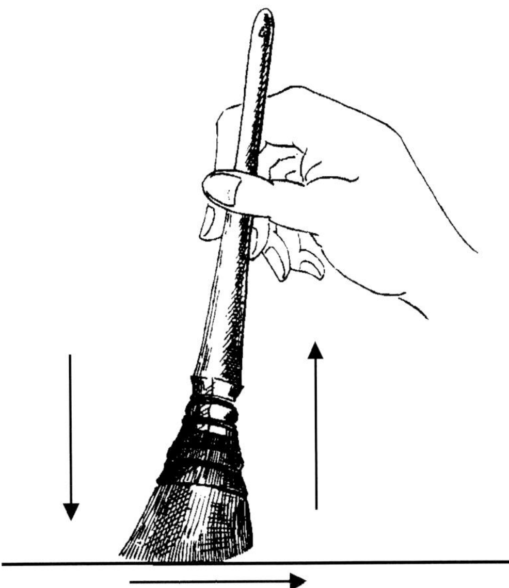

This drawing illustrates the 'down, drag, spring' motion that is used to 'walk' a brush.

Clearing stage

After applying the initial layer of ink you need to increase the contrast of the image, clearing the muddy highlights and strengthening the shadows. To do this you should change your action to a light, rapid dabbing movement.

Without recharging your brush, hold the bristles about 1in (25mm) above the print and dab gently down on to the surface, allowing the bristles to spread so that the whole working area of the brush is in contact with the print. Then allow the brush to spring a back to its original position just above the surface. In fact, you should help the brush to spring away from the surface of the print by almost snatching it up. This will ensure that the bristles leave the surface quickly and cleanly. Do not drag the brush at all during this stage. What you are trying to do is not to apply additional ink, but to redistribute excess ink from the highlight areas into the shadows. This will have the effect of both improving the clarity of your print and increasing its contrast. Use a flexible wrist action with this dabbing stage, see below left, and keep your arm still to avoid putting too much pressure on the bristles. It needs a light but firm touch.

Use the two brush actions – walking and dabbing – alternately to build up strength and contrast in your print.

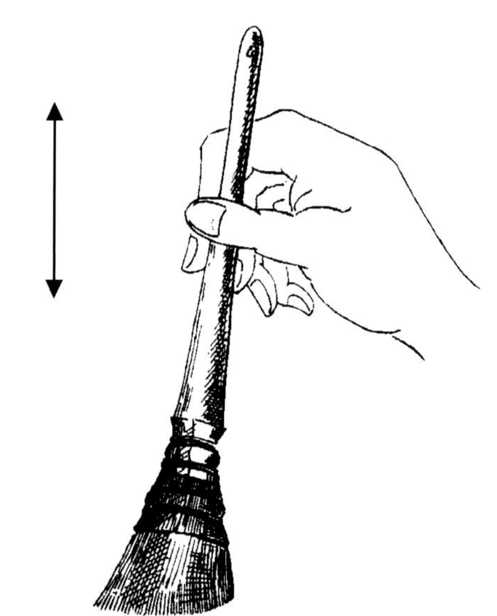

When the whole print is covered with a thin layer of ink, use a rapid dabbing action – without dragging – to increase the contrast of the image.

Re-moistening

Sometimes, especially when you first start bromoiling, you may find that the print does not clean up sufficiently while you are using the dabbing action. This is usually an indication that the matrix has started to dry out and that it needs to be moistened again.

To do this you should take a pad of cotton wool or a wide foam paintbrush, soak it with water and gently squeeze most of the water out. Wipe the entire surface of the print quickly but gently. Then immediately wipe the entire surface with your viscose sponge or a well-wrung-out chamois leather and then once again with a dry handkerchief or cloth to make sure that all of the moisture has been removed from the surface.

The effect of this re-moistening will be a dramatic increase in the contrast and clarity of the image. It is worth re-moistening the print in this way even if it has not begun to dry out. Indeed, this stage has now become a standard part of my inking procedure. You can, if you wish, place the bromoil in a dish of water and work on it with the cotton wool or foam brush under the water. But in order to do this correctly you will need either a flat-bottomed dish or a piece of Perspex laid in the bottom of the dish to provide a completely flat surface.

Intermediate inking

You can now use the dabbing brush action to add more ink to the matrix to build up density in your print.

Charge your brush with ink as you did before, but this time use the dabbing action to apply it to the bromoil rather than the walking action. You will find that you need to be quite a lot more gentle when applying the ink using this action compared to when you are using it to increase the contrast of the image. This intermediate inking should quickly build up the strength and contrast of your print. If you

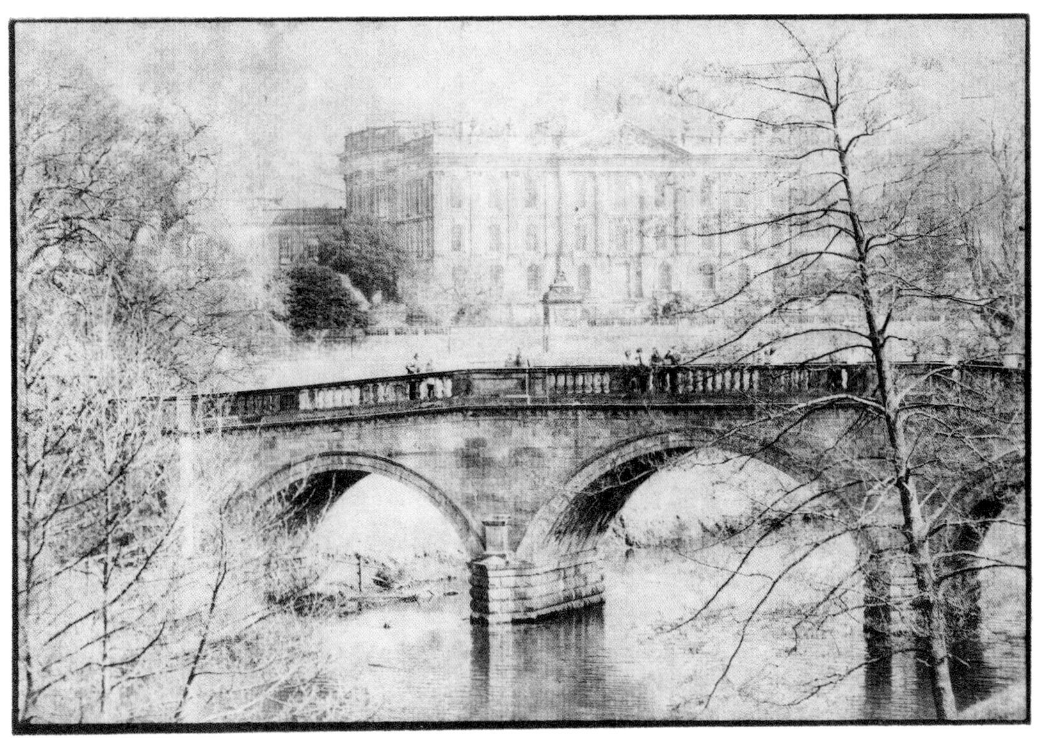

Secondary inking adds depth and contrast to the print.

find that the highlight areas of the image are becoming too muddy then use a vigorous dabbing action to clear them. You may also find that another re-moistening of the bromoil will help.

As you continue to build up the image you can work on specific areas of it. Use a smaller brush to add ink to the shadows and wet cotton-wool buds when you are lightening the highlights. Always be very careful to remove any water from the surface of the image before you start applying any more ink.

Final stages

When you have built the strength and contrast of your print to the point where you are making no further progress it is time to clean up the highlights and bring out any hidden detail in both highlights and shadows. To do this you need to change your brush action once again, this time to the hopping or sweeping action.

The hopping action is very similar to the dabbing action, but in this case you need to hold the brush quite loosely. Allow the handle to slide through your fingers and bounce off the surface of the print, then catch the handle on the rebound. For this stage of the inking process I use a fresh, clean brush, and I usually choose a more dome-shaped brush than the one I use for inking. Alternatively I use my home-made hopper (see below and *pages 82–3*) which I find does the job of cleaning highlights and bringing out detail very quickly and easily.

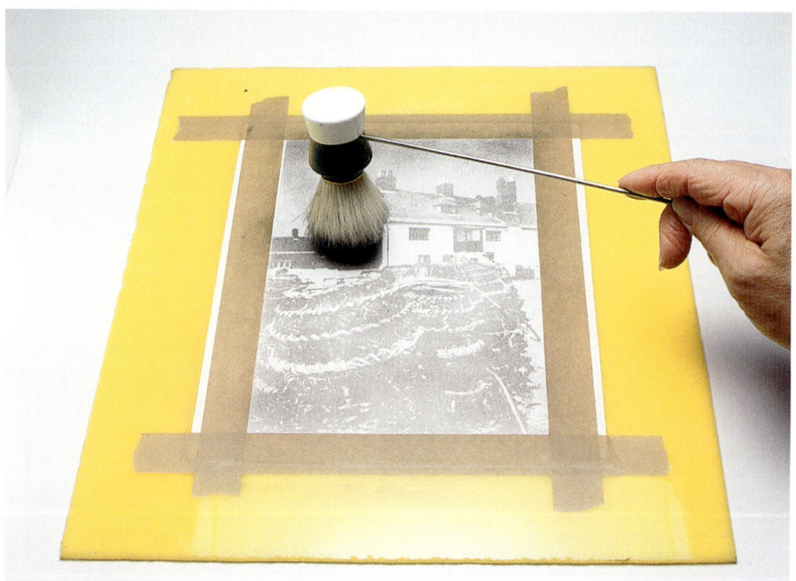

A home-made hopper makes cleaning highlights extremely quick and easy. Allow the bristles to bounce lightly on the surface of the print.

An alternative method is a gentle sweeping action, right, its only disadvantage is that you can smudge the ink, destroying the bromoil's characteristic crisp grain. By combining these actions you will eventually have a print that you are happy with. At this point, resist the temptation to work on it any further.

Finally, clean up the safe area of the print around the image area with wet cotton wool or a cosmetic sponge and remove any surface

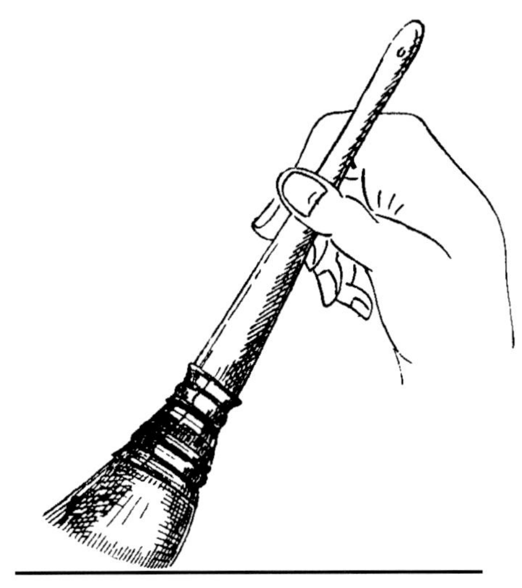

After using the walking and dabbing actions to build up strength and contrast use the hopping or sweeping action to clean up the highlights.

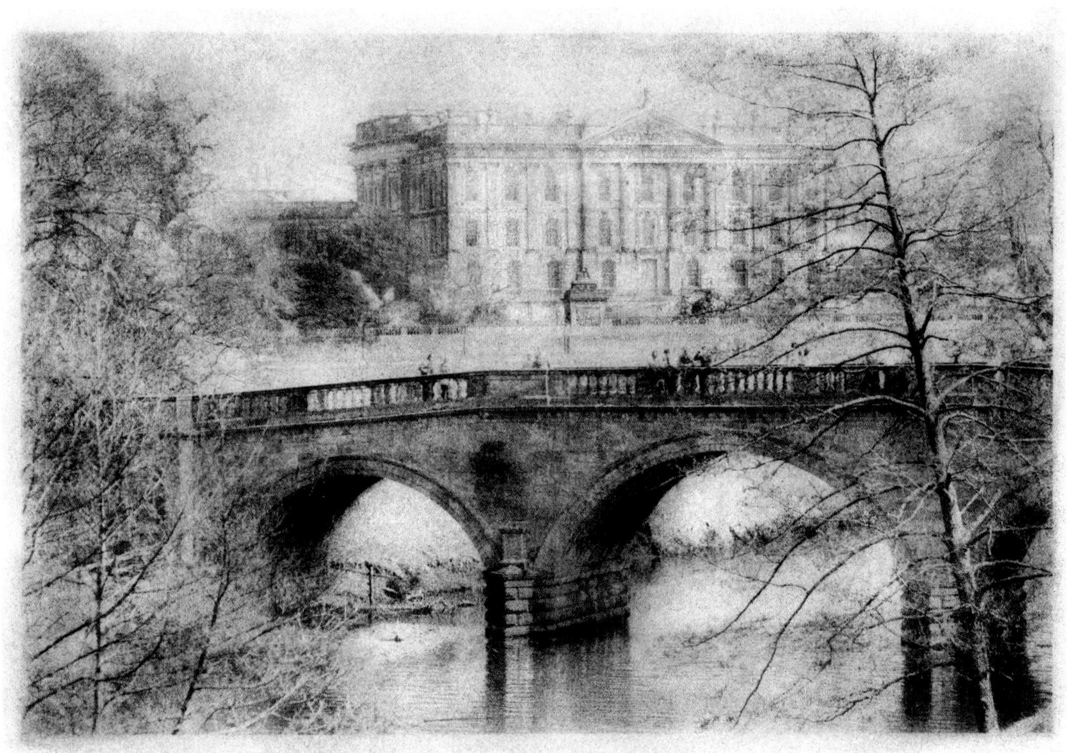

***Chatsworth*, Derbyshire. The finished bromoil after cleaning the highlights with the hopping or sweeping brush action. Original taken on 35mm Olympus OM-1 camera with 135mm lens using Ilford FP4 film and Microphen developer. Initial inking with GC&I 1803, finished with GC&I 1796 on Kentmere Bromoil paper.**

water. Of course, if you have taped the matrix to its support, with the tape abutting the image, you will not have to clean the safe area because the tape will have protected it.

Hang up the print to dry naturally. This should take a few hours, but it will be a day or two before the ink has set sufficiently to avoid smudging. Always handle the print with care and protect it between sheets of acid-free paper when you store it ready for mounting.

Using a roller

As an alternative method for the initial inking stage you can use a foam roller to apply the ink instead of a brush. Many of the old-school traditionalist bromoil workers frown on this method of inking, but they tend to forget that back in the early 1900s G. E. H. Rawlins used a roller to apply ink to his oil prints from which the bromoil process was derived. However, there is no one right way to ink a bromoil; that is part of the beauty of the process. Just go with what works for you. I do.

The main advantages of using a roller are that it is much faster than using a brush and it applies the first layer of ink much more smoothly than a brush.

You can use a roller for all the inking, but the finished print will be much smoother and almost photographic in appearance with more contrast. The roller tends to suppress the grain and softness which are the characteristics of a bromoil print. For this reason, many workers use a combination of both roller and brush. The roller is used for the initial application of the ink, while the brush is used in the later stages of application and for working up smaller areas of the print. In this way you can get the best of both worlds: a faster process with a great deal of control.

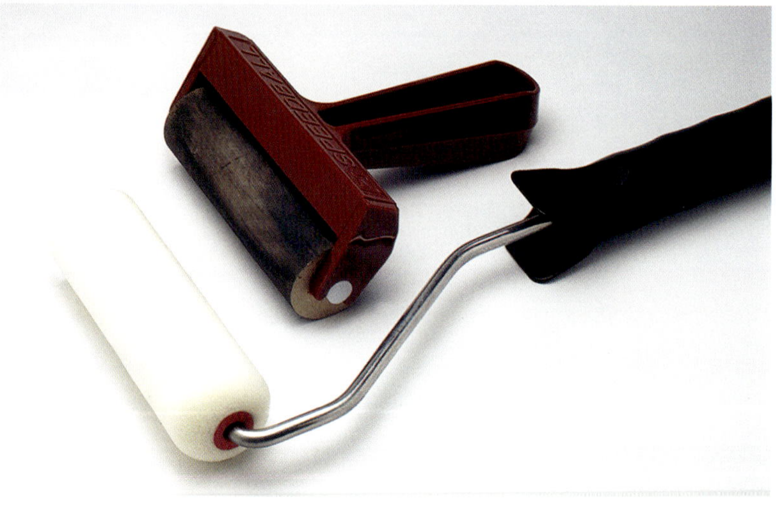

Many bromoilists use rollers either to ink a print completely or, more often, for the initial application of ink. Foam gloss paint rollers are the most suitable but, used with care, a soft rubber roller can work well.

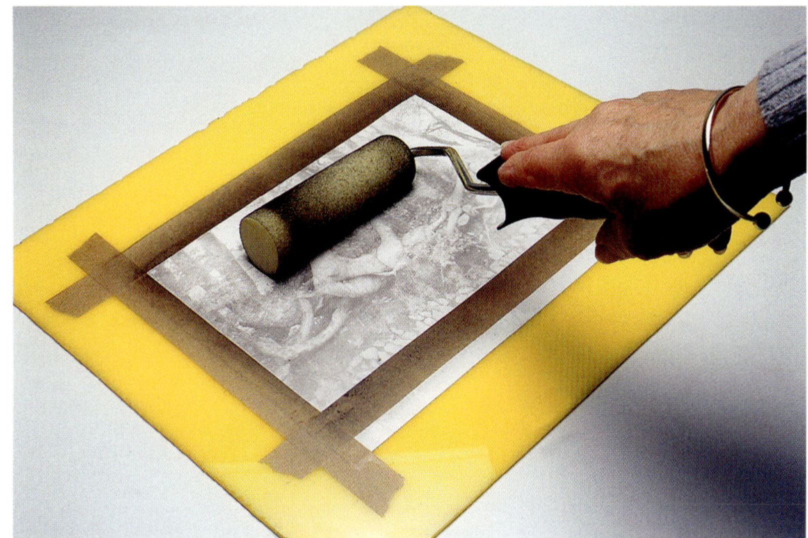

If you prefer to use a roller for initial inking, work over the whole area of the print slowly, applying even pressure, and rolling in one direction only.

As I mentioned earlier, the best kind of roller to use is the foam type sold at hardware and interior-decorating stores for applying gloss paint. They are about 4in (10cm) wide and are often sold in a pack containing one handle and two rollers. Additional rollers normally come in packs of two.

Working procedure

Using a palette knife or hard rubber roller spread the ink on your palette tile exactly as you would for brush inking. Next, using the hard rubber roller, transfer some of the ink to a clean area of the tile and roll it out into a thin patch. Then take a little ink from this thin patch on your inking roller and roll it out evenly on a clean tile or larger piece of glass. It is from this area that you should take the ink to apply to the matrix.

It is advisable to tape the matrix down on to the glass or Perspex support when using a roller for inking. This will prevent the matrix being picked up and wrapped around the roller as you work. Use gummed tape for this job. Take up a little ink on the roller and slowly, with pressure, apply the roller to the matrix, rolling in one direction only. Work over the whole matrix, starting at the top left and re-inking the roller as necessary. When you get to the bottom right, turn the print through 90 degrees and again work from top left to bottom right. Repeat this procedure until the print is back at its starting orientation.

Next, clean the roller by rolling it on to a clean tile. Then very rapidly and very lightly roll over the entire image area, this time rolling in both directions. This will quickly clear the image and any overlapping streaks should

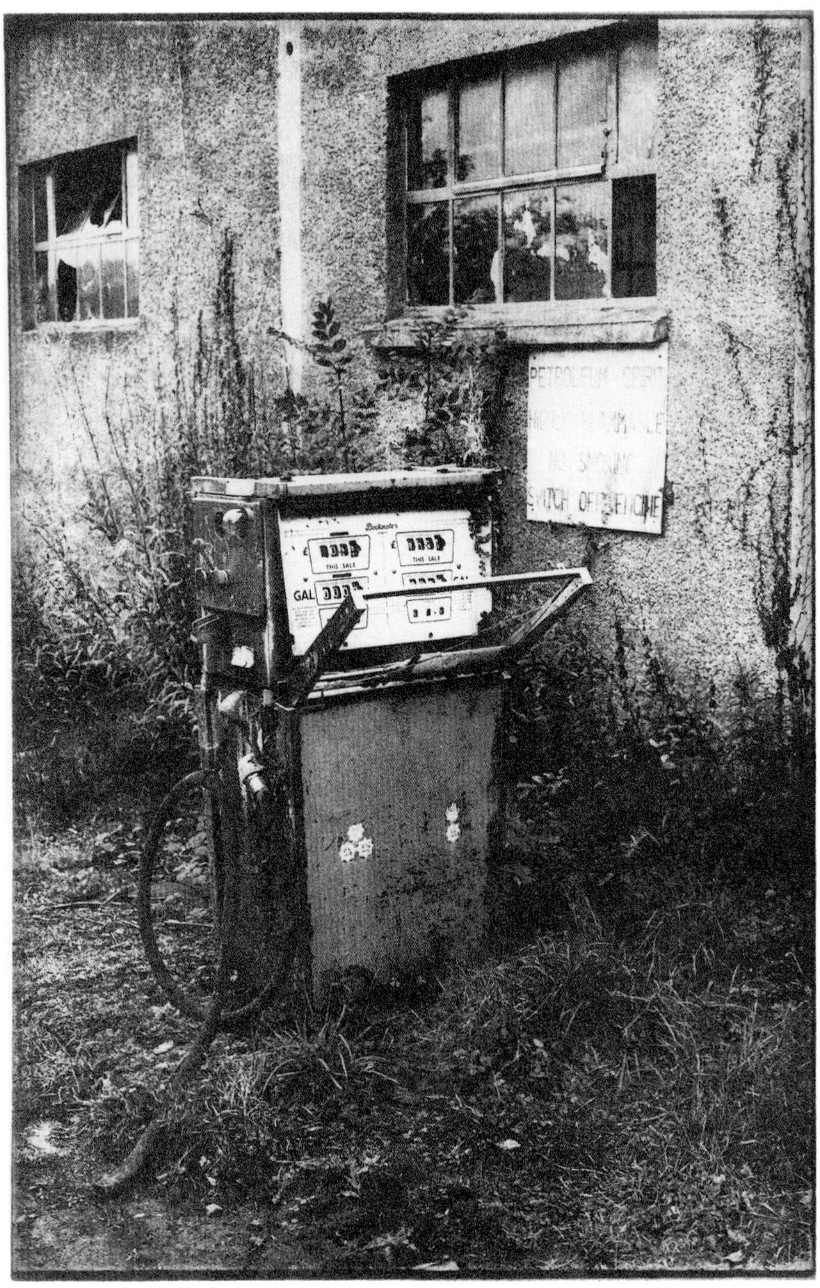

Abandoned fuel pump, Blackaller quarry, Dartmoor, Devon, England. Original taken on 35mm Olympus OM-2 camera with 28mm lens using Ilford HP5 Plus film and Pyro PMK developer. Inked with GC&I 1796 ink on Kentmere Art Document paper using a roller only to retain the feeling of a photo.

disappear. You can also use a fresh, clean roller for this job. Incidentally, you can use this light, rapid roller action instead of the dabbing brush action to clear a brush-inked bromoil after the initial inking. If the print is still rather muddy when you have cleared it with the roller, wipe it over with a wet foam brush or a pad of wet cotton wool, exactly as for brush inking. Then remove all surface water before you continue inking.

Build up the density of the image by applying more ink, clearing the print periodically with the light, rapid roller action, until you are happy with it. Alternatively, put aside your roller and continue inking up with brushes as I have already described.

Adding ink after drying

If you get to the point where the matrix appears not to want to accept any more ink, dry the print, leave it for a day or two, then re-soak it and start inking again. Quite often you will find that because the original ink has dried and hardened, the matrix will accept additional ink more easily.

Although early exponents of the bromoil process did not recommend this practice, it is now quite widely used. Nor does there appear to be any time limit on when you can do this. Even several weeks or months – years, maybe – later you will find that you can add more ink to strengthen shadows and add highlight details.

Knowing when to stop

One of the biggest problems, especially when learning how to ink bromoils, is knowing when to stop. It is easy to keep thinking that a little more ink might improve the picture, but then find you have gone too far.

This happened to me when I started bromoiling, so I made a conscious effort to avoid over-inking, but then found I had not taken the inking far enough. Fortunately, it is fairly easy to correct either of these faults. If you have not taken the inking far enough, you can simply re-soak the matrix later and add more ink. It is a little more difficult if you have over-inked the image, but you can remove excess ink by using the techniques that are described at the end of the next chapter and in Chapter 9.

When judging your bromoils, always do so in a good light – preferably diffused daylight – and always mask off the border around the image with L-shaped white cards in order to isolate the picture.

If you have any ink left on your palette and you intend to make more bromoils the next day, lay a piece of clingfilm or aluminium foil over the ink and seal the edges. This will prevent the air getting to the ink and will keep it at the right consistency.

Practice makes perfect

The techniques of inking with brushes and rollers covered in this chapter are much easier actually to do than they are to describe. You should find it quite simple to apply ink and to achieve acceptable results fairly quickly. However, you should not expect perfect results with your first bromoil. Like any other technique, especially one that relies on dexterity and judgement as bromoil inking does, the more you practise the better your results will become.

Aller Plantation

Like *Twisted Roots* (*see pages 66–7*), I took this photograph while walking on Exmoor, Somerset, England. But this picture presented the additional problem of the hazy distant tree trunks seen through the gap on the left.

Original taken on 35mm Olympus OM-1 camera with 50mm lens using Ilford FP4 film and Microphen developer. Inked with GC&I 1796 ink on Kentmere Art Document paper.

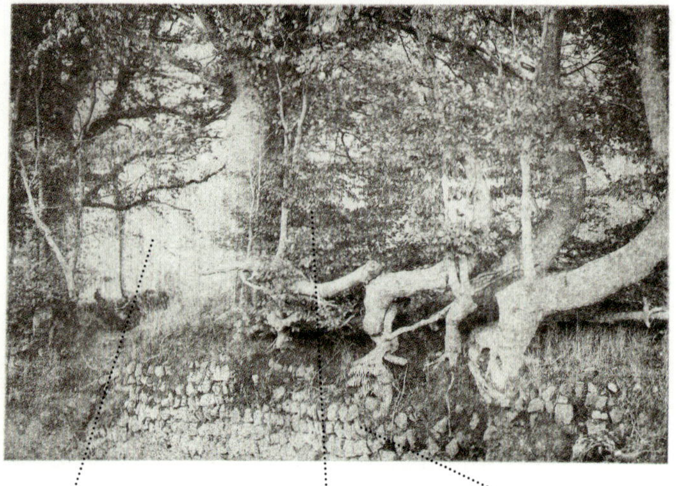

I chose Kentmere Art Document paper for this bromoil because I find that it handles light delicate tones, such as the distant tree trunks, extremely well

For the initial inking I used a foam roller to apply the ink and a second, clean roller to remove excess ink, building up the density gradually

For the dark tree on the left, the wall in the foreground and the leaves centre and right, I used a brush locally and cleaned up with a hopper

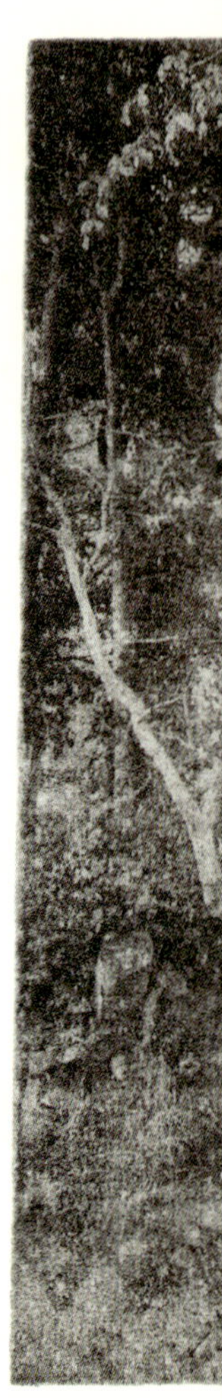

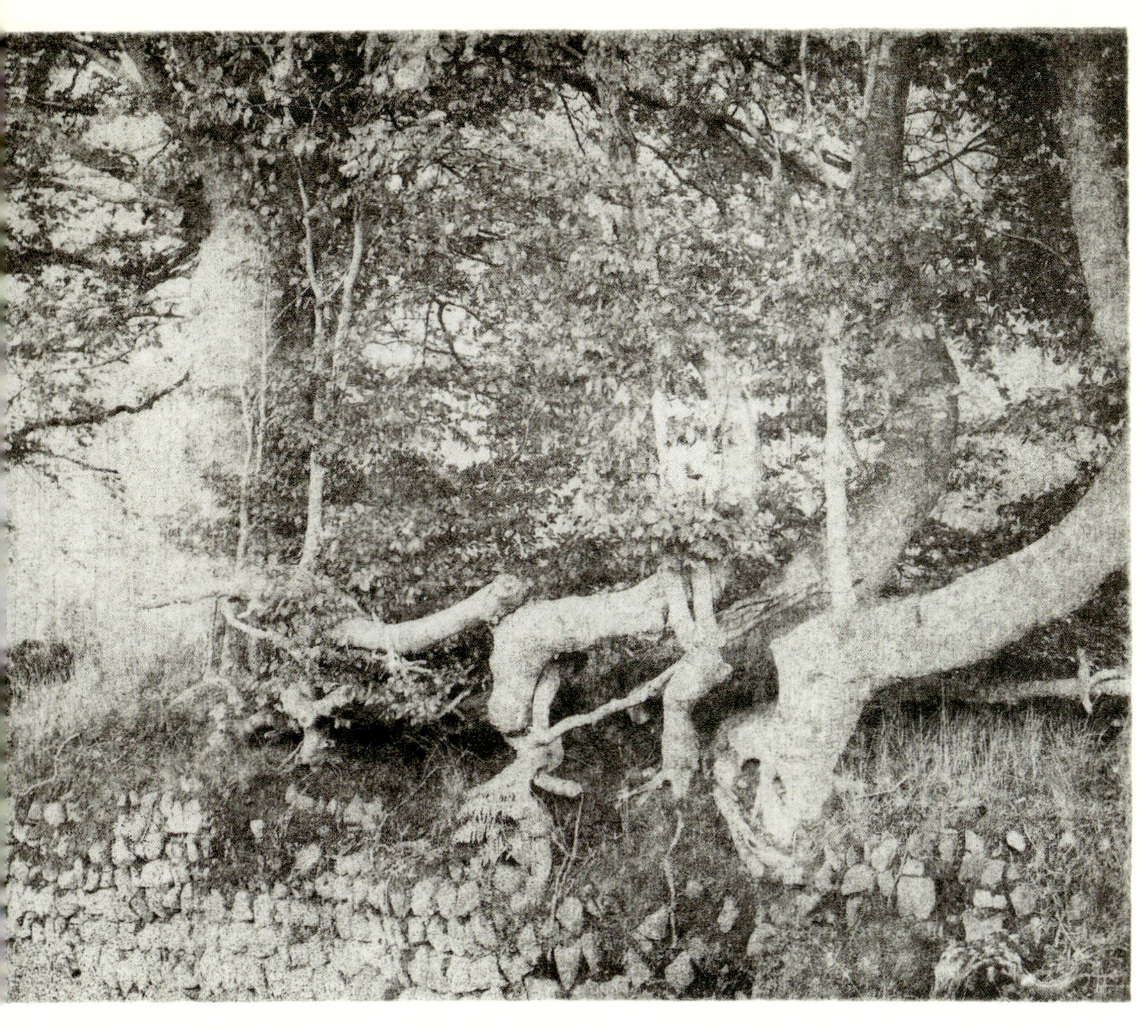

8 Advanced inking

Although the basic inking techniques using stiff ink straight from the can will be more than adequate to produce perfectly acceptable bromoil prints, additional, more advanced, techniques will enable you to create more individual results.

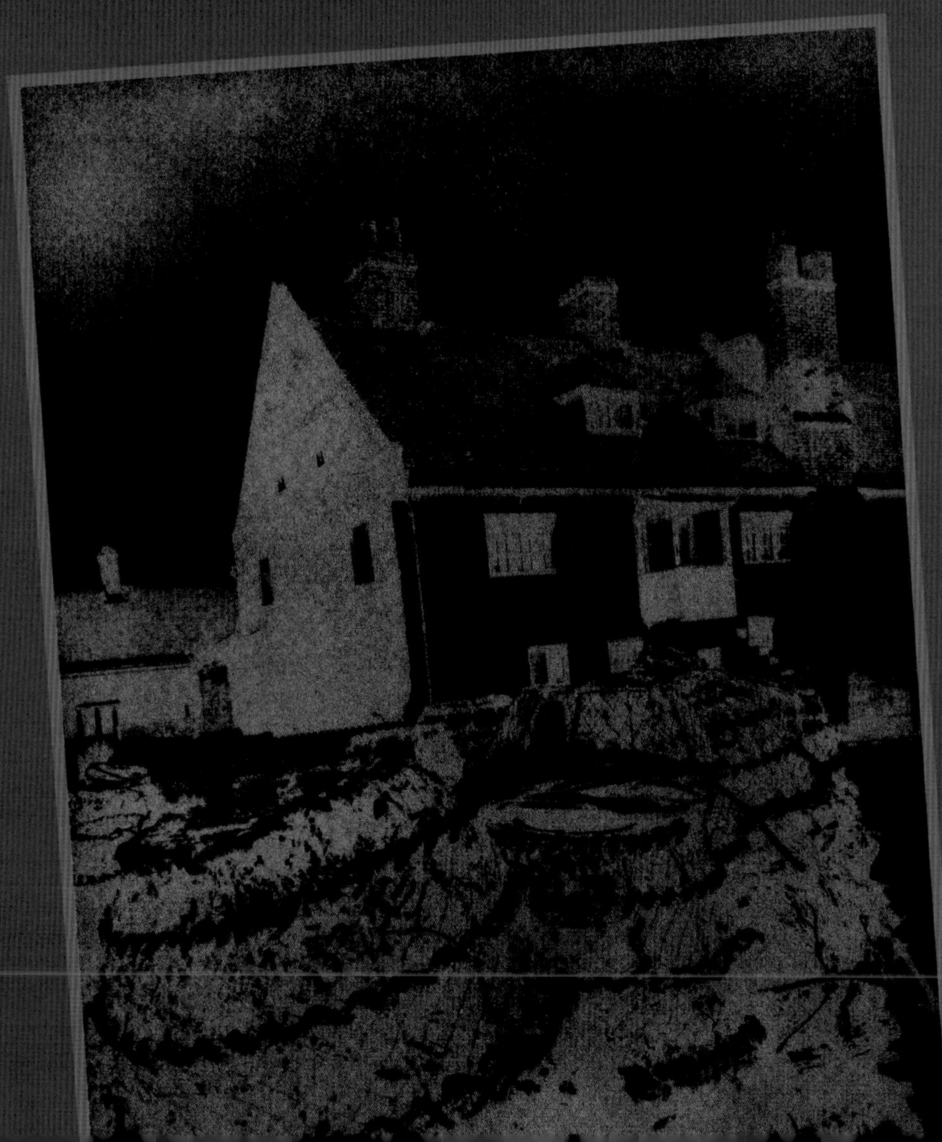

Basic inking techniques will produce an accurate reproduction of your original print, but by using inks of different consistencies you will be able to gain greater control over the final result. However, I must stress the importance of becoming proficient in the basic inking techniques before adding these more advanced methods to your repertoire. Many bromoilists use some of these techniques as a standard part of their bromoiling procedure, others use them occasionally for special effects, and yet others find that they achieve the results they want by using just the basic methods. As with so much in this fascinating process, there is no single correct way of achieving the effects that you seek.

HARD-INK TECHNIQUE

The basic inking method described in the previous chapter is essentially the hard-ink technique. Provided that you do not soak the matrix at too high a temperature it is possible to achieve prints with good contrast, plenty of shadow detail and a smooth, even grain. In order to achieve these characteristics it is almost essential to use brushes with stiff bristles for most of the inking. A softer brush may help to add highlight detail towards the final stages, but generally will not provide very successful results with the stiff ink used.

As I mentioned earlier, the most important factor in producing good results with the hard-ink technique is establishing the correct soaking time and temperature for the ink and paper you are using, and for the water supply in your area. But if you carry out the testing procedure I described, you should not find that you experience any undue problems, and it is possible to produce beautiful and delicate prints using just the hard-ink technique.

One point worth noting is that it is much easier using this method to ink up a matrix from an original print that is somewhat darker than usual. If I know that I want to make a bromoil using only the hard-ink technique, I give the print half a stop more exposure than usual. This gives more depth to the shadows and darkens the highlight detail, making the matrix much more receptive to the ink. But you do need to make sure that the matrix is thoroughly soaked before you start inking, so do not cut short this vital part of the process.

Adding softer ink

The technique of using a hard or stiff ink to begin inking the matrix and then changing to a softer one was first described in 1924 by Bertram Cox FRPS and F. C. Tilney. Their idea, basically, was to use a stiff ink to produce the required depth in the shadows and darker mid-tones, then change to a softer ink to build up detail in the lighter mid-tones and highlights. This method allows a great deal of control over the finished result, which can range from the soft, delicate almost grainless to a more robust, contrasty image.

Soak the matrix enough to allow the stiffest ink you have to be accepted to full depth by the shadows and darker mid-tones. Inks such as GC&I 1803 Senefelder's Crayon Black are ideal in this case. Use either a large, stiff brush or a foam roller. Be careful not to over-ink the shadow and dark mid-tone areas; stop when you have achieved full depth of tone, because the softer ink applied later will reinforce these areas.

Next, pour enough hot water into the soaking bath to raise its temperature by about 9°F (5°C). Place the partly inked matrix in this water and leave it to soak for about 10 minutes, making sure that it remains fully immersed and face up. This will increase the swelling of the gelatin and will enable you to bring out the highlight detail.

While the matrix is soaking, add a little softer ink to your palette – about the same amount as there is left of the original hard ink – and work the two together, mixing and spreading. GC&I 1796 Black is ideal as the softer ink or, if you wish to add a hint of colour to the print, you could use one of the many GC&I coloured inks.

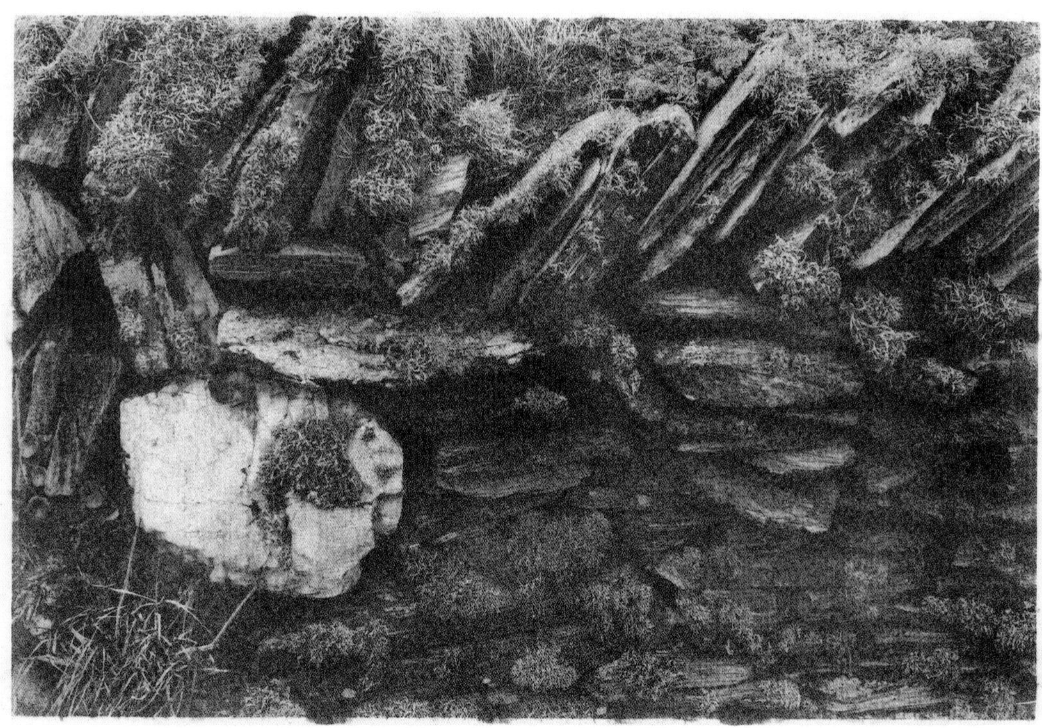

***Cornish wall*, Tintagel, Cornwall, England. This is an example of the mixed hard- and soft-ink technique. First the matrix was inked with hard black ink (GC&I 1803) and then with softer Burnt Umber (GC&I 1925) on Kentmere Bromoil paper.**

Alternatively, you can thin the original stiff ink by adding a single drop of linseed oil to it and mixing well.

Remove the matrix from the water and return it to the support. Remove all surface moisture with blotting paper and a viscose sponge, taking care not to smudge the ink on the matrix. Before you begin inking with the softened ink, use the hopping action with a clean brush to gently clear any muddiness that may be left after the initial inking.

Now start applying the softened ink. Concentrate initially on the lighter mid-tones and highlights, then work over the shadows and darker tones you have already inked to unify the tones. Clean up the highlights again using the hopping action. You may find that this removes all or nearly all of the ink in the highlights, but you will replace it during the next stage. Raise the temperature of the soaking bath by another 9°F (5°C) and soak the matrix for a further 10 minutes. In the meantime, add a drop of linseed oil to the ink on your palette and mix. After removing all surface water from the matrix again, apply the re-softened ink, concentrating initially on the highlight areas but once again working briefly over the whole matrix to unify the print.

You can use a softer brush for this final inking to give a softer gradation to the highlights, a light touch will get the best results. After a final clean up with the hopping action the print is ready to be hung up to dry.

One point about this mixed-ink method of inking is that you should never attempt to apply more hard ink to the matrix after you have applied the softened ink. If you do, the hard ink will lift off the softened ink. And if you intend to use hard ink again during the same working session – to ink another fresh matrix, for example – always use a clean brush to do so. If you use the brush with softened ink on it it will modify the fresh hard ink and you may not get the results you expect on your new print. You will, of course, also need to prepare a fresh inking tile for the hard ink because your original tile will have softened ink on it.

SOFT-INK TECHNIQUE

The bromoil process usually produces prints with a soft yet grainy etching-like quality, and it is this quality that most bromoilists find so attractive. However, if you want a more photographic appearance you can use the soft-ink technique. It is very useful if you want a very fine-grained result with plenty of gradation, but I must emphasize that the soft-ink technique is considerably more difficult to master than the hard- and mixed-ink methods.

Because you will be using only soft ink for this method you need to soak the matrix in quite warm water to achieve the necessary degree of swelling for the ink to be easily accepted. A good starting point for most papers is a temperature of about 104°F (40°C) and a soaking time of around 30 minutes.

To reach the correct ink consistency for this soft-ink technique you can either thin your normal hard ink or start with a softer one. If you normally use GC&I 1803 as your hard ink, take a pea-sized amount of the ink and spread it on your palette. Work it until it becomes smooth then scrape it into a small pile. Then, using a cocktail stick, add one drop of linseed oil to the ink and mix thoroughly. Repeat this procedure twice – so that you have added a total of three drops of linseed oil – working the mixture well each time. Try this as a starting point for your soft ink; you may find that you need to add a little more oil, but be careful not to add too much, just one drop at a time. If you use GC&I 1796 as your normal hard ink you will need to add rather less oil as the 1796 is slightly softer than the 1803. Start with just two drops of linseed oil added one drop at a time and mixed thoroughly. Perhaps a better way is to start with a softer ink rather than thinning a hard one. There are several inks of this softer consistency on the market, such as Lefranc & Bourgeois Typographic, with which it is worth experimenting.

As with the mixed-ink method, begin the inking with a large, stiff brush but using a gentle walking action to avoid overworking the ink into the softened gelatin. Alternatively, use a foam paint roller. Indeed, if you are trying to achieve a more photographic result it is a good idea to use a roller for much longer than you would with the hard- or mixed-ink techniques.

When you have the depth of the image almost to your liking, switch to a softer brush to finish, giving the print a smooth, fine-grained appearance. It may help to wait until the matrix has begun to dry before finishing the highlight areas of your print like this, to ensure the ink is retained by these very light tones. Finally, re-soak the matrix, remove surplus surface water, and work the whole print with a light hopping action using a clean brush or home-made hopper to clean the image and increase the contrast.

After using this soft-ink technique it is important to clean your brushes before using them for hard or mixed inks. Remove every trace of the soft ink using lighter fluid and dry them thoroughly. In fact, many bromoilists keep a separate set of brushes for the soft-ink method to avoid mixing the two consistencies.

A different way of inking

You can use the phenomenon of hard ink removing soft to your advantage if you plan it at the outset. Leonard G. Gabriel BSc described a method in 1930 that results in bromoils that are stronger and more vigorous than those produced by the soft-ink method. Yet, with a little experience, it allows greater flexibility in applying the ink. As with the normal soft-ink technique you need to soak the matrix at a high temperature – about 104°F (40°C) – for around 30 minutes to get a high degree of swelling in the gelatin.

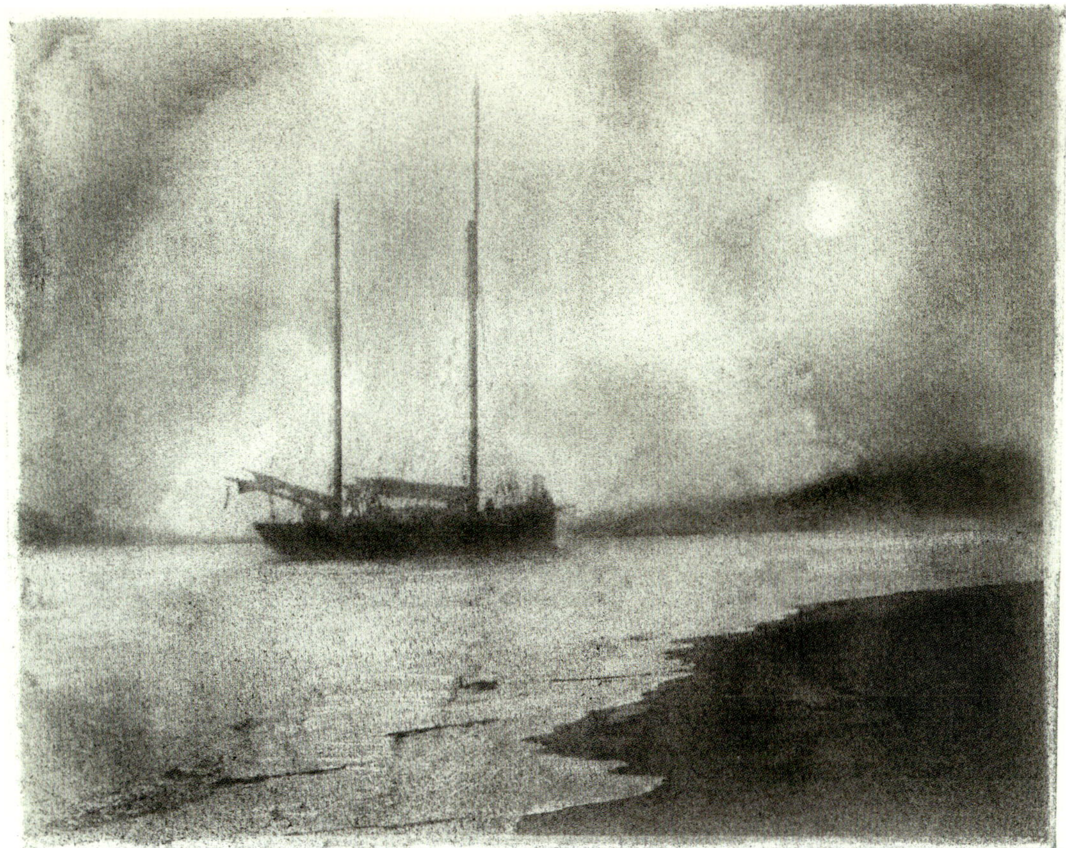

Schooner in the mist by Colin Ivison

Prepare two inking tiles, one with your hardest ink and one with either a soft ink or the hard ink softened as described earlier. Now apply the soft ink evenly over the whole matrix using the walking brush action or a foam paint roller. This will give a soft, misty-looking image with no great depth of ink in the shadows and no clear, clean highlights. Next, charge your brush with hard ink. While you can use the same brush for both ink consistencies, I think it is better to use a fresh one for the hard ink to keep the two consistencies separate. Apply this hard ink to the areas where you want to build contrast, using the dabbing action. The highlights should begin to clear and the shadows strengthen; as you progress the contrast will build. You can continue to work on the print with either hard or soft ink or, indeed, with an intermediate consistency made by mixing the two. In this way you can create exactly the contrast you want in any part of the print. Finally, work the whole area of the print with a gentle hopping action to clean the highlights and unify the image.

Removing ink

As already explained, the usual way to remove ink is with the hopping action. If you use a clean brush or home-made hopper and clean it every few strokes by dabbing it on a piece of paper you will remove ink from all parts of the image. However, if you charge the brush with a little ink first, you will pick up ink from the highlights and transfer it to the shadows, increasing contrast in both areas.

By using a large brush you can quickly clean the whole print or build contrast overall, while small brushes enable you to cover selected areas of the picture. In this way you can control the local tones and contrast; you can darken intrusive areas or lighten elements to which you want to attract the viewer's eye.

There are, however, other ways of removing ink to give local control. The simplest is to lay plain paper over the area you wish to lighten and rub it with your finger. The amount of ink transferred depends on how hard you rub. With practice it is quite easy to gauge how much pressure to apply to remove the amount of ink necessary to achieve the desired effect.

A variation of this technique is to use a scrunched-up ball of clingfilm. I was introduced to this by American master bromoilist Gene Laughter, who calls it the 'ink magnet'. Dab the ball rapidly on the over-inked area, turning it constantly to present a clean surface to the print. This evens out your inking removing excess ink from heavy areas of the print.

Another simple method is to use a small pad of cotton wool or small sponge. Soak it and then squeeze most of the water out, leaving it just damp. Using a stroking action, work carefully over the area you want to lighten. This method is useful for cleaning areas such as clouds and expanses of water, but be careful not to apply too much pressure, and remove all surface moisture when you have finished.

Finally, if you want to add individual highlights or lighten small areas then use an artists' putty eraser. You can knead a small piece of this eraser into a point that will allow you to pick out tiny details, or you can use a corner of the eraser block to lighten a larger area. With practice it is possible to exert a lot of control in this way; you can even remove detail, such as an intrusive figure, completely.

When you have used any of these methods of local ink removal, the work you have done can look obvious, so ink over the areas with a lightly inked brush and a very light dabbing action. Your corrective work will quickly blend in with the rest of the picture.

Control in inking

One of the joys of the bromoil process is the control it allows over the final print. Blank skies can have majestic cloud formations added, landscapes can become mountainous, the recession of planes, or aerial perspective as it is sometimes known, can be modified, and a host of other controls are possible, but I would advise becoming proficient in basic inking first. It is a good idea to practise these techniques on pieces of plain paper.

Clouds and mountains are best put in after you have dried the print and are usually added by using masks torn from newspaper. To add clouds, simply place the mask on the sky and add ink to the surrounding area using a softish brush. This will darken the sky, making the artificial clouds stand out. With practice you can create varying tones in the clouds to make them look even more realistic. If your negative already has clouds you can make things easier by burning them in when you make the original print. Make the sky area darker than you would if you were leaving the print as a straight bromide. You will find it easier to ink and you will have better control of the tone.

You can add mountains or hills in much the same way, but inking slightly darker for the nearer slopes and lighter for those more distant. You can also use this technique to modify the recession of planes in your pictures, masking each more distant plane while you add more ink to the nearer ones.

By roughly tearing newspaper to use as a mask you can add mountains to a landscape. This shows the results of the technique on a plain piece of paper.

MODIFYING INKS

In Chapter 6 I explained the importance of matching the stiffness of the ink you intend to use with the temperature of the water in which you soak the matrix, and, to a lesser extent, the time for which you soak it. If you stick to the guidelines I gave there you should find little need to modify the ink. However, there are sure to be times when you would prefer the ink to be a little stiffer or softer, and that is what I want to deal with here.

Stiffening the ink

If you use an ink such as Graphic Chemical & Ink 1796, which is one of the most popular for bromoil, you may want to stiffen it a little for the first inking. Personally, I prefer to use GC&I 1803, which is considerably stiffer, for the first inking and then move on to 1796. There are two types of stiffening media you can use for this job: those that need to be melted and those that do not.

The media that need to be melted are ordinary candle wax and powdered aquatint resin. Of the two I prefer the resin; the candle wax has a tendency to give the finished bromoil a slightly glossy appearance which I do not care for. The type of candle you use is not important, as long as it is not coloured, of course. Just light the wick, turn the candle on its side and allow a few drops of the molten wax to drip onto the ink and then mix them together thoroughly.

To use resin, first place the usual amount of ink on your palette. Then add a small amount of the powdered resin and mix them together thoroughly. Scrape the mixture off the tile and onto a metal spoon. Now heat the spoon over a lighted candle or a low gas burner.

You will find that the ink and resin mixture will melt quickly and form a homogenous mass. Pour the mixture on to your palette, leave it for a few minutes to cool and then spread it in the usual way. If you find that you have added too much wax or resin, you can thin the ink again, as explained in the following section.

Among the stiffening media that do not need to be melted are powdered French chalk, powdered household starch, magnesium carbonate and magnesium sulphate – better known as Epsom salts. To use any of these materials, just add a little to the ink and mix. If it is still not stiff enough, add more. The important thing is to make sure that the powders are really fine before adding them; there should be no problem with the chalk and starch, but you may need to grind the carbonate or sulphate using a pestle and mortar to make it fine enough.

Adding pigments

If you want to add a hint of colour to your ink you can stiffen it by adding powdered pigment either from artists' pastels or by purchasing pigment powders. Pastels are quite expensive,

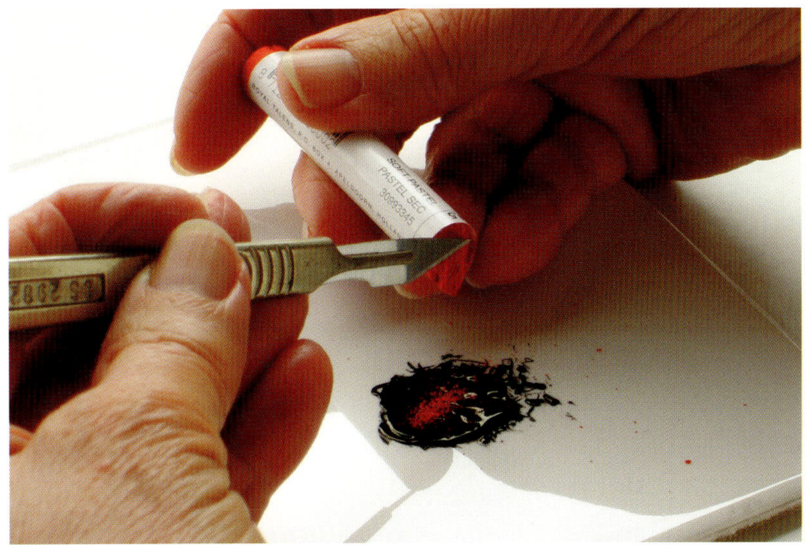

Ink can be stiffened and the colour can be modified at the same time by adding some powdered pigment in the form of powdered artists' pastel. Just scrape the pastel stick with a knife or scalpel.

so the less costly way is to use pigment powders. Buy fairly bright colours; when you mix them with black inks they will produce quite delicate shades. For example, a little cadmium red or primary red will make a warm brown and a small amount of ultramarine will produce a cool tone. Like the magnesium carbonate or sulphate, these pigments will probably need to be ground more finely before you use them.

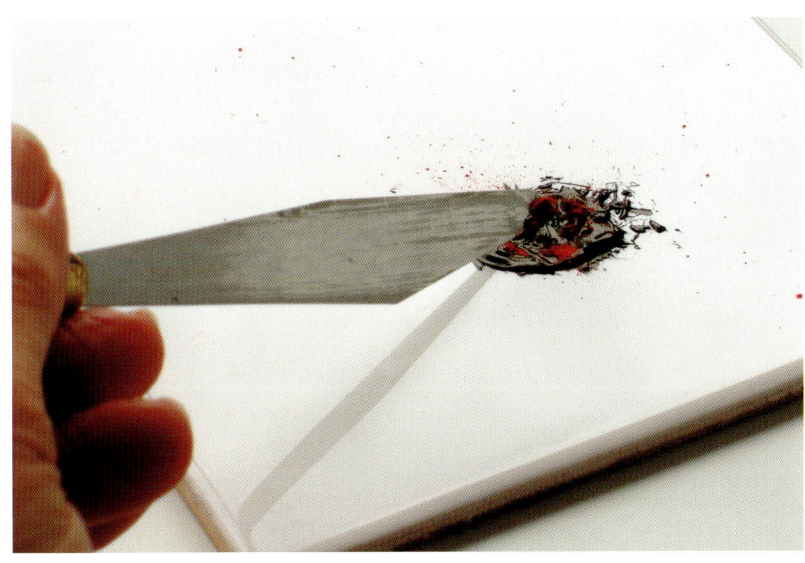

When you have enough powdered pigment, mix the ink and pigment thoroughly.

caution

Many pigments are very toxic and some are carcinogenic. When grinding and mixing ANY pigments ALWAYS wear rubber gloves, a dust mask and eye protection.

Thinning the ink

Perhaps the easiest and safest way to thin your ink is to use a similar ink but of softer consistency. For example, if your base ink is GC&I 1803, add a little 1796 to soften it just slightly. Or you can add a softer ink of a different colour to give the mixture a slight tint; most of the GC&I coloured inks are of softer consistency than 1803. Good colours to try are Burnt Umber, Litho Purple, Process Red and Process Blue.

A very small amount of artists' oil colour can also be used as a thinner that adds colour. But be careful, because just adding the tiniest amount you can of fairly bright colours should be enough.

The more traditional ink thinners are those used as media in oil painting. These include turpentine; linseed oil; stand oil, which is a heat-refined linseed oil that is thicker than ordinary linseed oil; plate oil, which is used in printmaking; poppy oil and megilp, a gel medium that also contains alkyd resin.

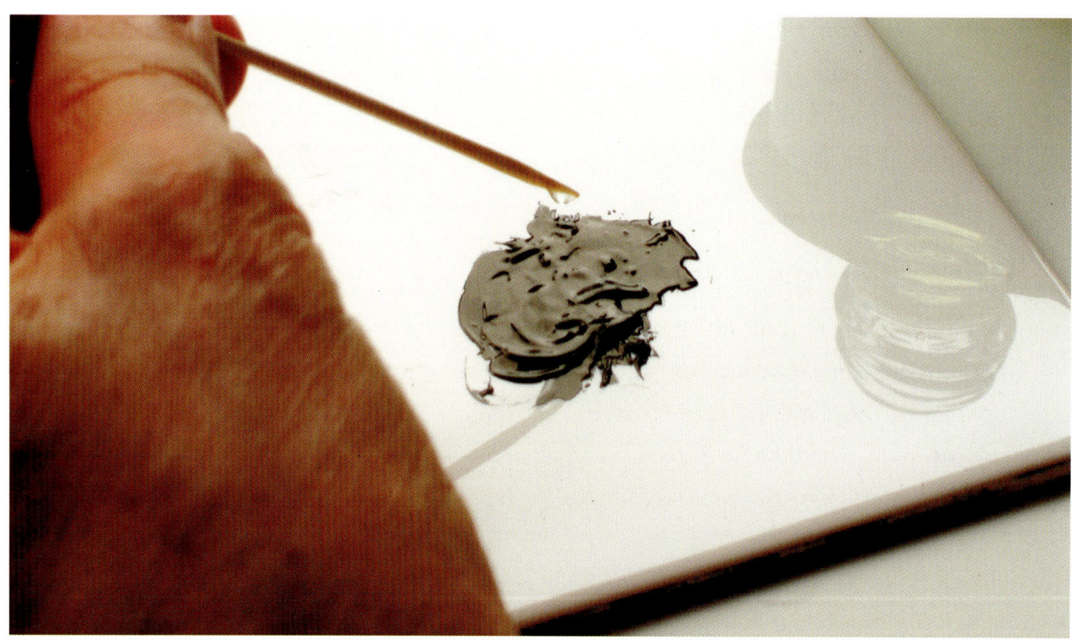

If the ink is too stiff you can thin it by adding linseed oil one drop at a time.

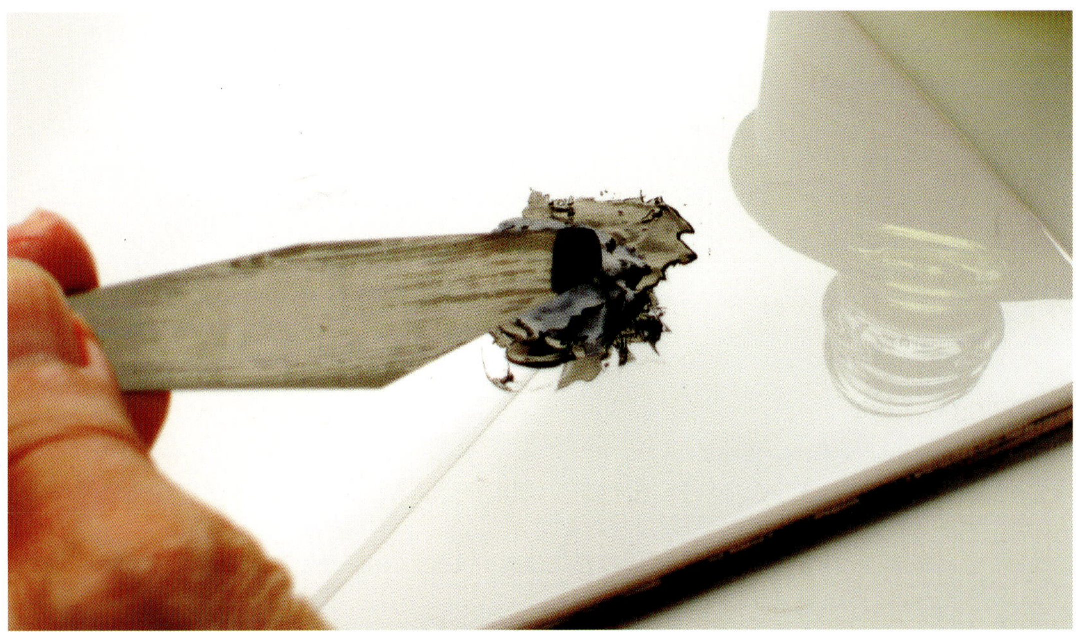

Mix the ink and the oil thoroughly and add more oil if necessary.

It is all too easy to thin ink too much, so take care. Add only a very small amount of any of these thinning media at a time and mix thoroughly. Use a cocktail stick to pick up just one drop at a time.

STORING YOUR INKS

Inks manufactured by Graphic Chemical & Ink Co are supplied in cans containing about 1lb (500 grams). They have a disc of oil-proof paper on the surface and the lid is secured by a length of plastic tape to keep the can airtight. When you have taken out the ink you need, replace the paper disc and plastic tape or the remaining ink will begin to harden. Actually, this is a useful dodge for thickening ink. Take the ink you need from the can and put it on your palette, then leave it exposed to the air for a few days before using it.

Some inks are supplied in small jars or tubes with screw caps. Always make sure to replace the caps securely to exclude the air. And keep the screw threads clean or you may not be able to remove the cap next time.

Lobster pots

This shot was taken at Mudeford in Dorset, England. The lobster pots seemed almost to demand the bromoil treatment, although the original colour slide also made a good picture.

Original taken on Olympus OM-2 camera using Fujichrome 100D film. An internegative was subsequently made using Agfa APX25 film and Rodinal developer. Inked with hard GC&I 1803 ink on Kentmere Bromoil paper.

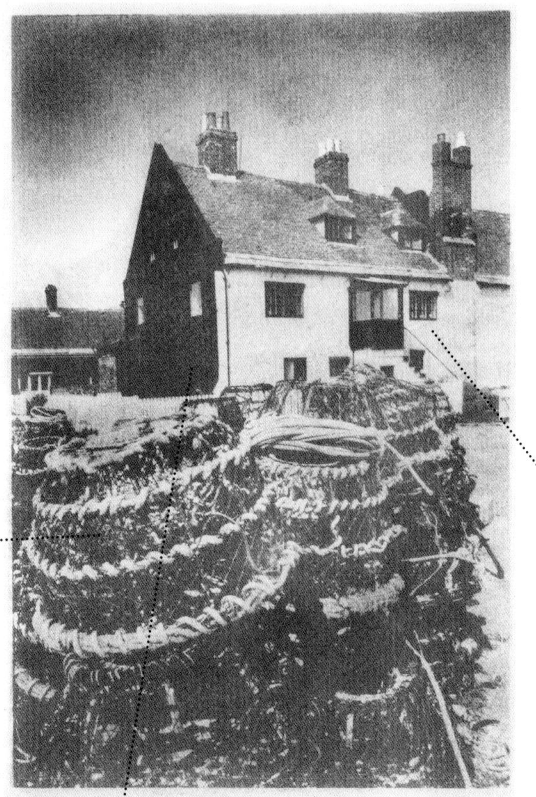

The matrix was soaked in water at a slightly lower temperature than usual to help maintain contrast and shadow detail with the hard ink

The dark areas of the print were built up with a foam roller and a stiff brush

Ink was removed from the highlight areas with a wet foam brush, then the print was blotted dry before being finished with a clean foam roller

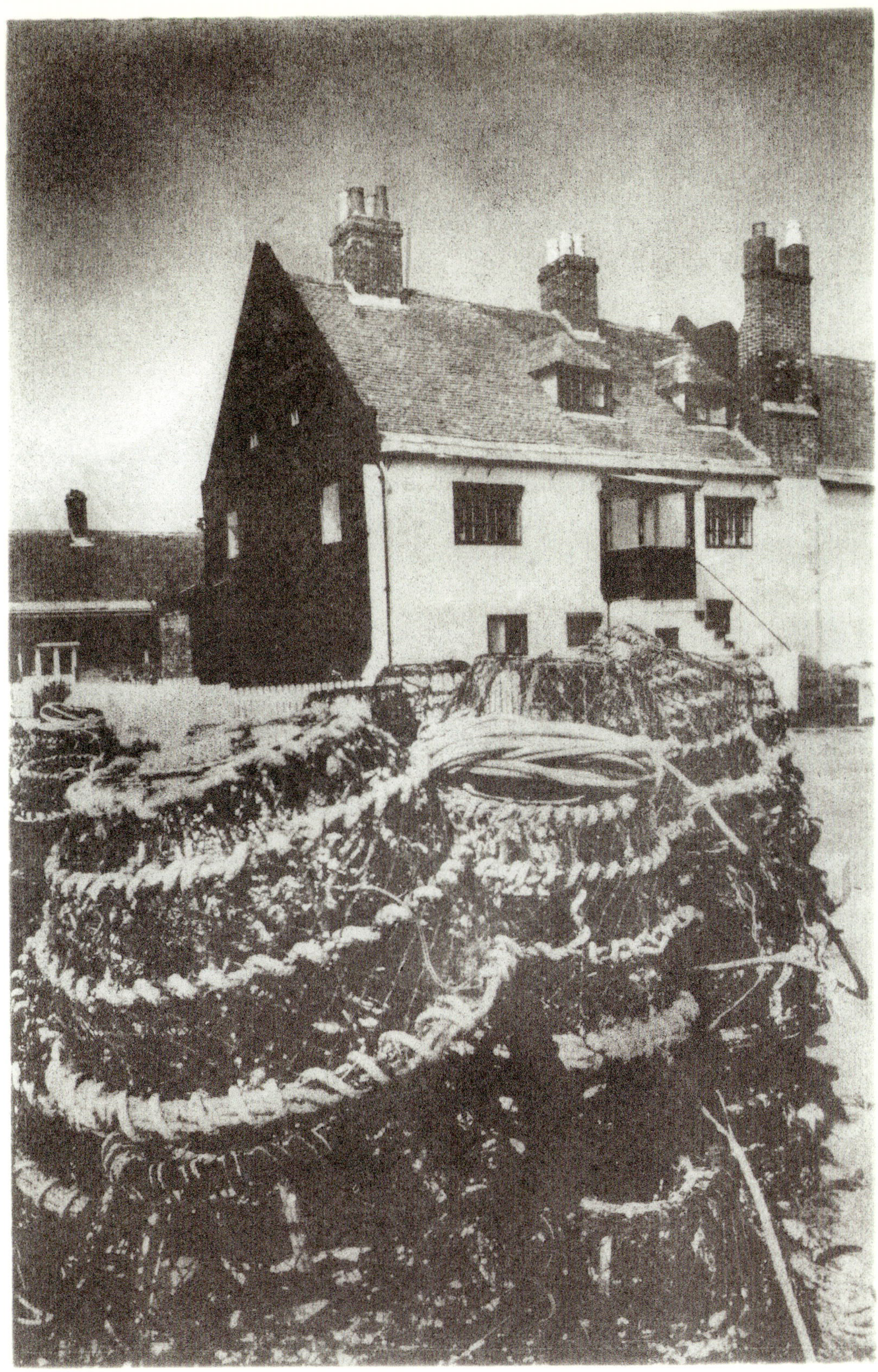

9 Afterwork

The process doesn't finish once you have inked your matrix – cleaning, retouching and mounting your finished bromoil can make an enormous difference to the final impact of the image.

Before you can carry out any afterwork on your bromoil you must make sure it is completely dry. Remember that a bromoil inked with soft ink or a combination of hard and soft will take longer to dry than one inked with hard ink.

Because exposure to air speeds up the drying process considerably, my own preferred method is to hang up the inked print on a line or clothes drying frame using wooden pegs at each corner. The pegs at the top anchor the print to the line and the bottom ones prevent – or at least minimize – curling. A moderate amount of heat will also accelerate drying, so make sure the room is warm. Alternatively, you can hang the prints in an airing cupboard. Either way the important thing is to hang the prints up, not dry them flat; that way you will avoid dust and other debris settling on the delicate surface. A novel way to speed drying is to place the print in a microwave oven on low power and set for ten seconds or so, but I would advise this treatment only if you really do need to dry your bromoil quickly.

Do not be in too much of a hurry to start working on your bromoils. Allow at least two to three days for hard ink to dry and set thoroughly and at least seven days for softer inks. If you are in any doubt, it is best to err on the side of caution. Remember that the inked surface is quite delicate and easily scratched, especially when not completely hardened. It would be a great pity to ruin an otherwise good print by trying to work on it too soon.

POST-INKING FIX

Some bromoil workers insist on re-fixing their prints after they have been inked, to remove every last trace of silver salts remaining in the emulsion. Personally, I have never found this to be necessary; if you take the proper time to fix and wash the matrix fully after bleaching and tanning, and use fresh fixer, you should have no problems. However, if you prefer to add this final fixing step it will certainly do no harm.

After drying the inked print thoroughly as described above, place it in a dish of water at room temperature and allow it to soak for about five minutes. While it is doing so, mix up around two pints or one litre of fresh fixer at normal print fixer strength. It is a good idea to use an acid fixer as this will also remove any last remaining traces of the greenish-grey stain in the bleached image beneath the ink.

Transfer the print from the water to the fixer and agitate it constantly but gently for five minutes if the fixer is a sodium thiosulphate bath, two minutes if it is ammonium thiosulphate. Because of the relatively delicate nature of the inked image, even after it has been dried for several days, do not be tempted to fix more than one print at a time to avoid the risk of scratching the ink image.

After fixing, wash the print thoroughly, using a hypo-clearing bath or 20 per cent sodium sulphite as part of the process if you wish, in exactly the same way as described in Chapter 4 for making the original bromide print. Finally, remove all surface water from the print with blotting paper and hang the print up to dry as before. When you are ready to start working on the print, fix it to a sheet of plywood or plate glass with masking tape to keep it flat.

CLEANING THE SURFACE

During the inking process it is inevitable that some broken hairs and other debris will be left on the surface of the print. Your first job is to remove these. Use either a very soft brush or soft cloth and very gently sweep the surface of the print. You will find that the debris will come away quite easily. I have found a soft watercolour wash brush or a cosmetic brush is ideal for this task. If you find a few of the hairs reluctant to leave the surface of the print with this treatment, use the point of a scalpel blade or craft knife to lift them carefully away from the surface. Then brush them gently away.

RETOUCHING

Like most prints, bromoils will usually show a few white spots that need to be retouched out. This is always a chore, but the good news is that bromoils are much easier to retouch than ordinary silver gelatin prints. To start with, it is extremely easy to match the colour of the retouching to that of the inked image; you simply use the same ink, but thinned considerably. If there is ink left on your palette after inking the matrix this is ideal. In addition you will need a fine sable spotting brush – a no. 0 or no. 1 is perfect – and a little of the lighter fluid you use for cleaning your brushes.

Moisten the brush with the lighter fluid, taking care not to get it too wet, and work the tip into the ink on your palette. If you do get too much lighter fluid on the brush just set it aside for a few minutes while fluid evaporates. Before applying the thinned ink to your print,

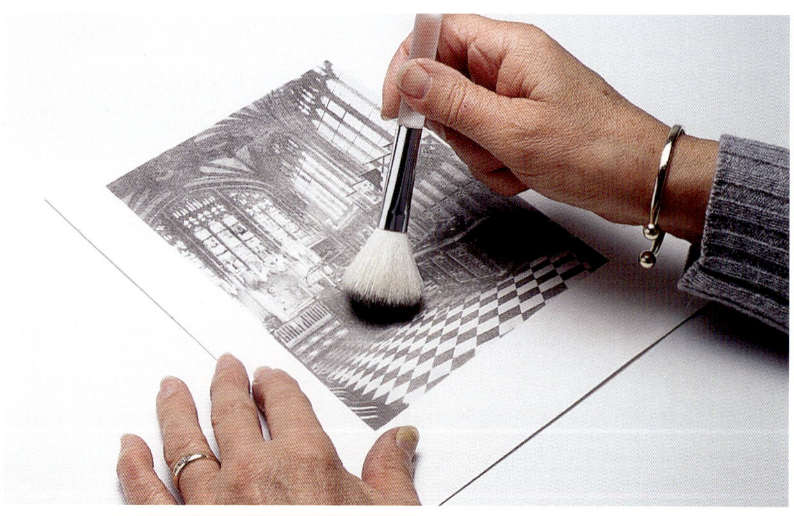

Use a soft brush such as this cosmetic brush to clean the surface of the print, removing broken hair tips and other debris.

> **tip**
>
> *Some workers use a sharpened lead pencil to retouch their work instead of thinned ink. I don't recommend this as the pencil leaves a fairly shiny finish, whereas the inked print is matt. As a result the retouching tends to look rather obvious.*

check its density on a plain piece of white paper. If it is too light add more ink until it reaches the tone you need; if it is too dark add a little more fluid. It is a good strategy to start with the spots in the darkest areas of the bromoil and then work towards those in the lighter areas, thinning the ink as you go. You will find the lighter fluid evaporates quickly so you will need to keep moistening your brush.

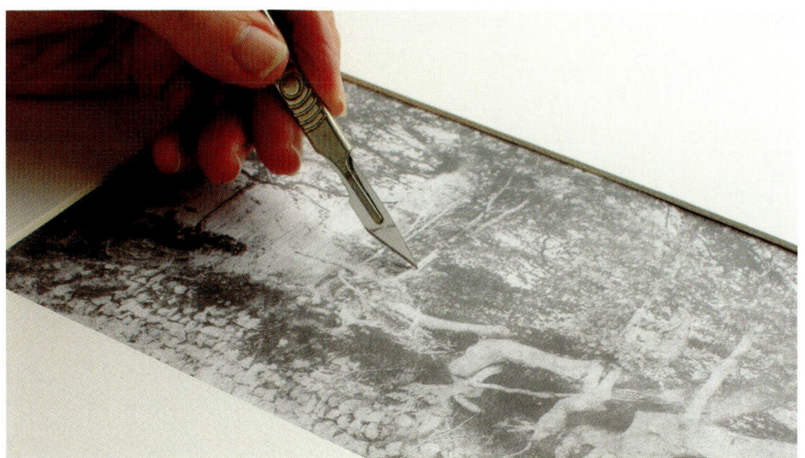

When your print is dry you can remove ink from the highlights to lighten them by scraping very carefully with a scalpel. Be careful, though, not to cut the surface of the print.

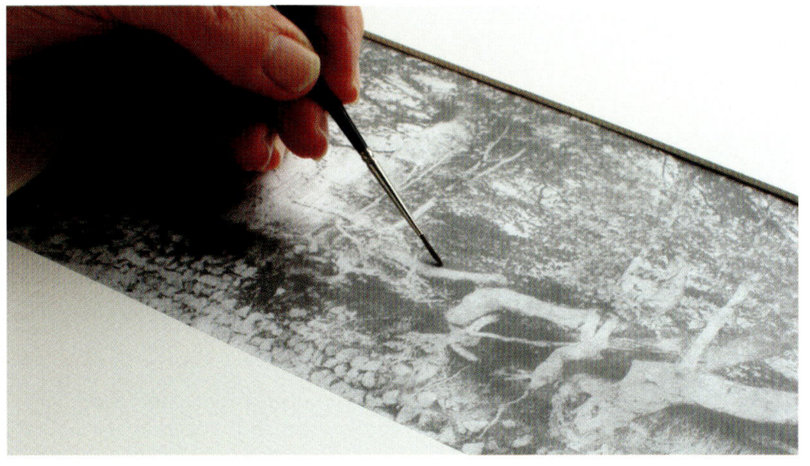

Small areas of shadow can be strengthened by adding thinned ink with a small watercolour brush.

If you prefer to use a pencil instead of thinned ink for your retouching, choose a charcoal or Conté pencil; both of these produce a matt finish that blends far better with the inking. But they will not, of course, match the colour of the inking as accurately as will thinned ink.

INKING A DRY PRINT

In Chapter 7 I explained how it is possible to re-soak a bromoil after drying and then add more ink to build the image further. The swollen gelatin will accept the extra ink in proportion to the tones of the original bromide print just as it does in the earlier stages of inking. However, applying ink to the dried print without re-soaking achieves a different effect. Because the gelatin is not swollen the print will accept ink evenly all over. This is a very useful technique that you can use to manipulate the tones in your bromoil, darkening areas that would not accept further ink when the matrix had been soaked. With practice, the possibilities offered by the dry-inking technique are enormous and were used to great effect by the late Norman Gryspeerdt FRPS. I touched on the technique in the previous chapter for adding clouds and mountains to your pictures. But even if you do not want to do this the technique is useful in a number of other ways.

One of the most useful applications of dry inking is to darken the edges of your prints. In conventional bromide printing it is quite common to give additional exposure to the edges and corners of a print to concentrate the viewer's eye on the main subject of the picture. You can achieve the same effect in a bromoil by inking along the edges and the corners of the dried print.

First apply lengths of masking tape around the border of the print so that they are aligned perfectly with the edges of the image. This will keep the borders or safe edges of the print clean. Now, using a very light and gentle dabbing action, apply a very little hard ink around the edges of the print and into the corners. Ink applied to a dry print is always more difficult to remove than it is to apply. You cannot use the hopping brush action to remove it as this simply distributes the ink over the whole surface to give a dirty, muddy appearance. But if you apply the ink a little at a time you can watch the density build and then stop when you have acheived the effect you want.

If you overdo it, you should remove some of the ink using a wad of clingfilm or by placing a clean piece of writing paper over the print and rubbing the affected area, as I described in Chapter 7.

You can use this edge-darkening technique to work on other areas of the print, too. If you have an area that is rather uneven, for example, a little ink applied to the dry print with a fairly soft brush will even out the tone quickly and easily.

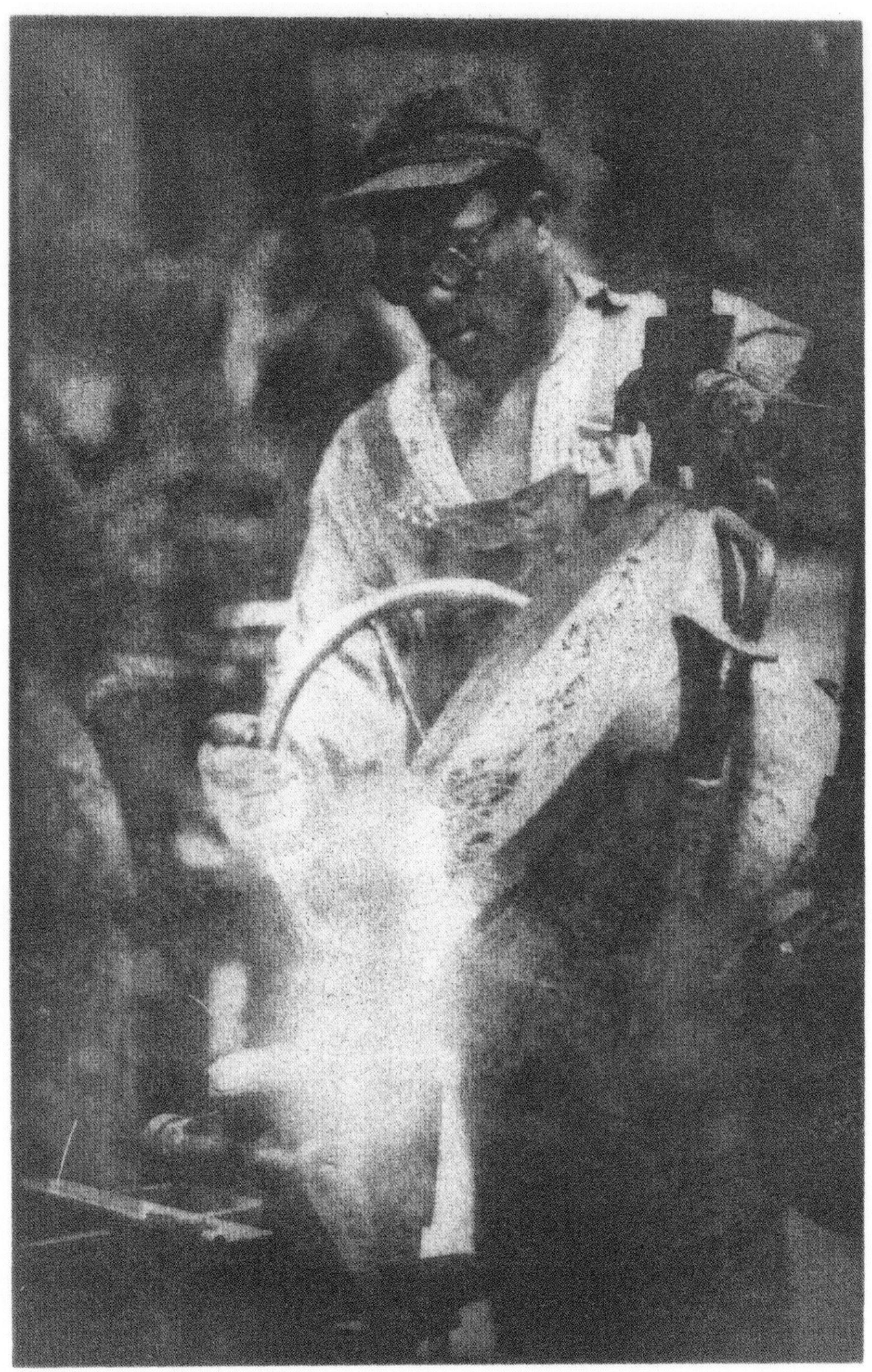

Foundry worker. I thought the dark, gritty atmosphere was ideally suited to the bromoil process. Original taken on a Prakticamat fitted with 135mm lens using Agfapan 1000 film and Rodinal developer. Inked with GC&I 1796 ink on Kentmere Art Document paper.

CLEANING HIGHLIGHTS

After your bromoil has fully dried and the ink hardened you may find small highlight areas that lack sparkle. It is less easy to brighten these areas using a kneaded putty eraser on dry ink than it is immediately after inking, but there are a couple of techniques that I have found to work on the dried print.

The first is to use a hard pencil eraser instead of the soft putty type. This is useful for brightening small areas, and if you shave the eraser to a point you can also work on very small highlights. I found a useful tool in a local art shop that allows me to do the same thing with more control. It is called a 'clay shaper' and looks rather like a watercolour paintbrush with a tapered rubber tip instead of bristles.

The other technique for cleaning highlights sounds a little more drastic, but used carefully is most effective. Use the point of a scalpel or craft knife very carefully to scrape away ink in the highlights to reveal the clean paper underneath. The trick is to scrape away a little at a time so that the cleaned area does not look obvious; if you overdo it, apply more ink and start again. And take care not to cut or abrade the surface of the paper.

Lightening larger areas

If you want to lighten a larger area of a fully dried bromoil, rub the area lightly with a dry paper kitchen towel or, for a more heavily over-inked area, a piece torn from a brown paper bag. The slightly rough surface of the brown paper acts as an extremely fine abrasive. With both of these materials, either screw the paper into a wad or wrap it around your finger and turn frequently to keep presenting a clean surface to the print.

American bromoilist Gene Laughter takes this technique to the extreme; he sometimes uses artists'-grade steel wool to work on the surface of his bromoils. But as he says, 'you have to ask yourself whether striations will enhance the print, because there is no turning back once you have started'.

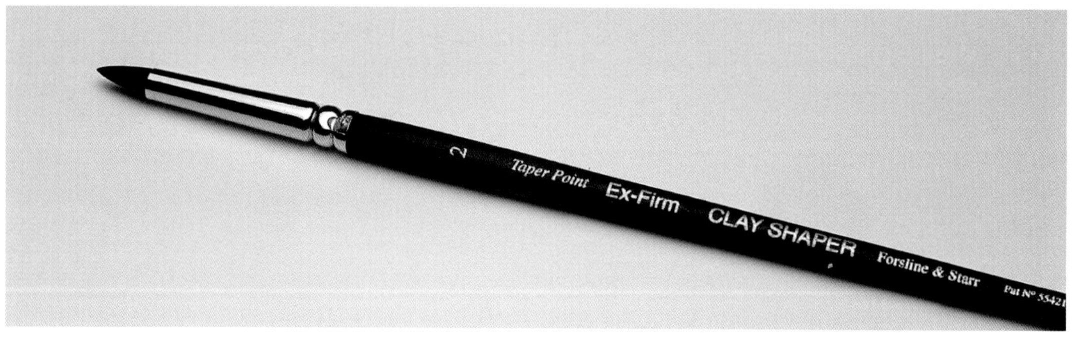

The clay shaper I have is an extra firm one that is very effective for cleaning the smaller highlights.

ADDING A BIT OF COLOUR

To me, bromoil has always been essentially a monochrome process and I do not greatly like colour bromoils, although some workers, such as Maija McDougal FRPS, have produced truly beautiful results in colour.

Having said that, though, I sometimes add a little coloured ink to the basic black to give a suggestion of tint to the picture. Generally I use a touch of red ink if I want the print to have a warm tone and blue if I want a cool-toned result. But this is done at the inking stage not as afterwork. However, you can add colour to your dried bromoil in several ways. The first is to use coloured pencils such as Marshall oil pencils. These are designed specifically for hand colouring photographs and blend in with the inked image very well indeed. Next, you can use oil pastels such as those manufactured by Sennelier. They are much softer than the oil pencils and you can spread the colour much more easily using your fingers.

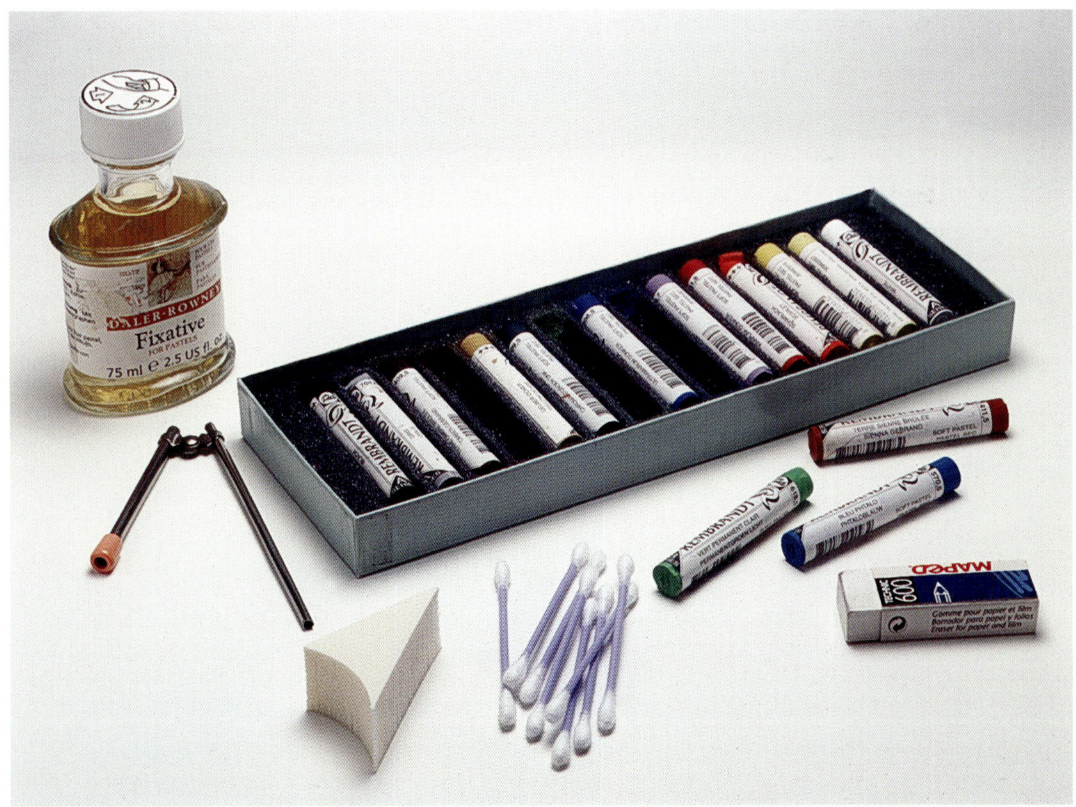

The equipment and materials necessary for applying colour to a bromoil, in this case using powdered artists' pastels.

But my favourite colouring medium is artists' soft pastel, again made by Sennelier and by other companies such as Royal Talens Rembrandt. These pastels are very soft – rather like blackboard chalk – and easy to work, either direct on to the print, spread with a finger or, best of all, as a powder scraped from the pastel stick.

With a scalpel or craft knife, gently shave the powdered pigment from the pastels; use a separate small container for each of the colours and limit your palette to just three or four colours – we are aiming for subtlety here.

Make sure that your bromoil print is lying flat on its support. If you have used the edge-darkening technique described earlier, leave the masking tape around the image to keep the borders of the print clean. If you did not darken the edges, apply tape around the image area now.

There are several useful tools for applying the colour to the print, including small balls of cotton wool, cosmetic sponge wedges and cotton-wool buds; I find the wedges best for large areas and buds for smaller areas.

Start with the lightest colour you want to use and apply it over the area you wish to colour. Use a light rubbing action and you will find that the colour spreads quite evenly. Dip the wedge or cotton wool into the colour frequently and do not worry about being too accurate at this stage as you will be cleaning up the print later. Indeed, if you are intending to colour the entire print it is a good idea to spread this lightest colour over the whole image area to unify the picture. Now apply the second colour, which should be the next lightest. Apply this more selectively though still in fairly broad areas, and use a clean wedge or cotton wool for each colour.

Continue with the other colours, applying them in progressively darker tones and increasingly selectively. Then, using another clean wedge or cotton-wool ball, blend all the colours to give balance to the print. Clean the highlights with a cotton-wool bud, a putty eraser kneaded to a point or a tool such as the clay shaper mentioned earlier. Wipe the point frequently to keep it clean.

Finally, because the powdered pastel colour can easily be rubbed off, spray the whole print with artists' pastel fixative. Then, when the fixative is dry, remove the masking tape from around the image and that holding the print to its support.

When colouring a bromoil, whether by oil pencil, oil pastel or powdered colour, aim to keep the effect understated. You are not trying to create an imitation of a colour photograph but simply to convey an impression of colour.

One technique that I use occasionally is to leave all the bromoil as basic black apart from a single area which I colour slightly with powdered pastel. This has the effect of emphasizing the focal point of the picture and attracting the viewer's eye to it.

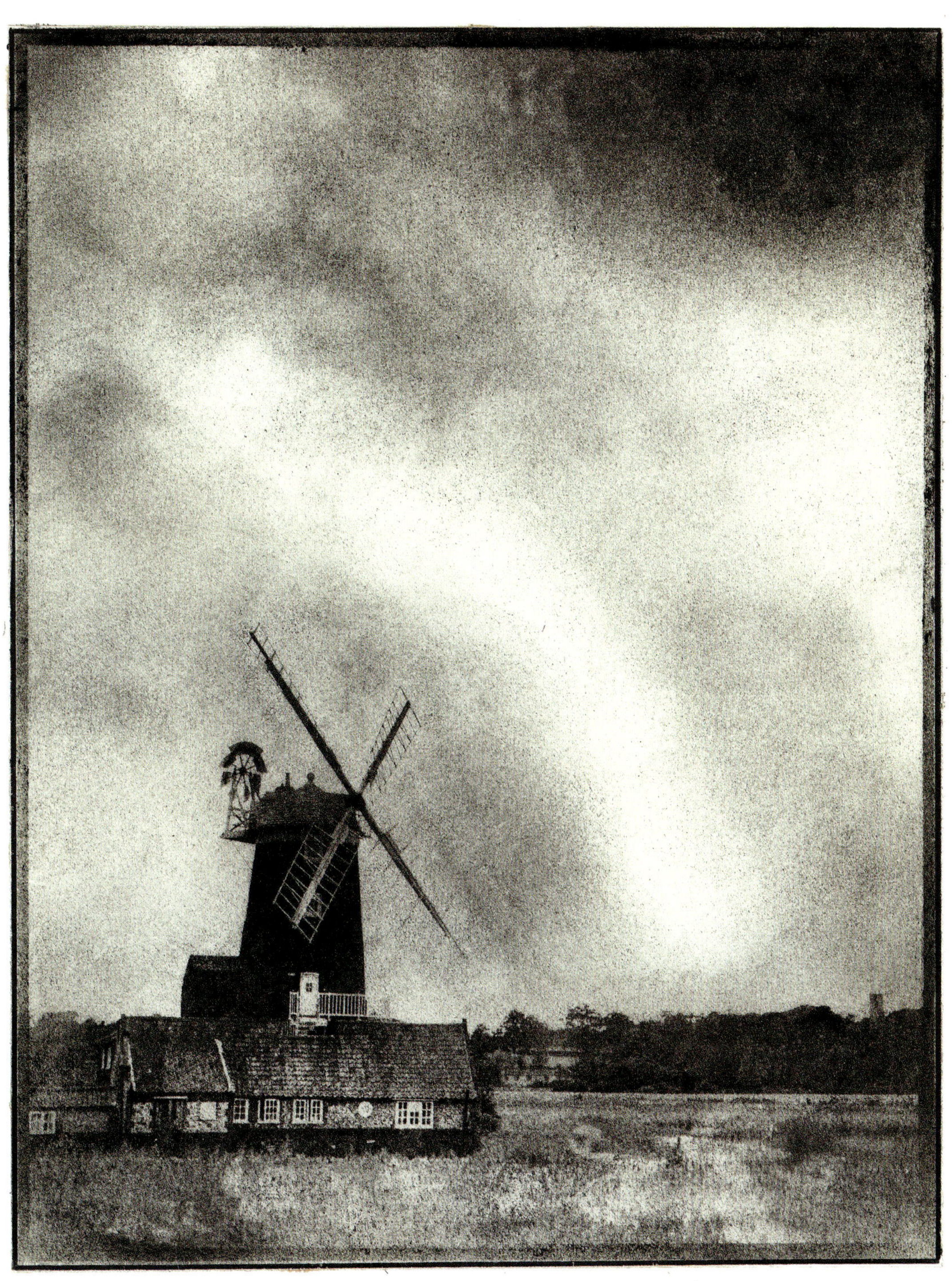

Cley Mill by Colin Ivison

Base tinting

Another way to add a little colour to your bromoils is to tint the paper base on which they are printed. You can use a variety of liquids, such as diluted photographic retouching dyes, food colourings, even tea and coffee. In fact, black coffee in particular gives a lovely range of sepia-like tints to the paper base depending on the brand that you choose. The working method for any of these colouring media is quite straightforward; I will describe the way I use coffee for tinting, but in fact the same procedure works with all the others. This method was first described to me by Gene Laughter.

First, soak the bromoil print in water at room temperature for about 20 minutes. Then transfer it to a dish of black coffee for about 30 seconds, with constant agitation. The exact tint you produce depends on the particular coffee you use and its strength.

Next, transfer the bromoil back to the water for a minute or so, then back to the coffee for another 30 seconds. Continue this procedure until you achieve the tint you want, then dry the print in the usual way. If you find that you have made the tint too dark, allow the print to soak in clean water for a few minutes to dilute it.

The reason for swapping the print back and forth between the coffee and plain water is so that the water absorbed by the swollen gelatin of the highlights will dilute the coffee while the shadow areas are more directly toned. This produces a deeper tint in the shadows than in the highlights, avoiding an overall flat coffee tone.

Naturally, if you want to add colour to your bromoil as described in the previous section, you must do it after tinting the paper base.

PROTECTING YOUR WORK

A bromoil print is a truly unique work of art and a great deal of skill goes into producing it. It is quite impossible to produce two identical prints, because each is the result of hand-applied ink combined with your own dexterity and judgement. So you should treat your prints with the care and respect they deserve.

When the ink is fully hardened and you have completed any afterwork, protect the image with a sheet of acid-free tissue paper and store it flat in a folder or box – again preferably acid-free. Do not place anything heavy on top of the prints, although you can store a dozen or so in each folder or box. Then leave them there until you are ready to mount them.

Mounting your bromoils

Bromoil prints are beautiful objects that deserve to be displayed properly, either in a portfolio or hung on a wall. Either way you need to mount your bromoils tastefully to show them off at their best.

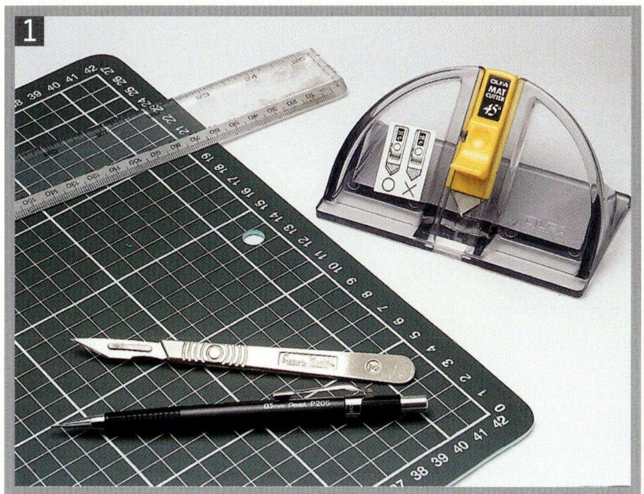

1 By far the most suitable way to present bromoils – or any other photographic prints for that matter – is behind cut-out mounts. And my view is: the simpler the better; after all it is the print that is important not the mount. Keep the mount plain and let the print speak for itself. You need a few simple tools such as a scalpel, angle cutter, cutting board, pencil and straight edge.

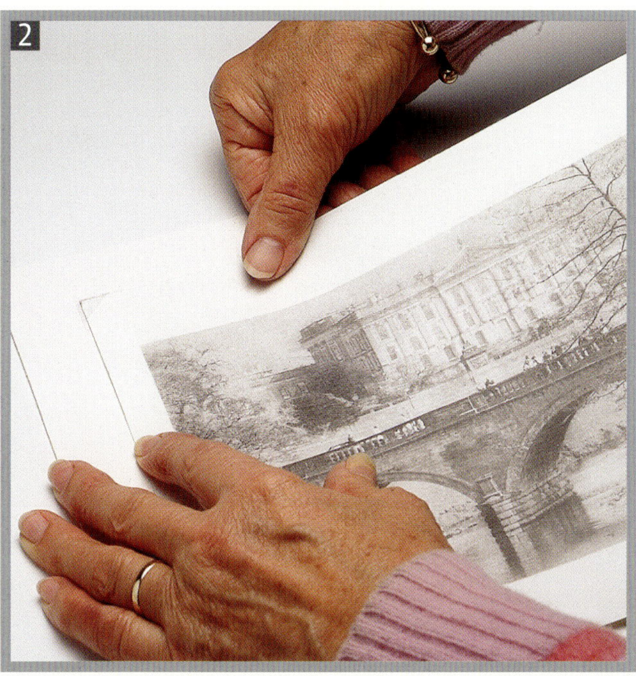

2 The first step is to mount the print on a piece of mounting board the same size as, or slightly smaller than, the cut-out mount. While you can dry mount the print using heat-sensitive tissue, or attach it with masking or gummed tape, I prefer to use photo-mounting corners like those you would use in a photograph album. The main advantages of these are that the print can be easily removed if necessary – if the mount should become damaged, for example – and they also allow the print to expand and contract, in response to changes in environmental humidity, without buckling.

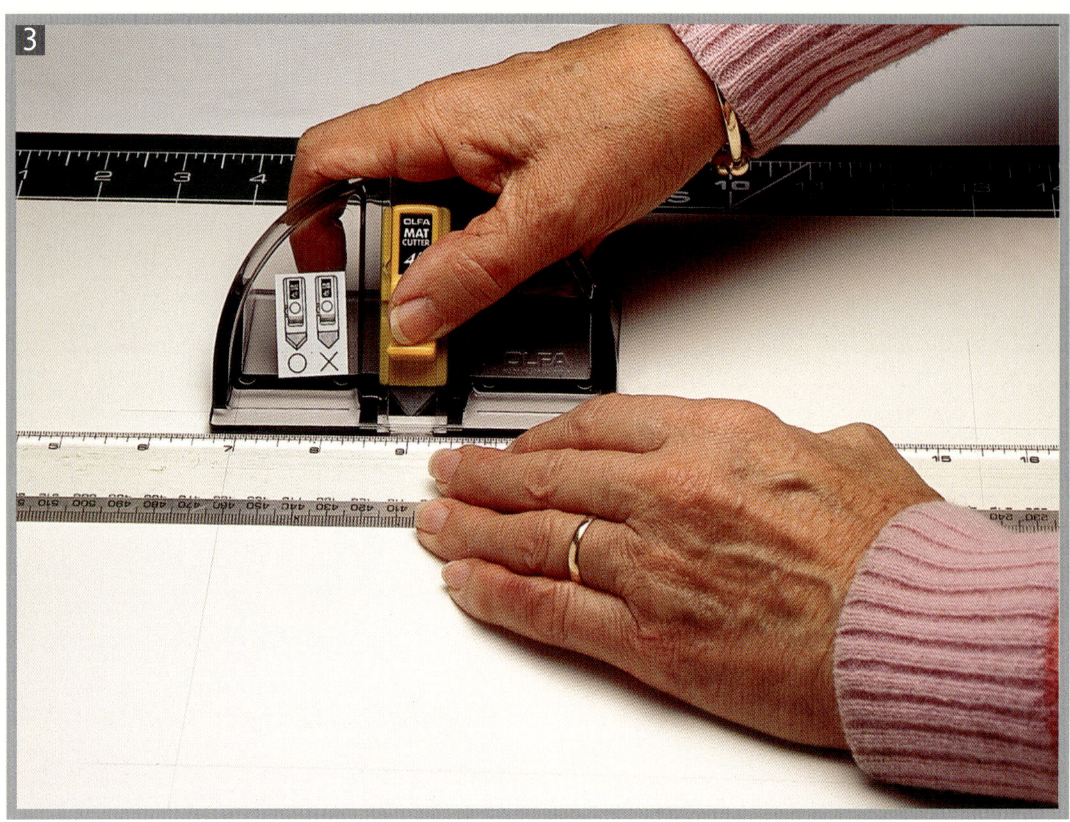

3 Next, cut out the window in the front mount. If you have kept the borders of the print clean, cut the window about 1in (25mm) larger than the image size. You can then title and sign the print in the bottom border and position it behind the window so that there is about 1/2in (12mm) of border showing all around the entire image.

Although you can use a scalpel to cut the window in the top mount, a proper mount cutter will give a more finished and professional appearance. These mount cutters, such as the Olfa, are quite inexpensive and will produce a neat 45° bevel on the window. Some, like the Maped, will cut at both 45° and 90°, although they are rather more costly.

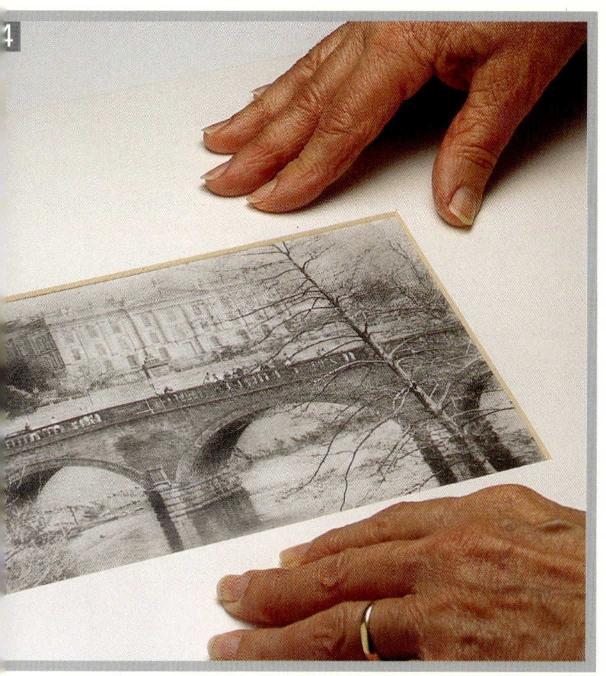

4 Position the window mount over the print before taping the two mounts together. Now attach the backing mount to the front mount. If they are both the same size, the easiest way is to fix a length of gummed tape on the inside of the top mount so that it projects above the top edge, then attach this to the backing mount so that the two mounts are hinged together.

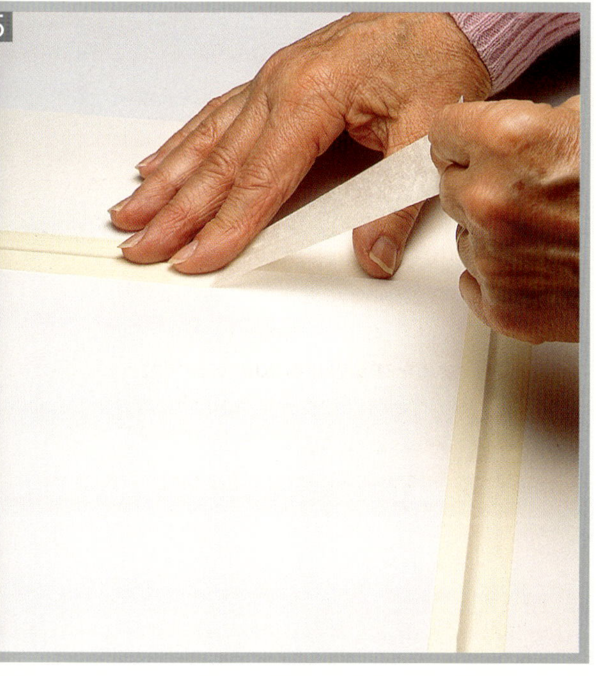

5 On the other hand, if the backing mount is smaller than the top mount, position the two carefully so that your bromoil is centred in the top mount window and fix it in place with a piece of masking tape on the back. Then turn the whole sandwich over and secure the backing mount to the top mount with four lengths of gummed tape.

Finally, fix a sheet of acid-free tissue to the back of the combined mount, towards the top edge, and fold it over the front of the mount to protect the image. Mounted in this way your bromoil will be safe from damage and will look its best to the viewer.

Disused quarry building

I discovered Blackaller quarry on the edge of the Dartmoor National Park when staying at the nearby village of Drewsteignton one October. It was an eerie spot full of abandoned machinery and vehicles, but provided a great location for photography.

Original taken on 35mm Olympus OM-2 camera with 90mm lens using Ilford HP5 Plus film and Pyro PMK developer. Inked with GC&I 1796 ink on Kentmere Art Document paper.

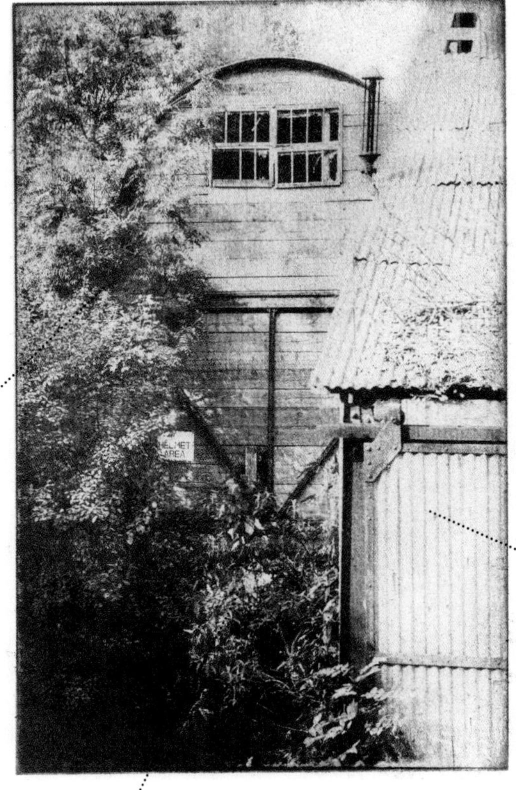

A major problem was the contrast of this picture, with deep shadows and bright highlights, tamed to some extent by the choice of developer

Extensive use of a wet foam brush and a hopper helped to keep the highlights fairly clean without losing detail

As I wanted a more photographic result, I chose to ink mainly with a foam roller, just finishing with a brush

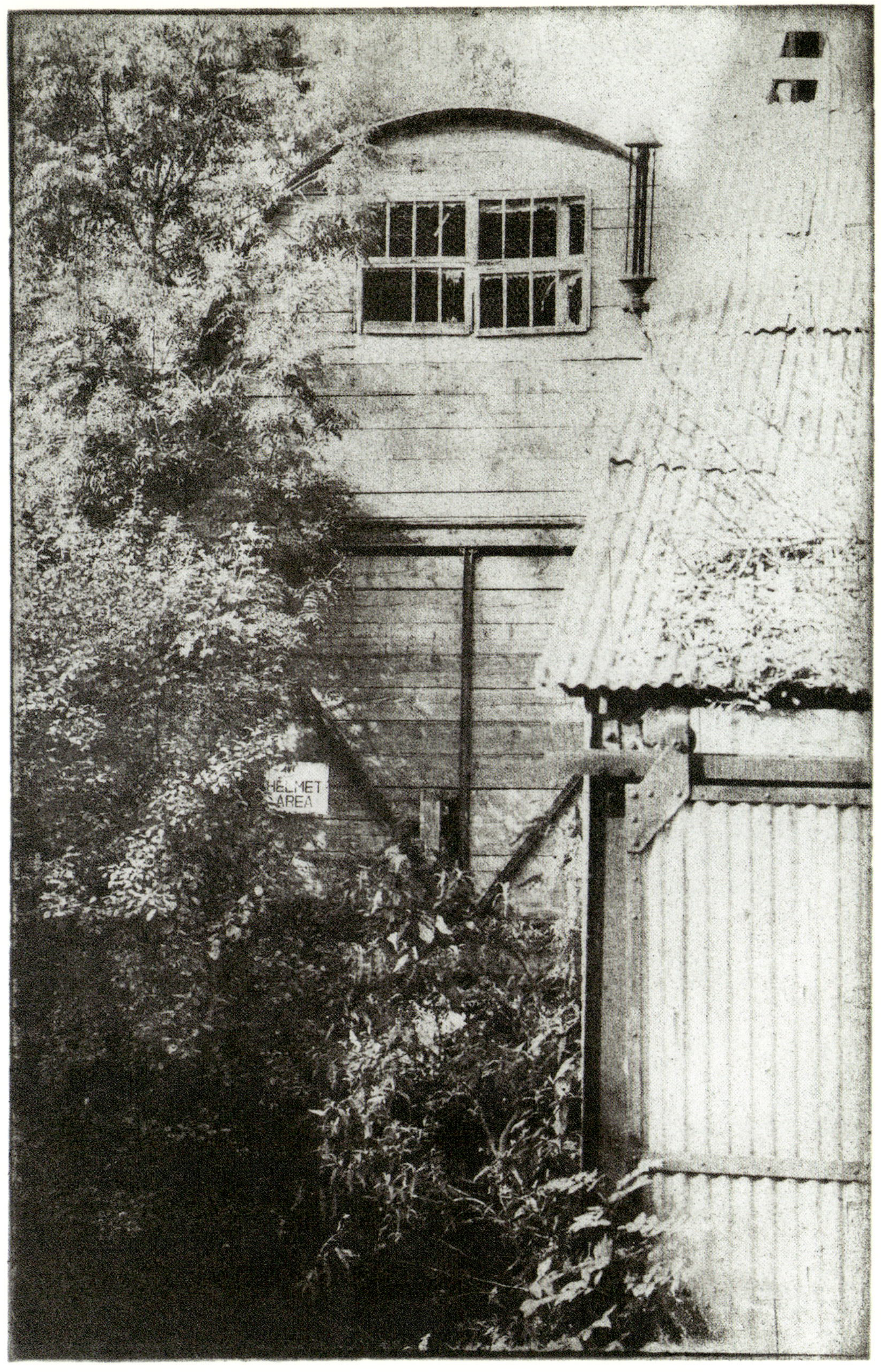
HELMET
AREA

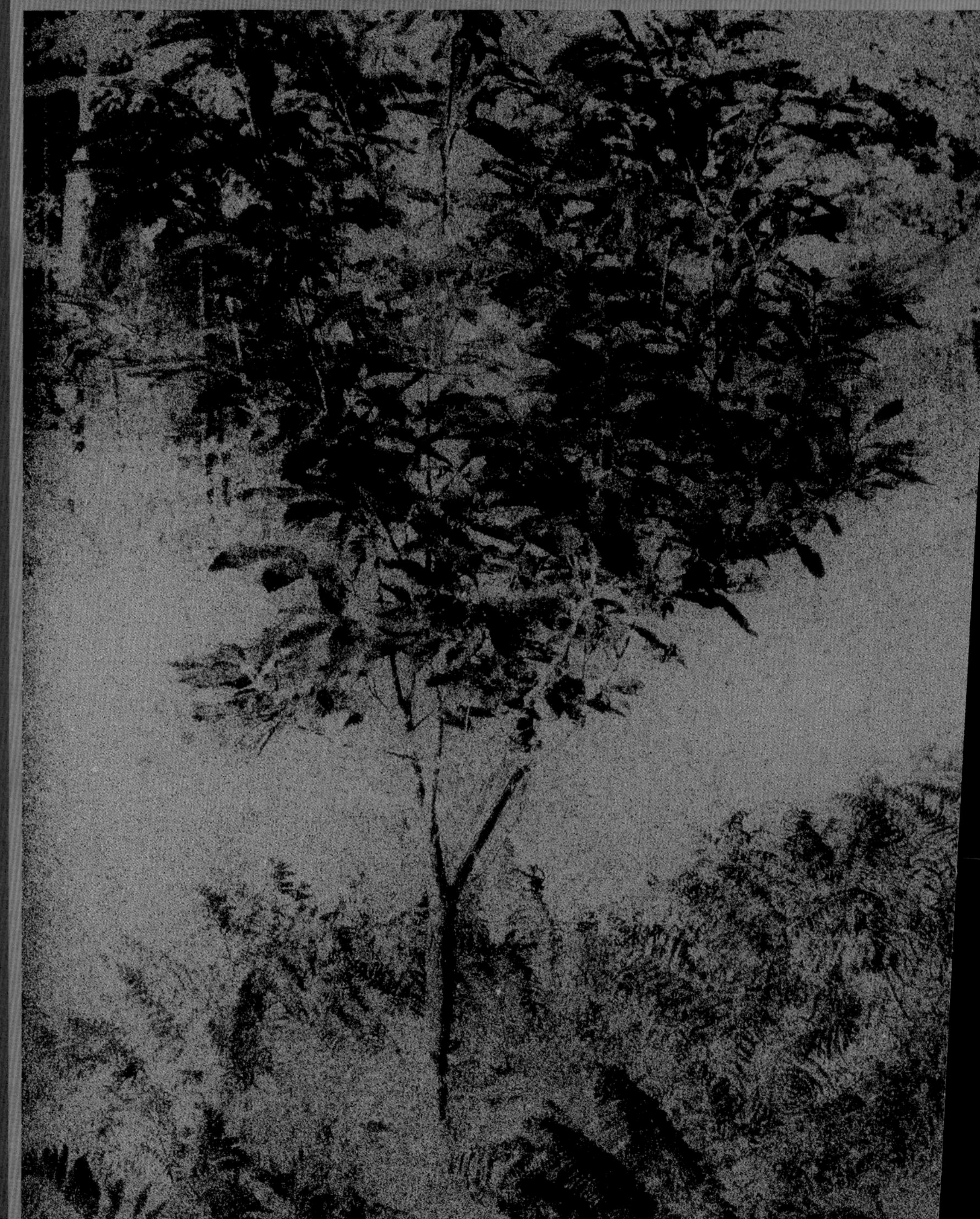

Part II

Some related processes

Bromoil is only one of a number of oil pigment-based processes. This section looks at bromoil transfer and other oil processes.

10 Bromoil transfer

Many workers consider the production of bromoil transfers to be the ultimate stage of the process. Whether you agree with this or not a bromoil transfer does offer some advantages.

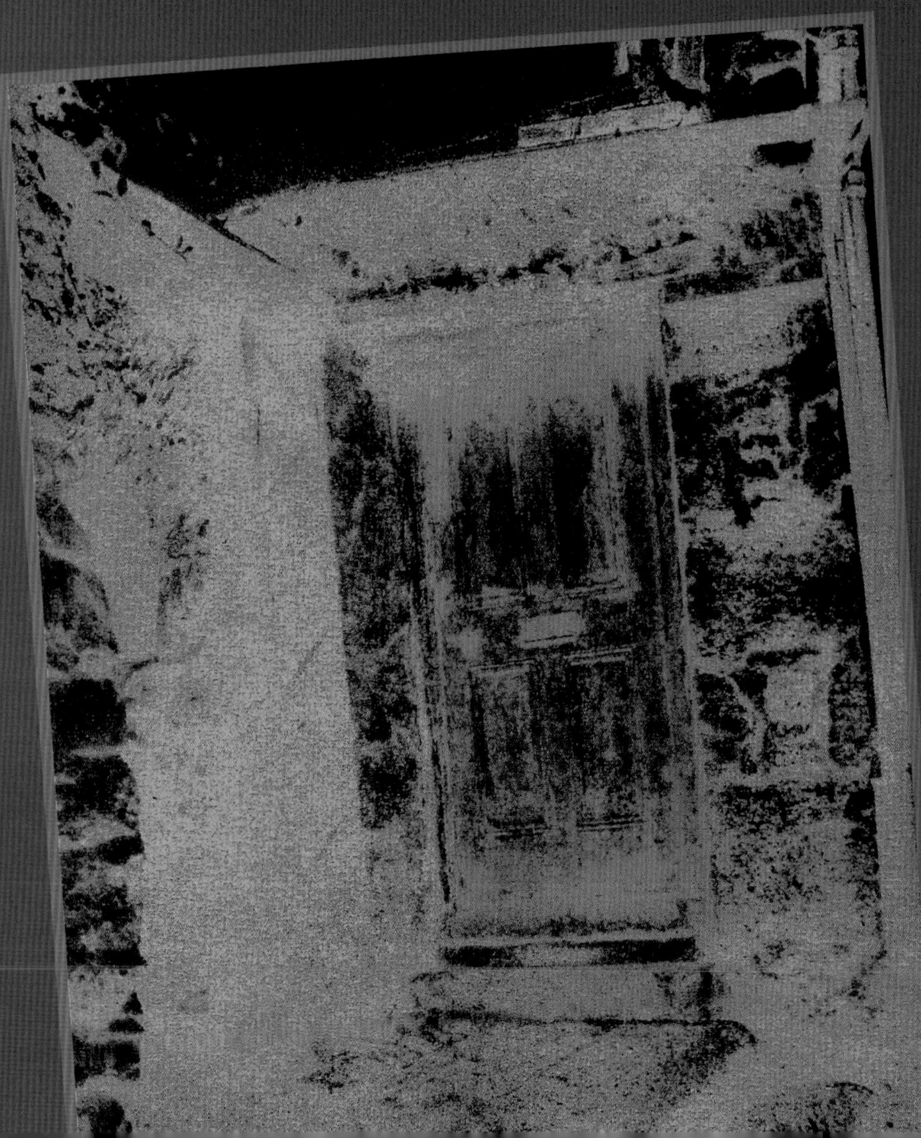

In 1933, G. L. Hawkins MC FRPS, wrote: 'I have never ... regarded the bromoil print as the finished picture. It seems to me that the natural and reasonable thing to do ... is to transfer the pigment image on to a new paper base.'

Personally, I do not share this view. I see the transfer process, which has a great deal in common with lithography, more as a means of printing reproductions of the original bromoil. However, a well-produced bromoil transfer can be a thing of beauty and offers certain advantages. Principal among these is that the final image consists solely of ink; there is no underlying gelatin on the paper. For this reason, the life expectancy of the bromoil transfer is as long as that of the paper on which it is printed.

There are, though, disadvantages as well. Something always seems to be lost in the transfer process – usually contrast. And although it is possible to compensate for this when inking the matrix, it is a further stage of complexity, which, unless you really are looking for longevity in your prints, is perhaps unnecessary. However, no book on bromoil would be complete without at least giving a mention to bromoil transfer.

WHAT IS BROMOIL TRANSFER?

When a matrix has been fully inked, the ink remains tacky for at least several hours. If you take the bromoil while it is in this state, place it face down on a piece of artists' watercolour or etching paper and apply very high pressure, the ink will be transferred from the matrix to the artists' paper. This process is known as bromoil transfer.

The original bromoil print acts, in effect, as a paper lithographic printing plate. After the transfer has been made the matrix can be re-inked and a further transfer made. This procedure can be repeated until the condition of the matrix has deteriorated to the point where the quality of the transfers is no longer satisfactory.

To get the necessary pressure to make this transfer you need some kind of press. And that is the main drawback of the process. Suitable presses tend to be fairly large, heavy and expensive, especially if you want to make large transfers. So in addition to finding somewhere to install it, you need to be making a considerable number of bromoil transfers to justify the cost of the press. Alternatively, you may know someone who already has one or perhaps there is a local art college with one they are prepared to let you use. There is, however, another way to produce transfers. Called 'spoon rubbing' it is a very cheap method, but more about that later.

The purpose-built Sinclair bromoil transfer press. Still the best buy if you can find one.

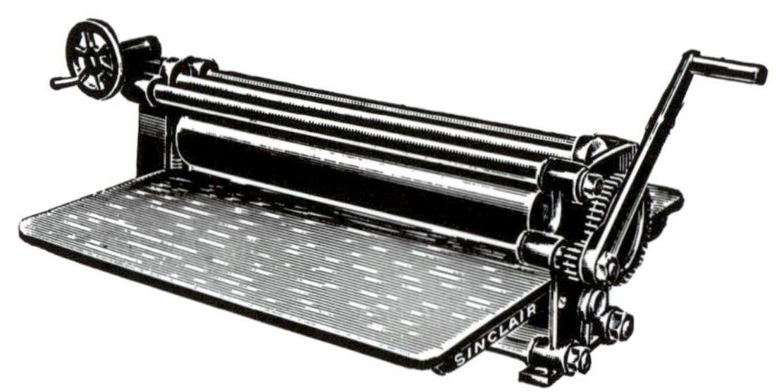

TRANSFER PRESS

Many years ago, Sinclair of London produced a press designed specifically for the bromoil transfer process. Sadly, this press is no longer manufactured, but they occasionally appear second-hand in the 'For Sale' columns of photographic magazines. If you want to get into bromoil transfer you can do no better than snap up one of these presses if you see one. The Sinclair press is very effective and extremely easy to use. The alternative is to use a small etching press. These are available from good printmakers' suppliers in a range of sizes from 9x15½in (23x40cm) up to 55x79in (140x200cm) or even larger.

You will also need a pair of zinc plates and two sheets of thick cartridge paper or thin Bristol board with which to sandwich the matrix and transfer paper as they pass through the press. Both the zinc sheets and Bristol boards should be the width of the rollers on your press.

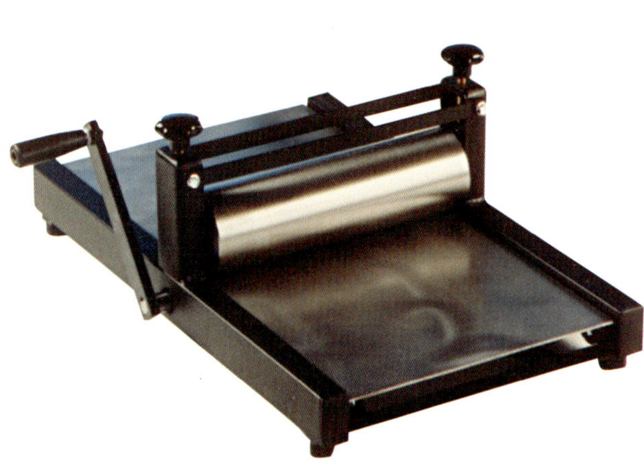

The small Norup Mini etching press made in Denmark. With a 12in (30cm) wide bed it is ideal for small transfers.

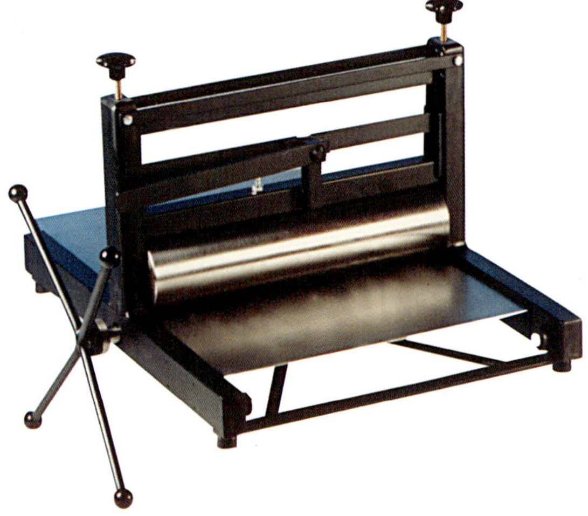

The Norup Midi etching press has a 16in (40cm) wide bed and a capstan type drive.

TERMINOLOGY / Bristol board

A Bristol board is a card that is normally used for mounting. It has two working surfaces and is usually a lighter weight than standard mounting or illustration boards. It is also possible to use high-quality Bristol boards for archival mounting purposes.

Making the matrix

The procedure for making the matrix for a bromoil transfer is exactly the same as that for making a normal bromoil print except for two very important differences. First, because the image will be reversed left to right during the transfer, you must make the original bromide print with the negative emulsion side up in the enlarger to give a reversed print. This will then be corrected during the transfer. And second, because a certain amount of contrast is lost in the transfer process, you need to make the bromide print rather more contrasty than for a normal bromoil. About half to one full grade harder is a general rule of thumb, but your own experience when making transfers will be a better guide.

When soaking and inking the matrix follow the same procedure as for a normal bromoil, although a light touch will make it easier for the ink to be transferred. If you pound the ink into the matrix it will not produce a good transfer. Try to use the hardest ink exclusively; only if you cannot produce sufficient depth in the shadows should you use any softer ink. Aim for a fairly contrasty result because some contrast is always lost in the transfer.

Transfer papers

You can use almost any good paper for the support, but an artists' watercolour or etching paper is best. Try Whatman, Somerset or Hahnemuhle papers with a smooth HP (hot pressed) surface to begin with as they are the easiest to use. When you have more experience you should try other, rougher, NOT (not pressed) surfaces to find your own preferences.

tip

Some workers have found that making the matrix on resin-coated paper helps to give a clean and easy transfer. As long as you ink the matrix very gently, this is a good method as the ink tends to stay greasy for a longer period. But you need to handle the inked matrix with great care as the ink will smudge and come off very easily.

The sandwich

The matrix and transfer paper need to be protected as they pass through the press and this is the job of the sandwich. First place a thin zinc sheet on the bed of the press; the zinc sheets may have been supplied with your press or you may have to buy them separately.

Next, lay a sheet of thin Bristol board on the zinc allowing a gap of 1in (25mm) or so at the leading edge. Follow this with the transfer paper and the inked matrix, placed face down on the transfer paper. Place a second sheet of Bristol board on top of the matrix, and finally the second zinc sheet, again allowing a small gap at the leading edge.

Before assembling the sandwich, give the matrix a few minutes' soaking in water at room temperature, blot the surplus water from the surface and quickly work over the whole matrix with a very light hopping action, *see page 90*. It may also help to produce a clean transfer if you dampen the surface of the transfer paper with water using a spray bottle. Then again wipe off surplus water and assemble the sandwich. This will also make it much easier to remove the matrix from the transfer paper after passing through the press.

tip

You may find that you need to add a little more packing to the 'sandwich' to get a good transfer. If you do, add a piece of printers' blanket between each of the Bristol boards and zinc sheets.

Making the transfer

Before you pass the sandwich through the press you must adjust the pressure to produce the best transfer. This is a matter of trial and error; there is no hard-and-fast rule. However, a useful guide to finding a starting point is to use a feeler gauge to set the distance between the upper and lower rollers. A suitable gap to start with is ten thousandths of an inch (0.025mm).

With the Sinclair bromoil press this is very simple as the pressure across the full width of the rollers is adjusted by a single hand-wheel. Simply insert the feeler gauge in the centre of the rollers and adjust until you can just pull the gauge out.

Etching presses, on the other hand, usually have two adjusting wheels, one at each end of the rollers. In this case you have to adjust one end roughly first, then the other and make fine adjustments until you have the correct gap set. It is also worth checking the centre of the rollers to make sure the correct gap is maintained across the full width of the press.

Insert the leading edges of the zinc sheets into the press and slowly turn the handle until the full sandwich is between the rollers. You will feel considerable resistance while doing this. Now, using a steady turning action, feed the sandwich through the press without stopping. This is vitally important as not only will stopping produce a line on your transfer, it will also damage the matrix rendering it useless for further transfers. Aim for a transfer rate of about 1in (25mm) per second. Leave the trailing edge of the sandwich between the rollers. It should not be difficult to achieve a steady rate if your press has a single handle to turn the rollers, but it takes a little practice if a capstan-style wheel is fitted. In this case turn with both hands so that the sandwich does not stop while you move your hand from one spoke of the capstan to the next.

When the sandwich has passed through the press, reverse the turning action so that it returns, finishing at its starting point. Then very carefully separate each layer and gently strip the matrix from the transfer paper. You should now be rewarded with a beautiful reproduction of your bromoil. However, unless you are extremely lucky, the transfer is likely to be less than perfect, so it is a question of re-inking the matrix, adjusting the pressure of the press so that it is slightly higher or lower, and trying again. If a considerable amount of ink is left on the matrix, the pressure of the press was set too low in the first place, but if the matrix is difficult to strip from the transfer paper, then the pressure of the press has been set too high.

Multiple-pull transfer

The description given of making a transfer is of a simple single-pull transfer. If you find that there is an insufficient depth of ink in the shadows, for example, you may want to try the multiple-pull method.

As its name implies, this consists of re-inking the matrix after the first pass through the press and then passing it through a second time, possibly following this with a third re-inking and transfer. The problem with this method is making sure that the images from the second and subsequent inkings are registered accurately with that from the first. A simple way of achieving this is to put small pencil registration marks on each edge of the back of the matrix and extending them on to the transfer paper. It is then a simple matter to line up these marks for the second and subsequent transfers.

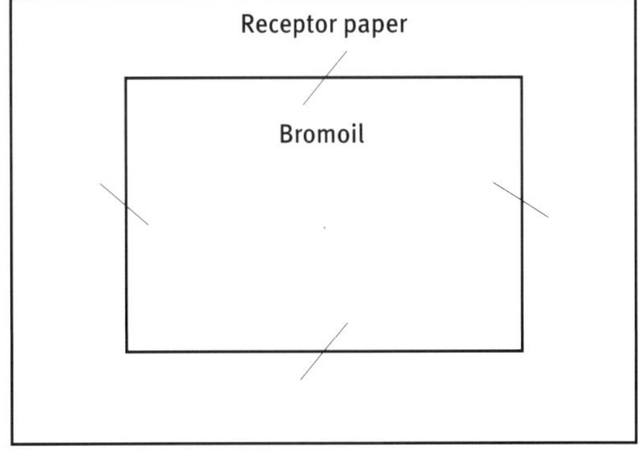

Extend the pencil marks from the back of the bromoil to the receptor paper for easy registration.

It is also a good idea, if you know from the outset that you want to make a multiple-pull transfer, to ink the matrix lightly and pass it through the press at a lower pressure than normal. This will stretch the matrix – which always happens in the first pass – and make registration easier. Use any spare piece of paper as the support for this stretching pull as it will not form part of the final transfer. However, if you ensure that the soaking of the matrix and the subsequent inking are carried out properly, there should be little need for multiple-pull transfers.

One instance where the multiple-pull method is essential, though, is if you wish to ink the matrix with different coloured inks for the second and subsequent pulls. This can produce spectacular results, but you need to have built a great deal of bromoil and transfer experience before moving on to this technique.

SPOON-RUB TRANSFERS

If you just want to try your hand at bromoil transfer without going to the expense of having to buy a press, the 'spoon rubbing' method is capable of producing surprisingly good results, especially with small prints up to about 10x8in (25x20mm).

In essence, the technique is rather like hand printing a woodcut or linocut. You simply place the inked matrix in contact with the transfer paper and rub the back with a spoon. You can use either the bowl of the spoon or its handle to give a range of control, and you need to exert a fairly large amount of pressure to obtain a good transfer.

Preparation of the matrix is exactly the same as for transferring by press. To prevent the matrix moving after you have placed it in contact with the transfer paper, you need to devise some way of clamping the two together.

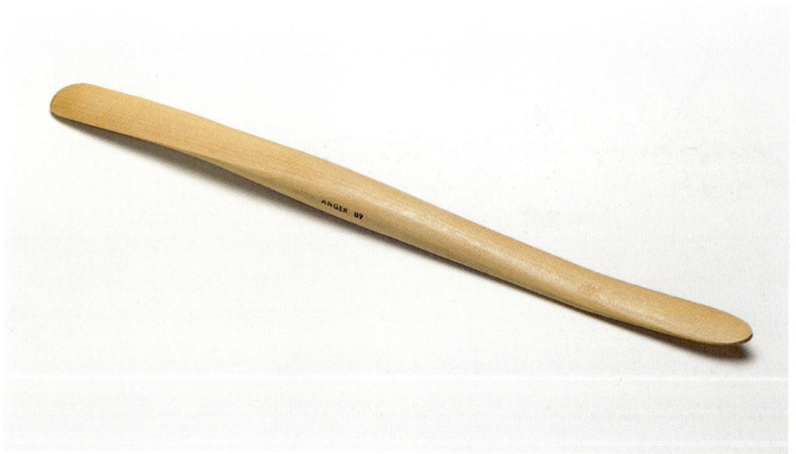

Instead of using a spoon, a boxwood burnisher gives you more control over the transfer.

tip

A better tool than the spoon, I have found, is a boxwood burnisher designed for use in book binding. The variety of shapes and edges on this tool gives more control over the transfer.

One solution is a home-made desk like that which used to be made by Sinclair of London. Take a piece of fairly heavy plywood or MDF (medium density fibreboard), drill and countersink two holes about ¼in (6mm) in diameter about 1in (25mm) from one end and 1in (25mm) in from each side. Take a length of $1in^2$ ($25mm^2$) softwood the same length as the width of the plywood and drill corresponding holes in it. Insert a countersunk bolt through the two holes in the plywood, drop the length of softwood on to these bolts, and put a washer and wing nut on each.

When the matrix and transfer paper are in contact, slip one end under the softwood pressure bar and tighten down the wing nuts to prevent the matrix from moving. A simple solution, but effective.

DIGITAL TRANSFERS

If making bromoil transfers simply as limited edition prints is your aim, and extreme longevity of the results is not a major issue, this technique may be of interest. It brings together both a historical process and a modern one.

First prepare your matrix, with the image right way round, ink it to your satisfaction as a bromoil print, not as a print for transfer,

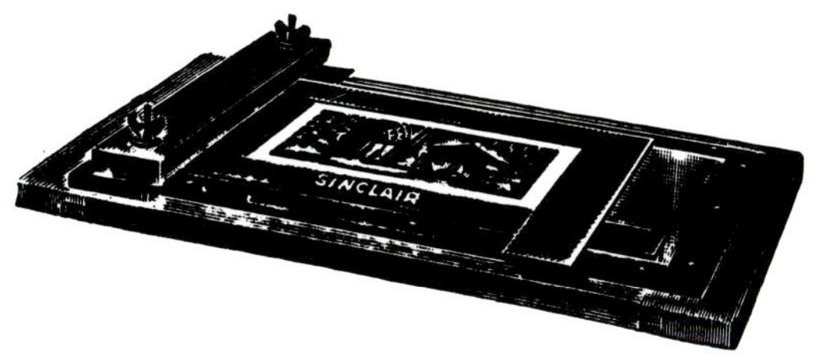

A simple transfer desk based on this design by Sinclair holds the bromoil and transfer paper firmly together for the spoon-rubbing method.

and allow it to dry. Then simply scan it into a computer on a flatbed desktop scanner. You can then work on it a little if necessary in Photoshop or other image editing software and print out as many copies as you wish.

Scan the original print at the 100 per cent scale setting and a resolution of 300 dpi (dots per inch). I have found it best to scan in RGB (red, green, blue) mode rather than greyscale as any slight tone or tint is then retained. Image editing with Photoshop is outside the scope of this book, but if you already use the software I am sure you will need no guidance from me.

One other point. Print out your digital transfer on a good quality 100 per cent cotton inkjet paper such as Somerset Enhanced, Bockingford or Hahnemuhle Photo Rag using all the ink colours, not just a single black cartridge. If you use a single black cartridge you are effectively reducing the resolution of your print because the difference between highlight and shadow areas can only be created by the variable spacing of the ink dots. This means that highlights have a lower resolution than shadows. By using all the colours there will be four or six dots of ink for each pixel, depending on whether you use a four- or six-ink printer.

If you want some degree of longevity – beyond ten years, say – use pigment-based inks instead of the more common dye-based inks. Although dye-based inks have improved in permanence in recent years, pigment-based inks are still superior from this point of view. Printing on papers that boast good archival values will also make your prints last longer.

I am quite sure that this hybrid method of producing 'transfers' will make many traditionalists throw up their hands in horror, but I am convinced that it is a useful technique to have in your bromoil armoury, as long as you do not try to pass it off as something other than a digital reproduction, of course.

tip

An alternative to using full-colour inks for black & white printing, albeit a more expensive one, is to use multiple black inks. These are known by a variety of brand names normally with the word black somewhere in the title. The variation of coloured inks that is necessary to print different tones in a black & white image can result in colour casts appearing. However, multiple black inks use a number of different-intensity black inks to provide a high resolution print without having to worry about colour casts occuring.

***Sloop Inn*, St. Ives, Cornwall, England. I shot this Ancient Pub on a home-made 5x4in pinhole camera using Ilford HP5 Plus sheet film developed in Pyro PMK and contact printed on to Kentmere Art Document paper. Inked with GC&I 17932 ink.**

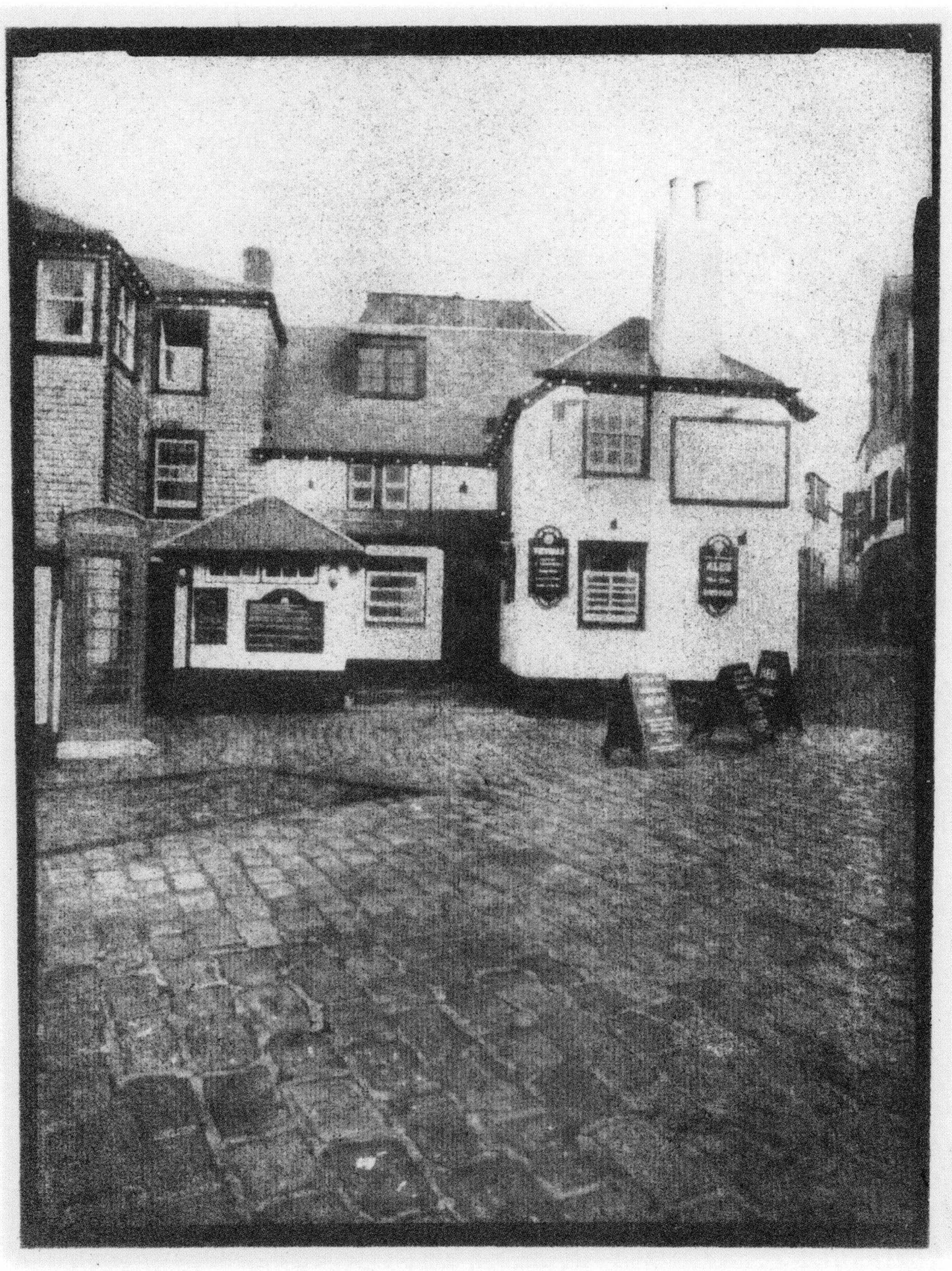

Roger's Door

As I was taking this photograph in one of the narrow streets of St. Ives, Cornwall, England, an elderly lady stopped and said: 'I see you're taking a snap of Roger's door.' Hence the title. Who Roger is or was I was unable to find out.

This is a 'digital transfer'. The original, which was stained with coffee and hand coloured in just the door area, was scanned into the computer on a flatbed scanner, then printed out on to high quality Somerset Enhanced paper using a six-ink inkjet printer.

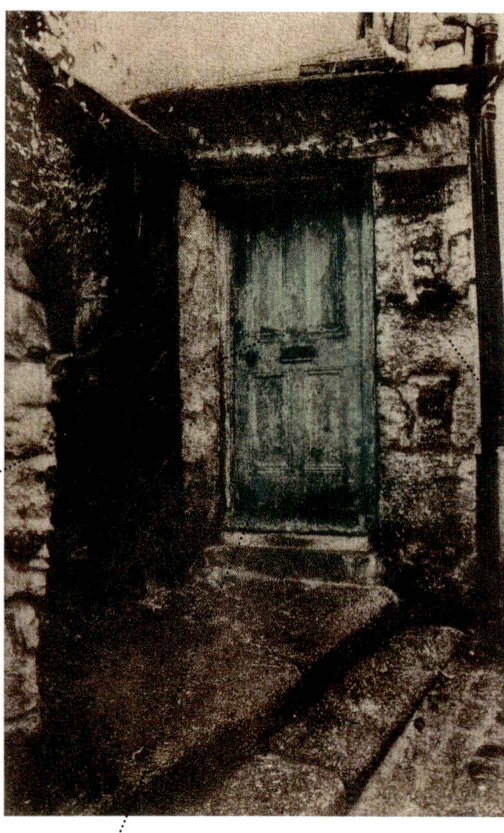

After drying, colour was added to the door area by scraping a little soft pastel on to the print with a scalpel and rubbing in gently with a finger

After first being soaked in water for some 20 minutes, the original bromoil was immersed in a dish of black coffee for about a minute to stain the base to a sepia colour

Cotton wool and a scalpel were used to clean up the coloured area, then the print was sprayed with fixative before scanning

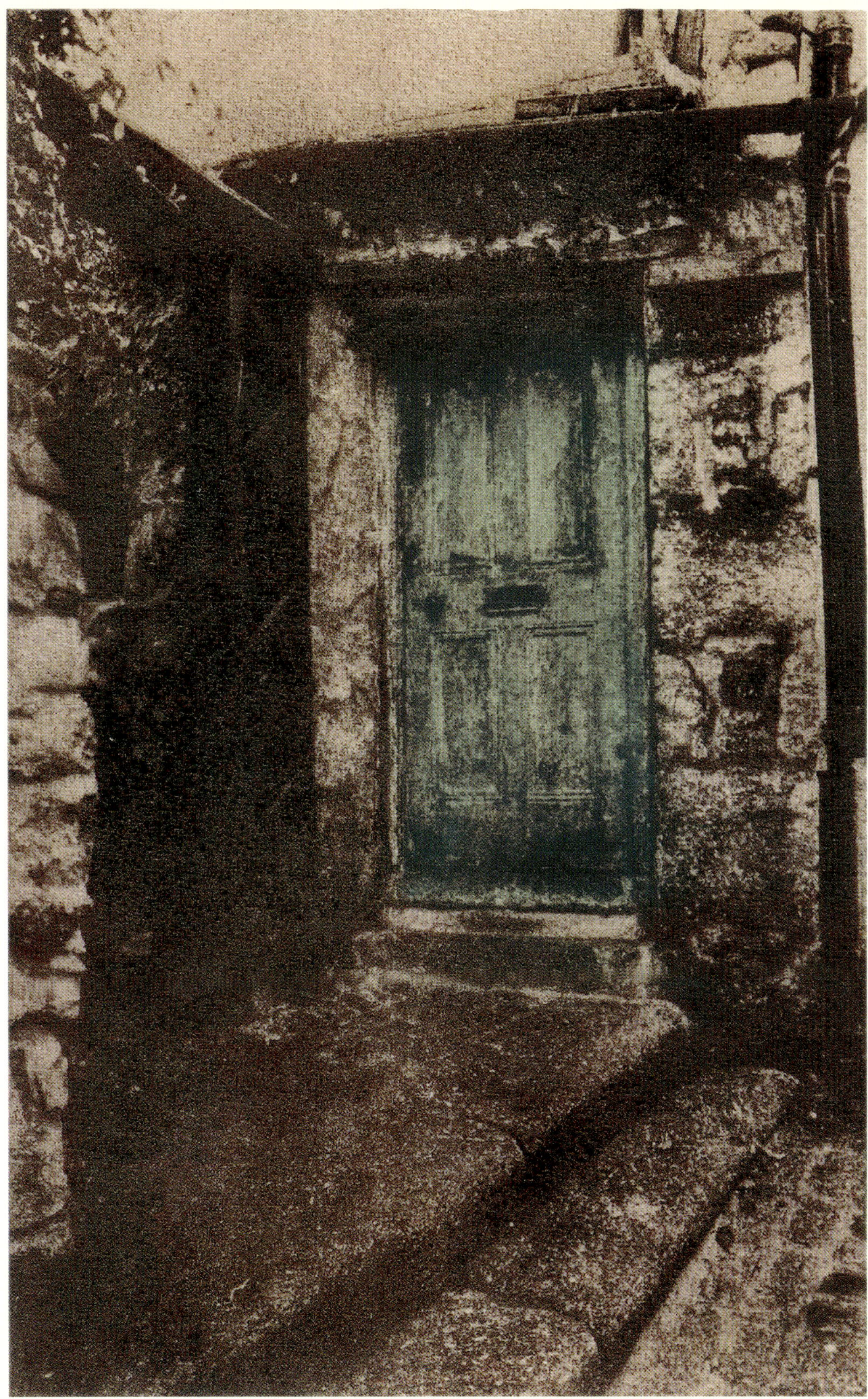

11 Other pigment processes

The bromoil process has evolved from oil printing and it is still possible to create beautiful pictures using this method and others such as Oleobrom and Bromotype.

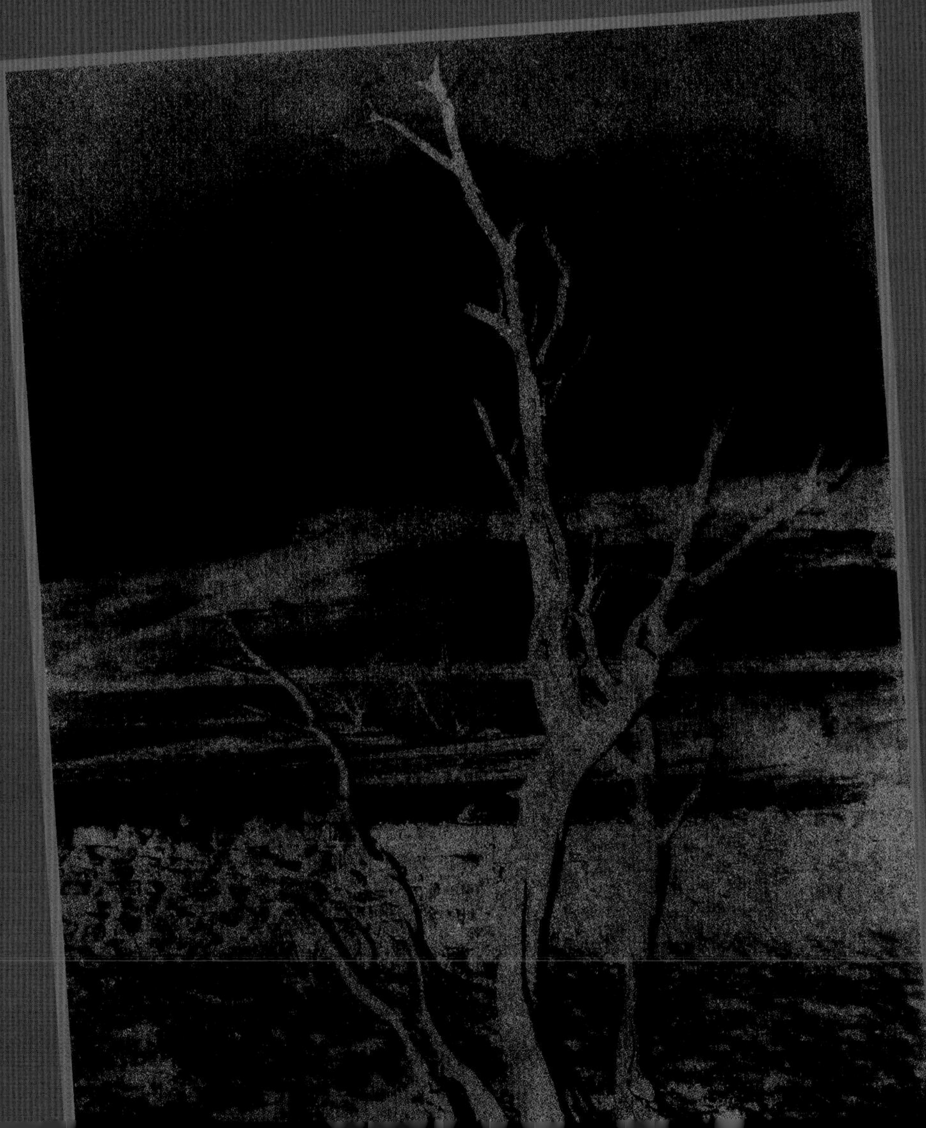

There are several other processes that use the principle of making a matrix that is differentially tanned, swollen in water and inked with a stiff, greasy ink. They bear a fundamental similarity to the bromoil process but differ in the detail. In this chapter I shall deal with the three most common of these processes.

THE OIL PROCESS

This is the process on which bromoil is based and was first perfected by G. E. H. Rawlins in the early years of the twentieth century. It was made popular by Rawlins – indeed it was originally known as the Rawlins Oil Process – and, later, by the French photographer, Robert Demachy and the Belgian, Leonard Missone.

The main difference between the oil and bromoil processes is the starting point. While with a bromoil you start by making a silver bromide print which you subsequently bleach and tan, with the oil process you print on to a dichromate-sensitized gelatin-coated paper which contains no silver. This eliminates the bromide print production stages and the bleaching and tanning steps.

However, the problem is that the dichromate-sensitized gelatin is extremely slow, so you cannot enlarge on to the paper; there is simply not enough light produced by the enlarger to expose the paper adequately. Instead, you need to expose the paper in contact with the negative to a strong ultraviolet (UV) source such as daylight or an artificial UV lamp. And this, in turn, means that if your aim is to make reasonably large prints you have to start with a reasonably large negative.

There are two ways of producing a large negative for oil printing. You can either make your picture with a large-format camera or you can make an enlarged duplicate negative from your 35mm or medium-format original.

When you make the exposure, the dichromate-sensitized layer is hardened or tanned in direct proportion to the amount of UV falling on it. So, just as when you bleach and tan a bromide print for bromoil, the shadow areas become extensively hardened and the mid-tones and highlights progressively less so. After exposure the paper is washed to remove the dichromate stain and then dried. It is now a matrix ready for soaking and inking.

So the whole process of producing the matrix is considerably shorter and quicker than with the bromoil process, and you need only one chemical – potassium dichromate. Added to this, most workers find oil prints much easier to ink than bromoils. This is because the gelatin is softer, so it swells quickly and accepts the ink readily.

Suitable papers

One of the major advantages of the oil process is that there is an enormous choice of artists' watercolour papers and virtually all are suitable for hand coating with gelatin. This gives you a wide range of paper surfaces, weights and colours to choose from. But it is best to avoid rough surfaces as it is difficult to achieve even sensitization with these.

My own favourite papers are Somerset Satin, Fabriano Artistico and Arches Aquarelle, but please test as many as you can to find your own preference.

Do not choose too light a weight of paper – 200 to 300gsm (grams per square metre) is about right.

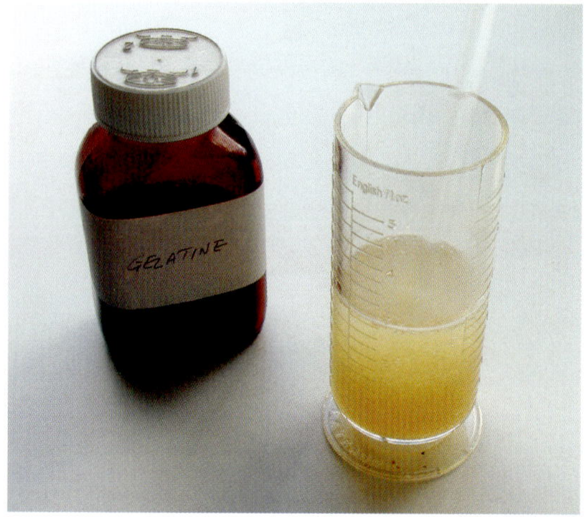

Prepare gelatin for coating artists' watercolour paper by first mixing with cold water. Then leave it to soak for 10 to 15 minutes.

Preparing the paper

The first stage in preparing the paper for printing is to coat it with gelatin. Ordinary cooking gelatin – unflavoured, of course – is perfectly suitable for this job and has the advantage of being available at any supermarket.

First make a seven per cent solution of the gelatin by adding 14 grams of the gelatin powder to 100ml of cold water in a glass beaker or wide-necked jar then make up to a total volume of 200ml. Allow this to stand for

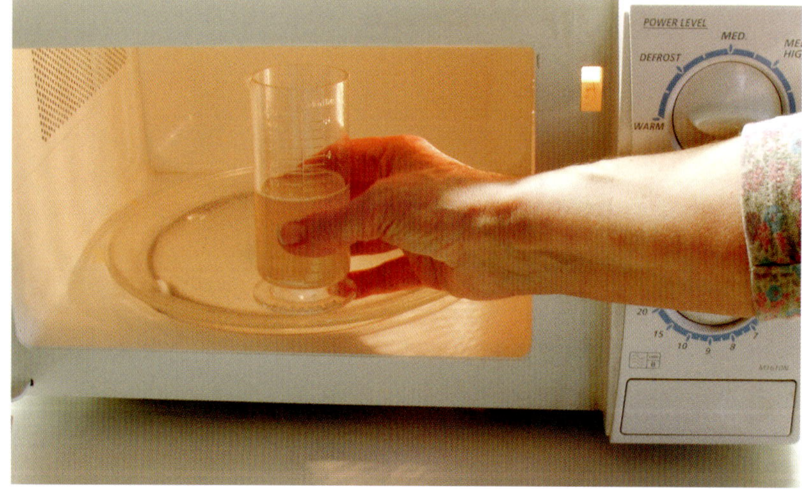

When the gelatine has soaked, place it in a microwave and heat for one minute on full power until the mixture is at approximately 100°F (38°C).

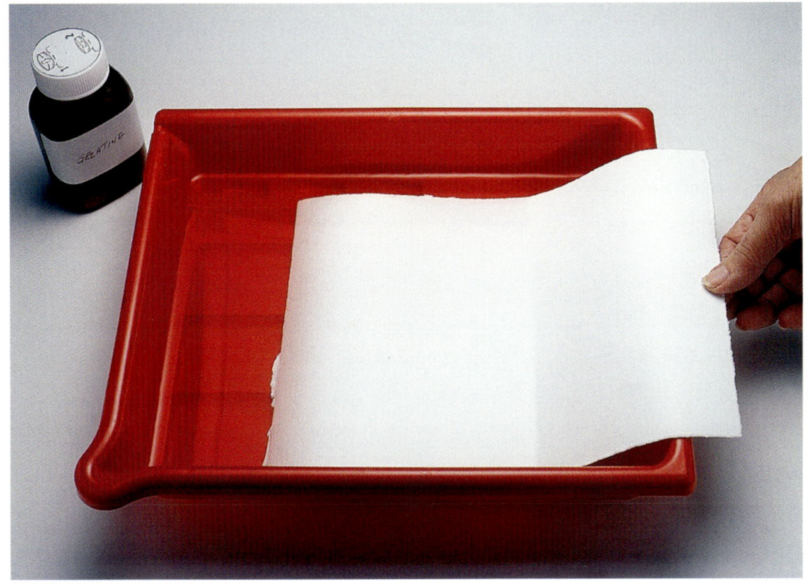

The base coat of gelatin is applied by immersing the paper in a dish of diluted solution for about a minute. When you remove the paper, drag it over the lip of the dish to remove surplus solution before hanging it up to dry.

about 10 to 15 minutes for the gelatin to absorb the water and swell. Now warm the gelatin solution to approximately 100°F (38°C). The easiest way that I have found to do this is to heat it in a microwave oven. Try one minute at full power as a starting point.

Take 50ml of this solution, dilute it with 150ml of warm water and pour it into a dish slightly larger than the paper you are using. I have based these quantities on the assumption that you will be making 4x5in (10x12cm) prints on paper about 6x7in (15x18cm). If you are making larger prints then you will need to increase the proportions required accordingly.

Slide the sheet of paper into the dilute gelatin solution and leave it for about one minute, making sure there are no air bubbles on the surface of the paper. Then remove the paper, allow it to drain and hang it up to dry. This forms the base coat of gelatin.

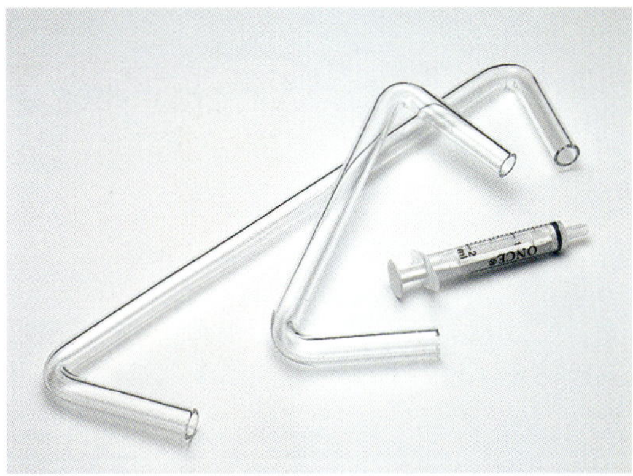

Glass coating rods make even sensitization easy. Use a 2ml syringe to measure 0.4ml of the potassium dichromate solution for a 4x5in (10x12.5cm) print, or 1.6ml for a 6x7in (15x18cm) print.

Once the paper has dried, warm the full-strength gelatin solution and coat the front surface of the paper using a wide foam brush. Work first up and down the paper and then from side to side. Hang up the paper and allow to dry. Then apply a second coat in exactly the same way, making sure that the coating is perfectly even. Hang up the paper and allow to dry thoroughly.

The next stage is to sensitize the coated paper. It is best to do this immediately before you want to make the exposure as the dichromate sensitizer will begin to harden the gelatin, albeit slowly, as soon as it is applied. Mix a three per cent solution of potassium dichromate by adding 3 grams of the chemical to 75ml of distilled or de-ionized water and then make up to a final volume of 100ml.

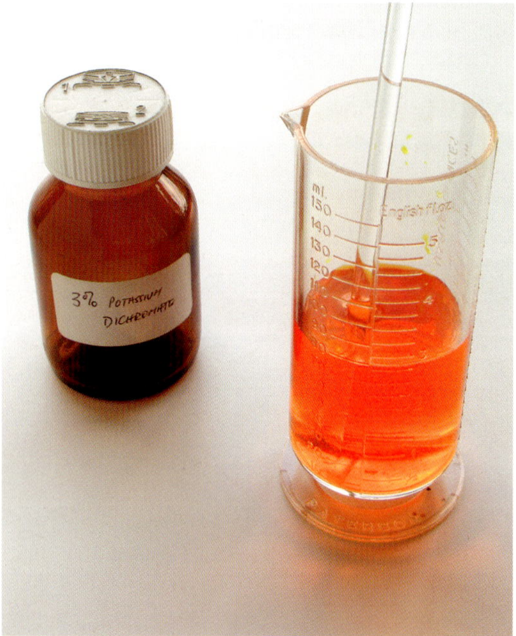

Mix a three per cent solution of potassium dichromate with which to sensitize the coated paper. Because potassium dichromate is very toxic, take great care when handling it.

caution

Potassium dichromate is a very nasty chemical. Not only is it toxic, it is also a suspected carcinogen. When mixing potassium dichromate solutions ALWAYS wear rubber gloves, a dust mask and protection for your eyes.

Mark out the area of your negative on the coated paper with small pencil marks. Then, using a wide foam or Hake brush, take up some of the dichromate solution and paint it on to the marked-out area of the paper. Try to work fairly quickly, as the gelatin may start to soften if you keep brushing, but strive to make the layer of sensitizer as even as possible. An alternative is to use a glass coating rod – sometimes called a puddle pusher – to apply the sensitizer. With practice it is possible to achieve a uniform layer very quickly. Work in a room with subdued lighting to avoid fogging the paper.

Hang the sensitized paper in a dark cupboard to dry; it should take no longer than an hour. Once it is dry, expose the paper immediately to avoid it deteriorating.

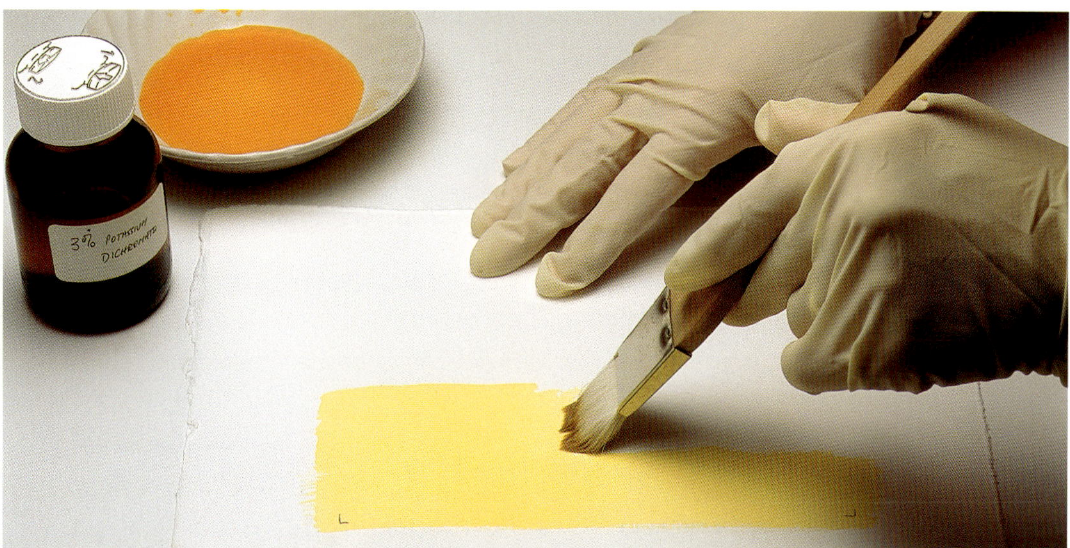

After coating the paper with gelatin, sensitize the area to be covered by the negative with a 3 per cent potassium dichromate solution. You can use a Japanese Hake or Jaiban brush for this.

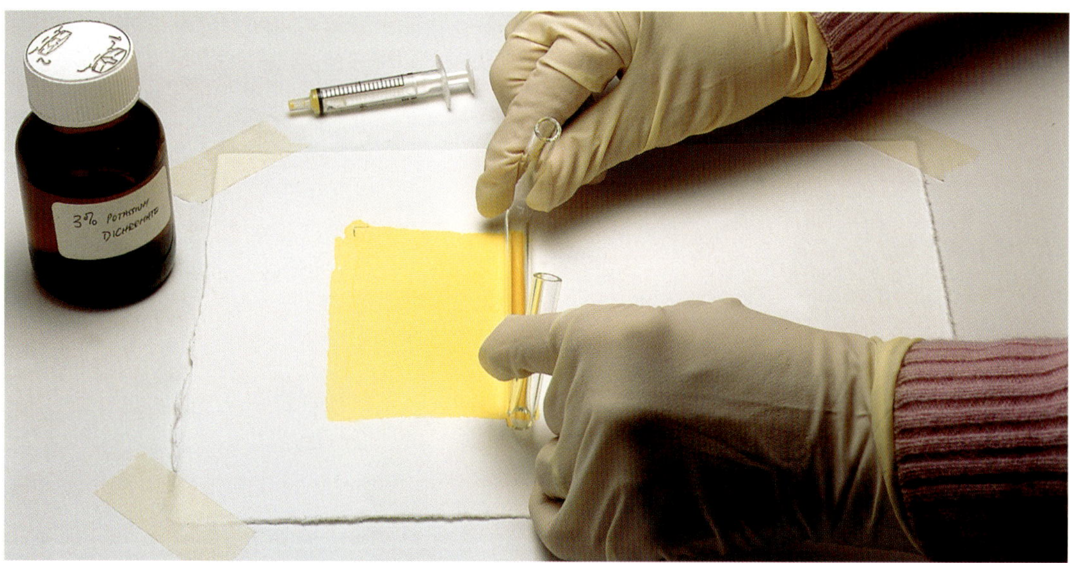

Alternatively, use a glass coating rod. Squeeze out the solution from the syringe into a bead covering the full width of the area to be coated. Then place the glass rod in this bead and pull slowly towards you. When you reach the end of the negative area, hop the rod over what is left of the bead of solution and push it away from you. This should provide an even coat of sensitizer very quickly.

Making the exposure

Place the sensitized paper on a sheet of plate glass and align the negative carefully in the sensitized area. Any negative that will produce a good print on grade 2 bromide paper should be suitable. Now lay another sheet of plate glass on the negative to hold it in place. You can, if you wish, use large bulldog-type clips to clamp the two sheets of glass with the paper and negative between them. If you have a contact printing frame large enough to hold the negative you can, of course, use that.

Take the sandwich outside into daylight – diffused sunlight is ideal – and leave it for about 15 minutes. Instead of daylight you can expose to a suitable UV source such as a sun lamp. My own UV source is a facial tanning unit I bought very cheaply at a garage sale. It contains six fluorescent UV tubes and is perfect for exposing oil and other UV dependent prints up to about 11x14in (28x36cm). Again, try a 15-minute exposure time to start with. Alternatively, you can make a test strip for your first attempt, giving exposures of 5, 10, 15, 20 and 25 minutes.

At the end of the exposure time, take the sandwich back into subdued light and remove the paper. You should be able to see a faint image in the dichromate-sensitized area. The correct exposure is the one that has just produced detail in the highlights, but this is not too easy to judge until you have built a little experience.

Washing the matrix

Wash the paper in running water as soon as you have made the exposure to remove the yellow dichromate stain. While the stain remains the paper is still sensitive to light and will start to fog. The length of wash will depend on the particular weight of paper you used, but it should be at least half an hour, preferably in an archival washer. You can also wash in several changes of water. Fill two dishes with clean water and immerse the print, which is now a matrix, in the first for five minutes. Then transfer it to the second dish for another five minutes. While the matrix is in the second dish, empty the first and refill it with fresh water. Continue the procedure of washing the matrix in alternate dishes for five minutes in each for at least six changes.

After washing, drain the matrix and hang it up to dry, weighting the lower corners in order to avoid curling.

tip

Sometimes, even after prolonged washing, a small amount of dichromate stain will persist. It is quite easy to clear this by immersing the matrix in a 5 per cent solution of sodium metabisulphite or potassium metabisulphite for three to five minutes. Follow this with another wash for 15 minutes in running water or four changes of fresh water.

Allow the matrix to dry thoroughly for a few days before you ink it. You can leave it for several weeks or even months and it should still ink satisfactorily.

Soaking and inking

As with normal bromoil prints you will need to establish the best soaking time by trial and error. I have found that half an hour at 68°F (20°C) gives me good results.

Traditionally, oil prints were inked with rollers rather than brushes, and they do seem to accept ink from a roller very readily. However, if you prefer to use brushes or a combination of both, you should experience no problems. But because the gelatin is not hardened you will need to use quite a light touch with your brushes to avoid damaging the gelatin. Although the procedure of coating and sensitizing your own paper may at first seem daunting, the results make it worth persevering with. Prints produced by the oil process have a truly hand-made feel about them, as indeed they should.

THE OLEOBROM PROCESS

Introduced in the late 1920s by Wellington & Ward Limited, the Oleobrom process is essentially a different way of inking up a matrix, although a review in the *British Journal of Photography* said that it 'may be described as Bromoil so altered and improved as to form a new printing medium...', however, the end result is a pigmented image that is extremely similar, if not strictly speaking identical, to a normal bromoil.

When Oleobrom was launched, the manufacturers included a special Oleobrom paper, which they said was essential to the success of the process. It seems that this paper was simply an ordinary (for the time) non-supercoated bromide paper that had been hardened during manufacture. Most papers that are suitable for bromoil, such as Kentmere Art Document, are extremely similar to this and will produce very good results. It is also possible to produce excellent results on resin-coated paper.

Making the matrix for an Oleobrom follows exactly the same procedure as for a bromoil, so there is no need to repeat it here. It is in the inking that the real difference lies.

When you are ready to ink the matrix, do not soak it. Instead, super-dry it as described in Chapter 4. Then put it on a piece of plate glass or Perspex and hold it in place with small pieces of masking tape.

Now charge a foam paint roller with a medium-to-stiff ink – GC&I 1796 is ideal – and coat the dry matrix uniformly with ink until the white paper base is just visible. Bromoil Circle member Kirk Toft LRPS, who has become an expert in the Oleobrom process, suggests that the inked matrix now be put aside for two or three days to allow the ink to stiffen a little, but you can omit this stage if you wish.

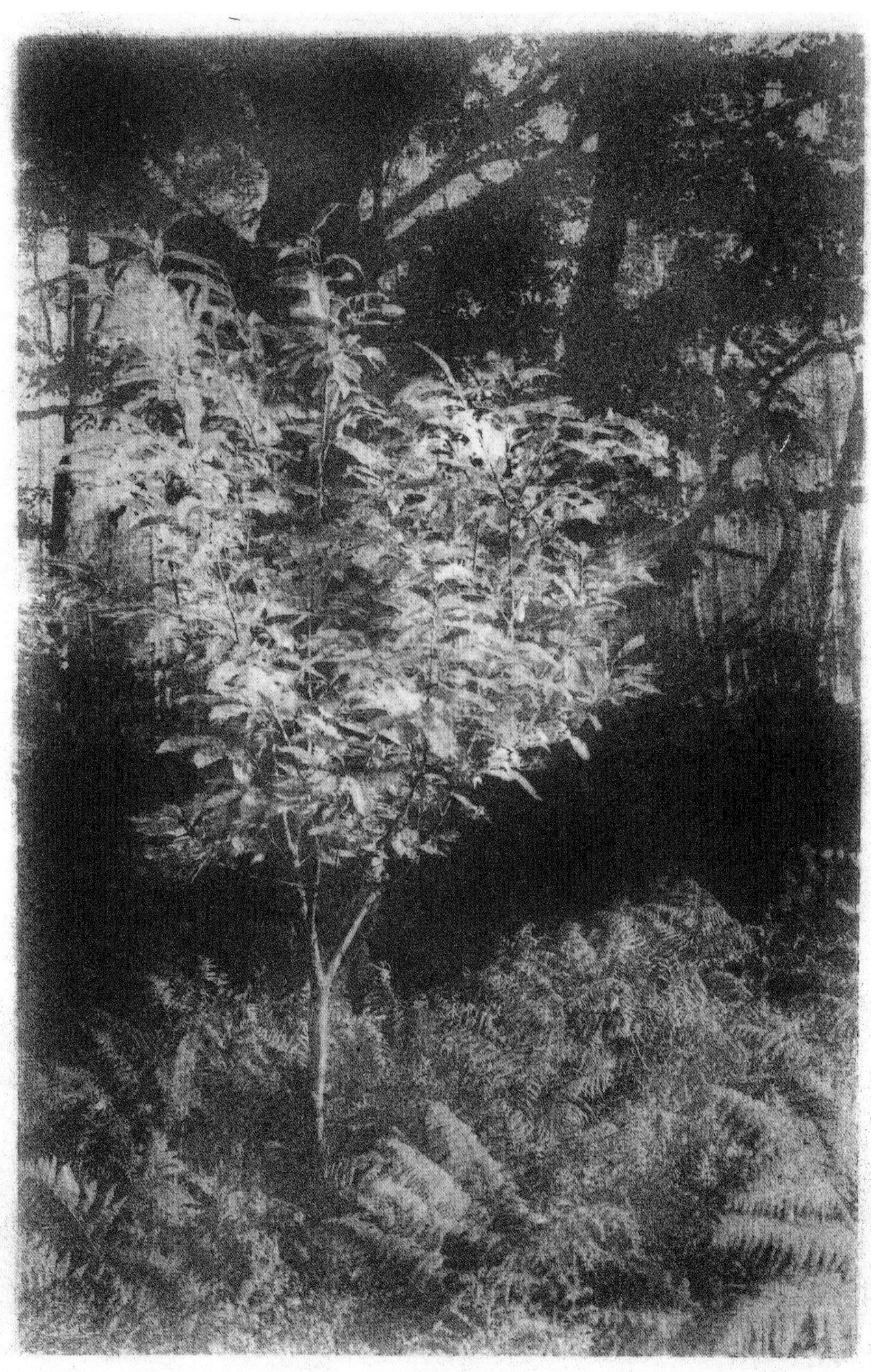

Autumn, Exmoor, Somerset. Made by the Oleobrom process inked with GC&I 1796 ink on Kentmere Bromoil paper. Original taken on 35mm Olympus OM-1 camera with 50mm lens using Ilford FP4 film and Microphen developer.

Fill a dish with water at about 75°F (24°C), immerse the matrix in it, still attached to its support, and leave it for about ten minutes. Then, while it is still in the water, run a clean foam roller over the whole matrix, back and forth, several times. This will quickly clear the surplus ink leaving the highlights clean but the shadows well inked.

Remove the matrix from the water, blot off all surface moisture and apply more ink with the first roller. Then return it to the dish of water and clean it again. Repeat this procedure until the print has achieved the depth of ink that you desire. Then, if you wish to, you can finish off the print with brushes in the usual way. Using small brushes will also ensure that you have a degree of local control; you can use small rollers in a similar way, but brushes will give you greater flexibility.

The results produced by the Oleobrom process tend to be more photographic than normal bromoils, with very fine grain. They are extremely quick and easy to produce and offer a good alternative appearance for suitable subjects, such as portraits.

THE BROMOTYPE PROCESS

Bromotype is, strictly speaking, an oil-reinforcement technique and is also known as Bromaloid. It is an ideal method for strengthening the tones in prints which have been made rather too light in tone and look washed out.

The first stages of making the matrix are identical with those for producing a normal bromoil, but after the bleaching and tanning stage do not fix the matrix. Instead, redevelop the image in a rather more dilute developer than you used to make the bromide print – Kodak D-163 diluted 1:5 instead of the usual 1:3 is ideal.

Wash the redeveloped matrix in running water for about five to ten minutes and then fix it. Finally, wash for a further 30 minutes, before drying and super-drying it. The rest of the soaking and inking follow the usual bromoil procedure. However, because it is an oil-reinforcement technique, inking the matrix using a foam roller will retain a more photographic appearance.

As you apply the ink you will, at first, see little change. Then, as you proceed, the image will gradually undergo a subtle change in both contrast and colour as the print takes on the colour of the ink you are using. Continue inking until the print attains the appearance you want. The process gives more robust shadows than a normal bromoil and beautiful vibrant highlights, thanks to the underlying silver image.

Dead tree

Intrigued by the angular shape of this tree against the soft hillside in the distance, I shot this picture at Rosedale in North Yorkshire, England, in beautiful early morning March sunshine.

This oil print was made from a digitally produced enlarged negative which was, in turn, made from a colour negative original. Inked with GC&I 1796 ink.

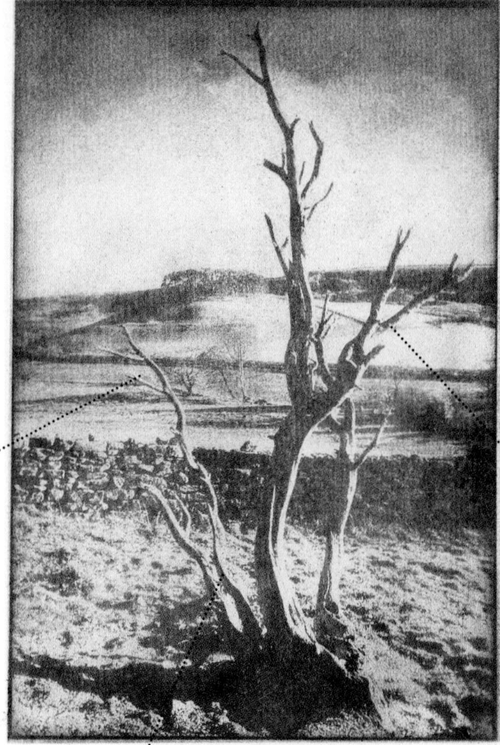

Making digital negatives from colour originals allows you to control the tone range of the negative – rather like using a colour filter with black & white film, but after taking the photograph

The rather soft contrast of the original was boosted in the computer to give a more dramatic effect

A matrix made by the oil process is often easier to ink than a bromide print that has been bleached and tanned

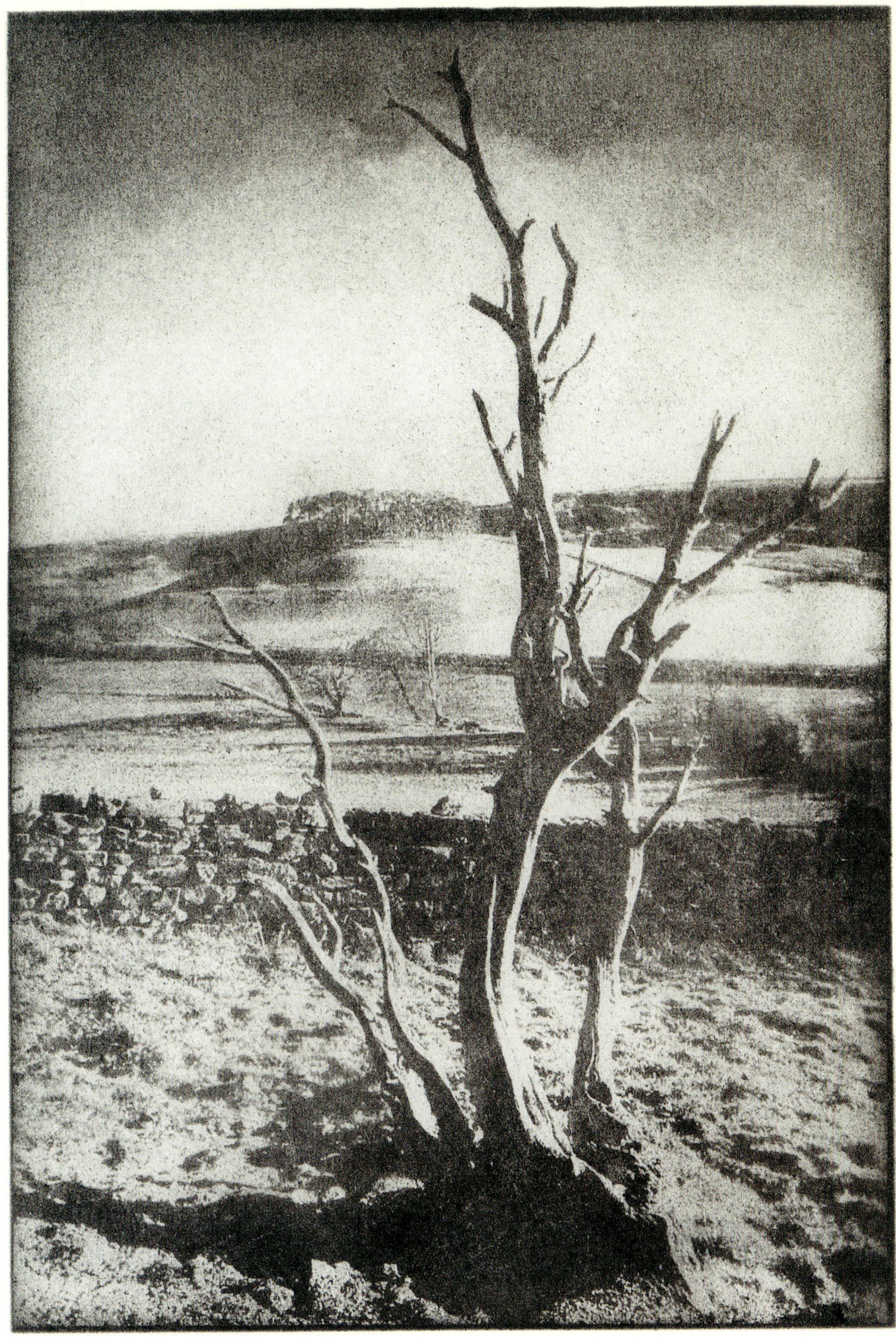

12 Making enlarged negatives

Paper for oil printing must be exposed by contact and therefore demands a negative the same size as the print will be. There are several ways to make the enlarged negative, both by traditional methods and digitally.

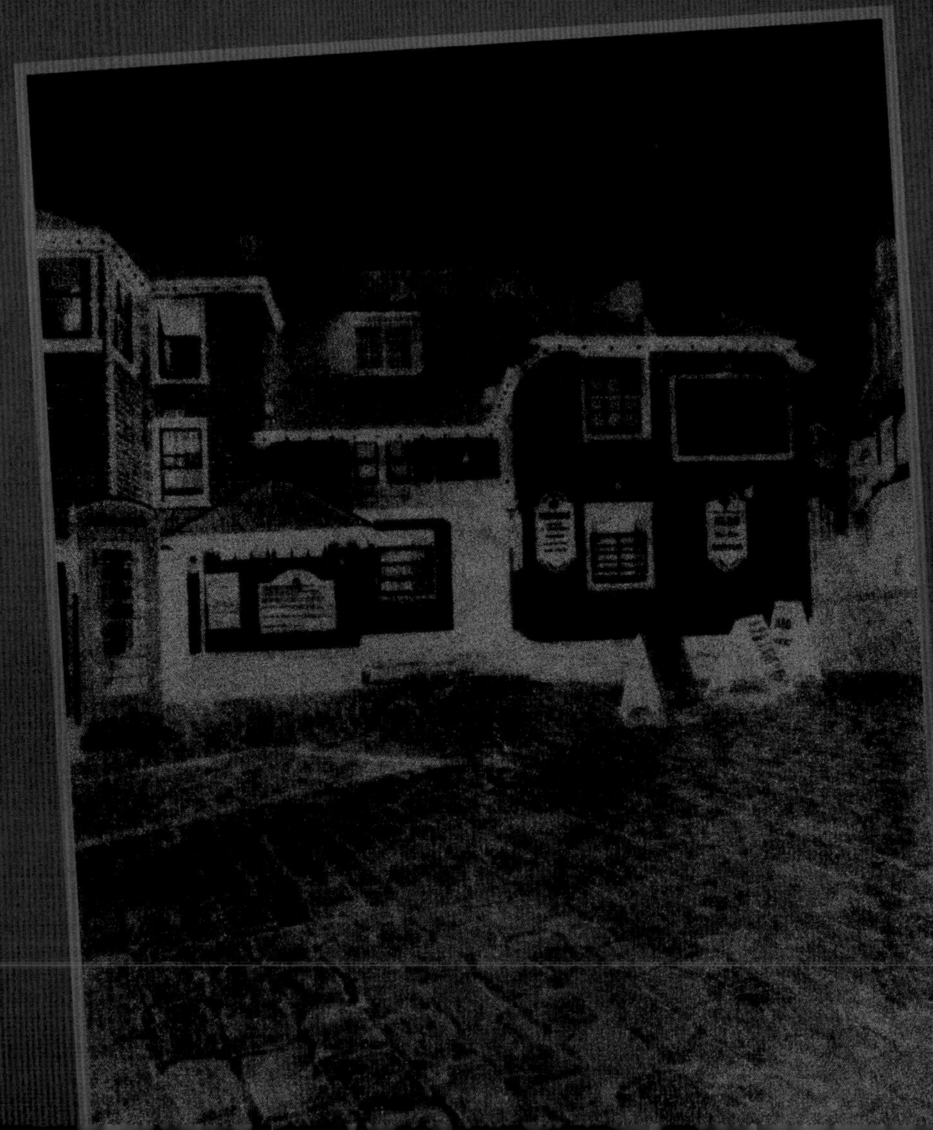

Because the self-sensitized paper used for making oil prints is so slow, you cannot expose your negatives on to it using an enlarger. Instead, you have to expose by contact to an ultraviolet source such as daylight or a UV lamp. This means that you need a negative the same size as your finished print. And that, in turn, means that unless you have a large-format camera you need to make an enlarged duplicate negative.

There are three ways to make enlarged negatives: one way is to make an enlarged positive and then contact print a negative from it; or you can do it by direct reversal processing large-format film; or digitally, by using a computer and inkjet printer.

LITH FILM

The simplest and least expensive way to make enlarged duplicate negatives is to use lith film. This film, which is designed for use in the graphic arts industry, is normally developed in a special two-part developer to produce an extremely high contrast positive or negative with just two tones – black and clear film. However, by developing it in an ordinary print developer such as Kodak Dektol or D-163 at bromide paper dilution, you can produce a high-quality continuous tone positive or negative.

Making enlarged negatives suitable for oil printing is a two-stage operation. The first stage is to expose a sheet of lith film under an enlarger containing your original 35mm or medium-format negative. Use lith film of the size that you want your finished print to be; one of the advantages of this specialist film is that it is available in a wide range of sizes.

When exposing the film, first place a piece of thin black paper in your enlarger easel and lay the film on top of it. This will prevent the light that passes through the film from reflecting back from the white focusing surface of the easel to cause fogging. The emulsion side of the film is the lighter side.

Make a test strip in the usual way, giving exposures ranging from two to 20 seconds, in two-second steps, at f/11. Develop the film in print developer at bromide paper dilution for five minutes at 68°F (20°C). Stop, fix and wash as usual, then examine the resulting film positive. Choose the best exposure – for a 35mm negative enlarged to 10x8in (25x20cm), an exposure of about eight seconds at f/11 will be about right. Now expose another sheet of film at this exposure, process and wash it before hanging it up to dry.

tip

Because the film is orthochromatic you can handle it and process it in dishes by the light of a red safelight. But it will be fogged by a normal amber safelight as used for enlarging paper.

TERMINOLOGY / Orthochromatic

An orthochromatic film is one that is sensitive to the entire visible spectrum except deep orange and red light. Orthochromatic films were the norm until panchromatic materials, which are sensitive to the entire spectrum, were introduced.

Today, orthochromatic films are used almost entirely for special graphic arts applications such as copying and in lithographic printing. It is their copying qualities that make them ideal for making enlarged negatives.

Because orthochromatic films are insensitive to red light they can be safely handled and processed by the light of a red safelight, whereas panchromatic films need to be processed in total darkness.

When this positive is dry, place it in contact with a second sheet of film – emulsion to emulsion with the positive on top – under the enlarger and place a sheet of plate glass on top to hold the film and positive in close contact. Make sure you have removed the original small negative from the enlarger and expose the contact sandwich for approximately 10 seconds at f/11, but make tests to find the best time for your enlarger.

Once again develop in print developer at bromide paper dilution for five minutes at 68°F (20°C). Complete the process and dry. The result should be a continuous-tone large-format negative of slightly higher than normal contrast, but ideal for oil printing.

You will not be able to buy lith film off the shelf at your camera shop; it is usually only available to special order and the normal pack size is 100 sheets. However, some mail-order companies offer unbranded or own-brand lith film in smaller quantities and at very much lower prices than the big brand names. This film is just as good as that which you will find in major brand boxes.

REVERSAL PROCESSING

It is also possible to reversal process lith film to eliminate the intermediate positive stage. This is a more complex process than that described above, but it does only use one sheet of film for each negative instead of two.

The first step is to expose the film in an enlarger exactly as described above, but remember that because the film is reversal processed, more exposure will produce a lighter negative and less exposure a darker one. Process to the following procedure.

You will find the formulas for the processing solutions in the Formulary, *see page 165*.

Reversal processing procedure at 68°F (20°C)	
First development	5 mins
Stop bath	1 min
Bleach	3–5 mins
Wash	5 mins
Clear	2 mins
Wash	5 mins
Re-expose*	30 secs–1 min
Second development	5 mins
Wash	5 mins
Fix	3 mins
Wash	10–15 mins

*To re-expose the film, place it in a white developing dish of water and suspend a 100 watt lamp about 18in (45cm) above it. Expose each side of the film for at least 30 seconds; more exposure is better than less as it is impossible to overexpose at this stage.

tip

The second developer is exactly the same as the first. In fact you can retain the first developer after use and use it as the second.

THE DIGITAL SOLUTION

If you have a computer, a copy of Adobe Photoshop and a colour inkjet printer you can make your enlarged negatives digitally. Ideally, you should also have a film scanner, but this is by no means essential because most good processing labs will scan your negatives to a CD for you. So let us start by assuming that you already have your picture as a digital file.

First adjust the tonal range of the image as a positive in Photoshop using the Levels and Curves controls. I find that increasing the lower end of the tonal range slightly opens up the shadows to give more detail. To do this, open the Curves dialogue box (Image›Adjust›Curves), position the cursor on the straight line and click and drag it until the Input and Output figures both read 60; now change the Output figure to 75. If you have Preview ticked you will now see the image brighten slightly in the shadow areas.

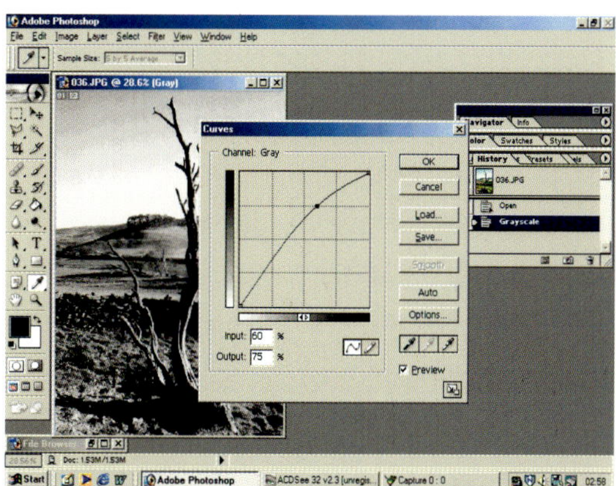

Using the Curves control in Photoshop to adjust the tonal range of the positive.

When you have finished adjusting the image, burning in and dodging any areas you feel could be improved, sharpen the image using the Unsharp Mask filter (Filters›Sharpen› Unsharp Mask). Set Amount to 100 per cent, Radius to 2 pixels, and Threshold to 5.

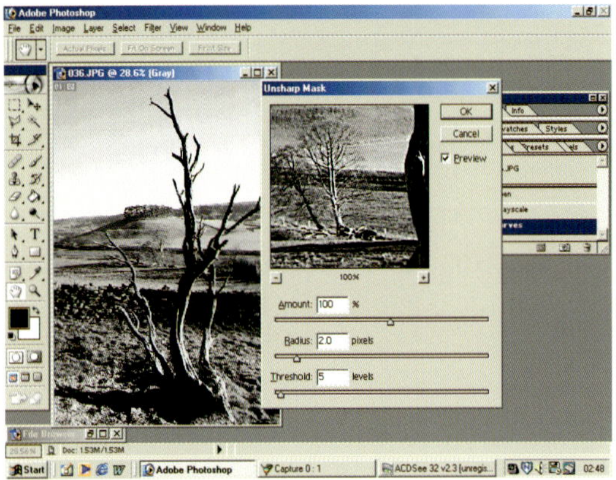

Sharpen the image using the Unsharp Mask filter.

Next, set the size of the image to the negative size you want (Image›Adjust›Image Size). The important thing to remember here is to have the Constrain Proportions box ticked but not the Resample Image box. Set the units to either centimetres or inches as you prefer, and type in the width or height you want your negative to be. The other dimension will change to maintain the correct proportions.

Now you are ready to make your negative by inverting all the tones in the image (Image›Adjust›Invert). You can now just print out the negative on to transparency material, but I prefer to add one further step to the process by 'colorizing' the image. This overcomes a problem when printing onto transparency material at high resolution using just black ink. Because there is so much black ink in the highlights it tends to puddle on the transparent material, which has a slightly sticky surface to retain the water-based ink.

Colorizing the image converts it to a reddish colour – the colour of a safelight – and this acts as extra density to the ultraviolet used to expose oil prints. This means that the dense black ink is not necessary to provide good highlight detail.

To colorize your negative, first change the mode to RGB (Image›Mode›RGB). Then select Image›Adjust›Hue/Saturation and click the Colorize box. You will see the image colour change from a greyscale to a reddish colour; the Hue slider moves to the far left and the reading in its box becomes '0' (if it does not, adjust it to '0') and the Saturation slider moves part-way to the left and has a value of 25. You can increase this if you find it necessary. Now save the file.

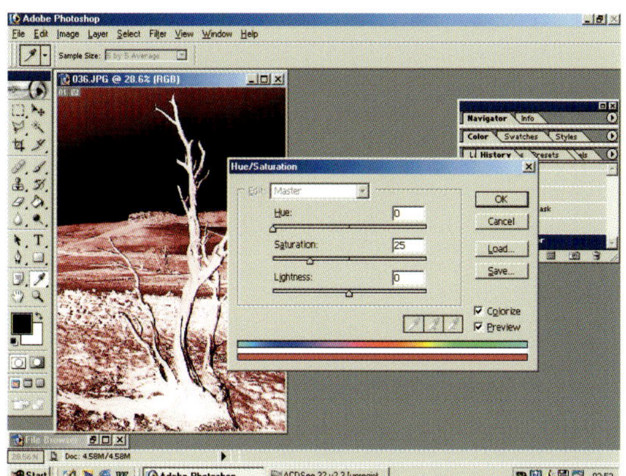

Colorize the negative image by ticking Colorize in the Hue/Saturation dialogue box and adjust the Hue and Saturation sliders to give the colour that you want.

An alternative way to achieve a similar result is to use Indexed Color. This second method is, however, a little more complicated than the first. You will first need to make sure that your image is a positive in Grayscale mode; if you find that it is not, change to this mode now (Image>Mode>Grayscale). When the dialogue box asks if you want to discard the colour information, click OK. Next convert the image to Indexed Color (Image>Mode>Indexed Color). Then select the Color Table (Image>Mode>Color Table) and a Color Table dialogue box opens. Make sure that the Table box reads Grayscale and change it if it does not.

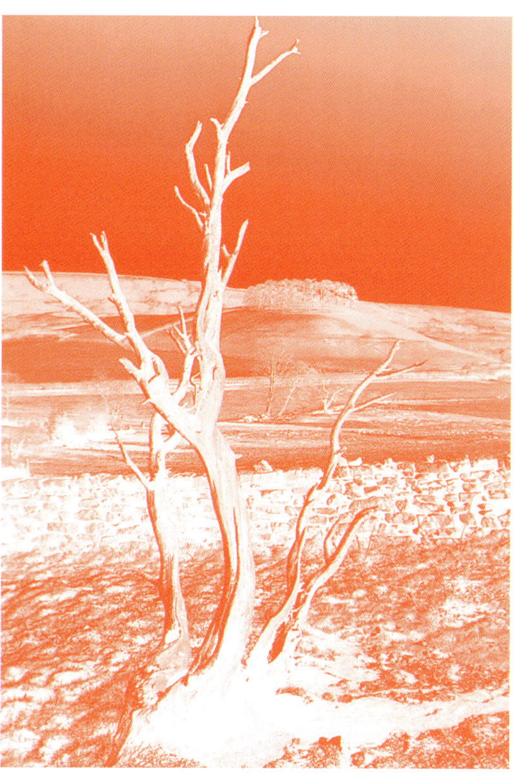

This enlarged negative was made as described in the text using a computer and inkjet printer.

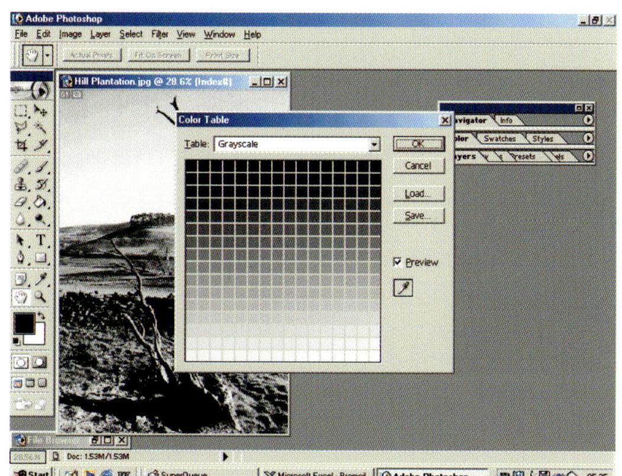

Select the whole tone range in the Color Table dialogue box.

Now select the whole tone range by clicking in the top left-hand corner and dragging to the bottom right-hand corner. Then press OK. A Color Picker dialogue box will now open. At the bottom right is a series of boxes marked C, M, Y and K. Type '0' in all four CMYK boxes and press OK. Yet another Color Picker dialogue box will now open. In this one, type '0' in the C and K boxes and 100 in the M and Y boxes, then press OK. The image on your screen will now change to a red and white negative. Save the file.

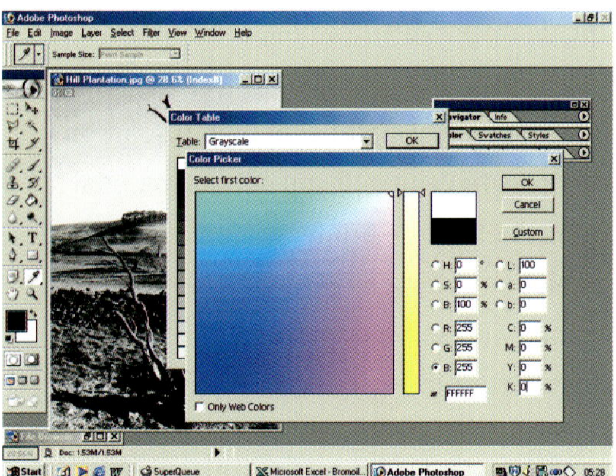

Type '0' in all four CMYK boxes in the Color Picker dialogue box.

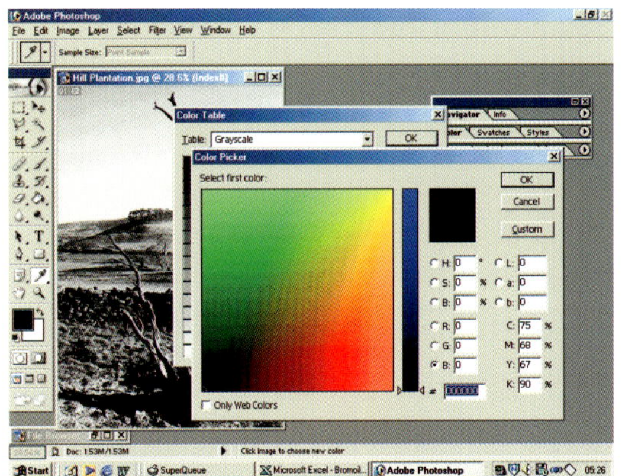

This is the Color Picker dialogue box.

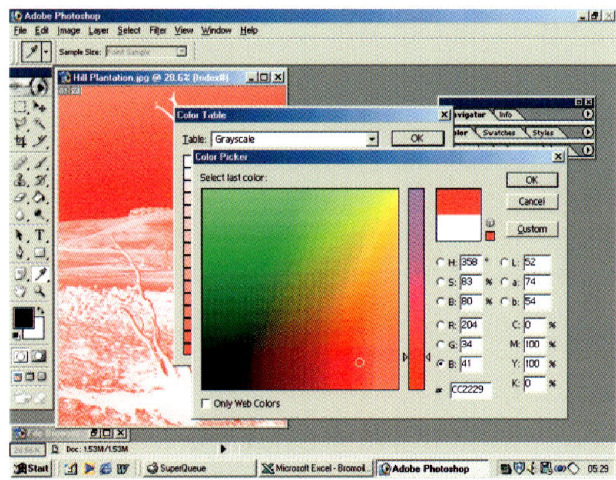

In the new Color Picker dialogue box that opens, type '0' in the C and K boxes and 100 in the Y and M boxes.

The final step is to print out your negative. To get your printer to print successfully on to transparency material at high resolution you have to lie to it. If you set the material to Transparency, the printer will default to a resolution setting of 360 dpi – also shown as Normal with some printers. But you want to print at 1440 dpi – Photo on some printers. So to get around this problem, you need to tell the printer you are printing on Photo Quality Inkjet Paper. This will allow you to set the resolution to 1440 dpi – Photo.

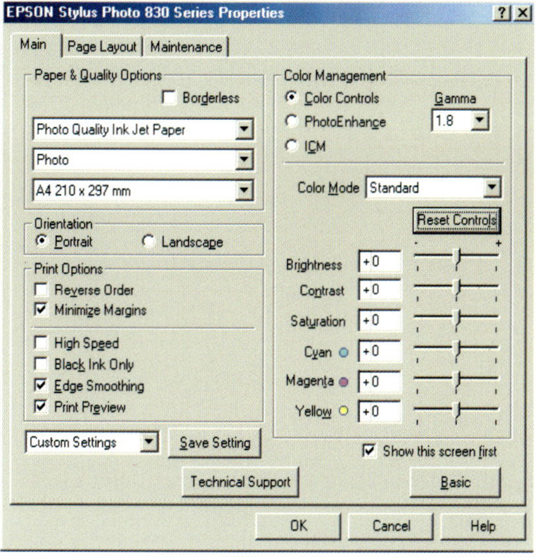

Be sure to set your printer to Photo Quality Inkjet Paper to allow you to set the resolution to 1440 dpi.

tip

At each stage give your files a different name, for example bromoils1.tif, bromoils2.tif and so on. This means that if you have made a mistake you will not have overwritten the previous stage and you will not have to go back to the beginning.

If you want to know more about making enlarged negatives digitally, I can do no better than recommend that you read the book *Making Digital Negatives for Contact Printing* by Dan Burkholder. It goes into great detail about tailoring the negatives for the particular process for which you want them, and contains a host of hints and tips.

Appendices

This section gives the formulas for all the solutions you are likely to need in the production of bromoils and oil prints. Some of these formulas I have already given in the relevant chapters, but for the sake of completeness I have repeated them here. The terms used in the book are also explained in the glossary, while there are also lists of further reading and useful contacts.

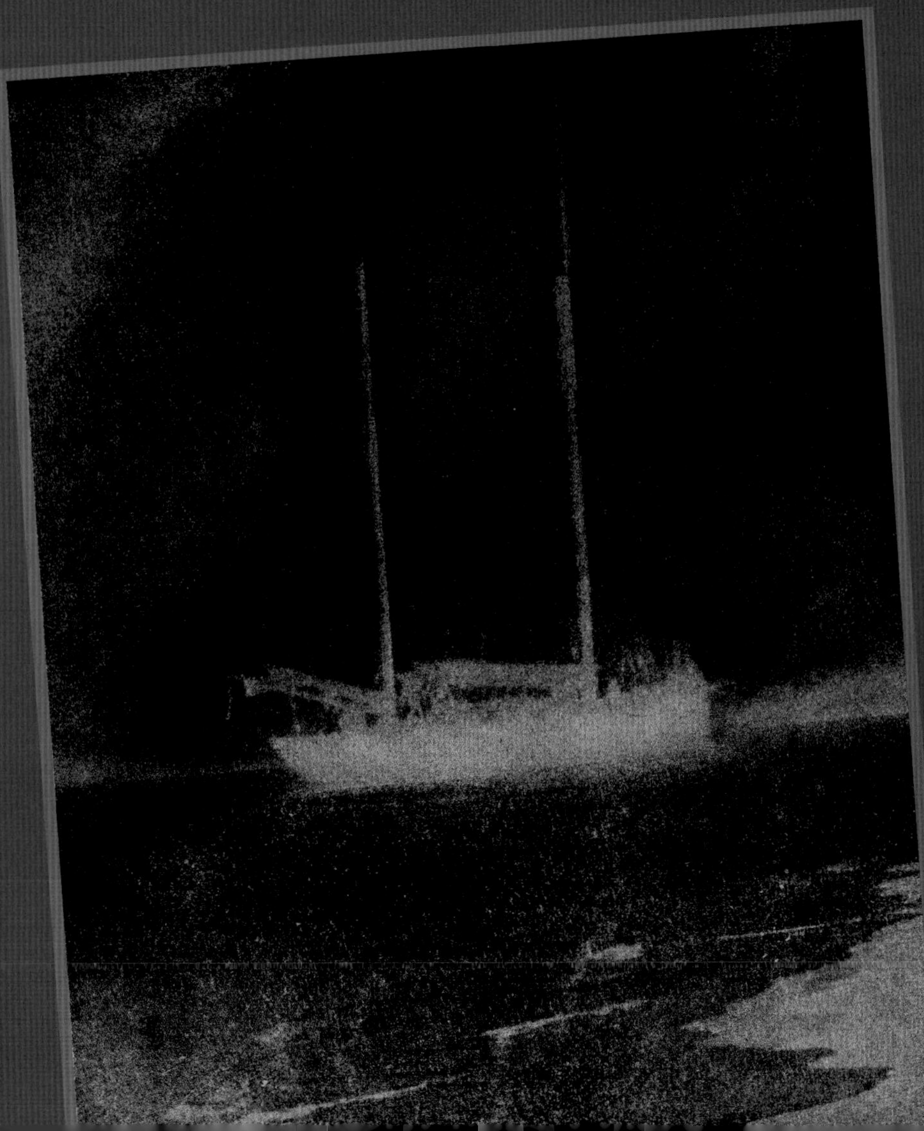

Formulary

First, a few words about safety in handling and mixing chemicals. Some of the chemicals used in photography are potentially quite dangerous. Potassium dichromate, for example, is very toxic and a suspected carcinogen, metol and amidol can cause skin irritation and dermatitis, and sulphuric acid is highly corrosive to both skin and clothes. Others are fairly innocuous. However, it pays to treat all chemicals with respect.

- When weighing, handling and mixing chemicals always wear rubber gloves, a dust mask and eye protection.
- Do not use domestic spoons for handling chemicals; use either a plastic or metal spoon or spatula kept exclusively for the purpose.
- Keep all chemicals out of the reach of children and pets.
- Keep all chemicals in clearly labelled jars and bottles. Never use old soft drinks bottles to store liquid chemicals.
- Never eat, drink or smoke anywhere near where you are handling or using chemicals, and that includes your darkroom.
- Clean up spillages immediately.
- Always use print forceps when handling prints in solutions.
- If you get chemical splashes on your skin, wash the affected area in plenty of clean, warm water immediately.
- If you splash chemicals into your eye, wash immediately with an eye bath and seek medical advice.

FILM DEVELOPER

Kodak D-23

A simple, versatile soft-working developer that can be used full strength for semi-compensating or diluted for true compensating effects.

Metol	7.5 grams
Sodium sulphite, anhydrous	100 grams
Water to	1 litre

Development times 6–10 minutes at 68°F (20°C). Use Kodak D-76 times as your starting points.

Windisch compensating developer

This classic compensating developer gives good results with a wide range of films.

Metol	2.5 grams
Sodium sulphite, anhydrous	25 grams
Water to	1 litre

Development times 18–20 minutes at 68°F (20°C).

Pyro PMK developer

My developer of choice for slow, medium speed and fast films, it gives amazing negative quality with superb sharpness and tonal control.

Solution A

Distilled or de-ionized water	400 ml
Metol	5 grams
Sodium bisulphite	10 grams
Pyrogallol	50 grams
Water to	500 ml

Solution B

Distilled or de-ionized water	700 ml
Kodalk (sodium metaborate)	300 grams
Water to	1 litre

For use take 1 part A and add to 100 parts of water, stirring. Then add 2 parts B. Development times at 70°F (21°C) are:

Ilford FP4 Plus	12 mins
HP5 Plus	13 mins
100 Delta	9 mins
400 Delta	11 mins
Kodak Tri-X	14 mins
T-Max 100	12 mins
T-Max 400	15 mins
Agfa APX 25	11 mins
APX 100	13 mins
APX 400	16 mins

PRINT DEVELOPERS

Amidol developer

The classic developer for bromoil, amidol gives neutral tones but has a very short dish life and stains easily.

Sodium sulphite, anhydrous	25 grams
Potassium bromide	0.25 gram
Amidol	6 grams
Water to	1 litre

Kodak D-163 developer

A good all-round neutral tone developer for print work, I find it is perfect for bromoils.

Metol	2.3 grams
Sodium sulphite, anhydrous	75 grams
Hydroquinone	17 grams
Sodium carbonate, anhydrous	65 grams
Potassium bromide	2.8 grams
Water to	1 litre

For use dilute 1:3 and develop fully.

Kodak D-165 soft gradation developer

Softer working than D-163, this developer is another good choice for bromoil work and gives neutral tones.

Metol	6 grams
Sodium sulphite, anhydrous	25 grams
Sodium carbonate, anhydrous	37 grams
Potassium bromide	1 gram
Water to	1 litre

For use dilute 1:3 and develop for 2 minutes at 68°F (20°C).

Kodak D-72 (similar to Dektol)

An alternative to D-163 giving broadly similar results, but different dilutions can produce different contrasts.

Water at 120°F (50°C)	750 ml
Metol	3 grams
Sodium sulphite, anhydrous	45 grams
Hydroquinone	12 grams
Sodium carbonate	68 grams
Potassium bromide	2 grams
Water to	1 litre

Dilution can vary from 1:1 to 1:4 depending on the contrast you want. Develop for 2 minutes at 68°F (20°C).

Kodak D-52 (similar to Selectol)

A warm-tone developer that gives different contrasts according to dilution.

Water at 120°F (50°C)	500 ml
Metol	1.5 grams
Sodium sulphite, anhydrous	21.2 grams
Hydroquinone	6 grams
Sodium Carbonate, anhydrous	14.5 grams
Potassium bromide	1.5 grams
Water to	1 litre

Dilute 1:1 to 1:3 and develop for 2 minutes at 68°F (20°C).

STOP BATHS

Kodak SB-1

Suitable for a wide range of films and papers.

Water	1 litre
Acetic acid, 28%	48 ml

Kodak SB-8

Similar to SB-1, but without the vinegar odour.

Water	750 ml
Citric acid	15 grams
Water to	1 litre

FIXERS

Plain hypo

As simple a fixer as you can make, its non-hardening properties make it ideal for bromoil work, but dish life is fairly limited.

Sodium thiosulphate (hypo), crystals	480 grams
Water to	2 litres.

Use fresh and undiluted. Do not keep overnight. Fix for 1 minute at 68°F (20°C).

Kodak F-24 Non-hardening acid fixer

A good general-purpose non-hardening fixer for both papers and films, especially those developed in Pyro PMK.

Water, at about 120°F (50°C)	500 ml
Sodium thiosulphate, crystals	240 grams
Sodium sulphite, anhydrous	10 grams
Sodium bisulphite	25 grams
Water to	1 litre

You can use 25 grams of citric acid instead of the sodium bisulphite. This will eliminate much of the odour associated with fixers. Fix for about 5 minutes at 68°F (20°C).

BLEACH-TAN SOLUTIONS

Venn's two-bath bleach-tan

If you prefer to keep the bleaching and tanning operations separate, this formula is the one to choose.

Solution A – Bleach

Copper sulphate, 10% solution	250 ml
Potassium bromide, 10% solution	13 ml

Solution B – Tan

Potassium bromide, 10% solution	70 ml
Potassium dichromate, 1% solution	30 ml
Water to	250 ml

Bleach the print in Bath A for 30 seconds at 68°F (20°C) or until only a yellow image remains. Drain and transfer, without rinsing, to Bath B for 4 minutes at 68°F (20°C).

Gilbert Hooper's bleach-tan

A good all-round solution favoured by many members of the Bromoil Circle of Great Britain.

Copper sulphate	25 grams
Potassium bromide	25 grams
Potassium dichromate	1.25 grams
Sulphuric acid, 10% solution	10 ml
Water to	400 ml

Add the sulphuric acid to the water first, then dissolve the rest of the chemicals. For use, dilute 1:10 and treat the print for 10 minutes at 68°F (20°C).

Trevor Jones's bleach-tan

Another combined solution, very similar to Gilbert Hooper's, but without the acid.

Copper sulphate	35 grams
Potassium bromide	35 grams
Potassium dichromate	1.5 grams
Water to	500 ml
Dilute 1:9 for use.	

LITH FILM REVERSAL SOLUTIONS

Developer

Use any standard print developer at bromide paper dilution.

Stop bath

Use any standard stop bath, but it must be fresh.

Bleach

Water	700 ml
Potassium dichromate	50 grams
Sulphuric acid, concentrated	50 ml
Water to	1 litre

Dissolve the dichromate in water before adding the acid. Alternatively, use 500ml of 10% sulphuric acid instead of 50ml of concentrated acid. In this case, dissolve the potassium dichromate in 400ml water, add the 10% acid, and add water to one litre. Use diluted 1:9.

Clearing solution

Sodium metabisulphite	25 grams
Water to	1 litre

Fixer

Water at about 50°C	600 ml
Sodium thiosulphate, crystals	240 grams
Sodium sulphite, anhydrous	15 grams
Acetic acid, 28%	48 ml
Boric acid, crystals	7.5 grams
Potassium alum	15 grams
Water to	1 litre

CONVERTING UNITS OF MEASURE

Weights and volumes have been represented in metric units as this better illustrates the percentage nature of the solutions made. Internationally available chemicals are often marked in both metric and imperial, as are a number of measuring devices. If you wish use imperial measurements then you convert on a part-by-part basis, However, the following short summary provides guidelines.

10 grams	=	0.353 oz
1 oz	=	28.350 grams
10 ml	=	0.338 floz
1 floz	=	29.574 ml
1 litre	=	2.113 pint
1 pint	=	0.568 litre

Making percentage solutions

For some solutions, such as bleach-tan, it is very convenient to have the constituent chemicals mixed up as percentage solutions. This means that, instead of having to weigh and mix powdered chemicals each time you need a new working solution, you simply pour the appropriate amount of each percentage solution into a measuring jug, add water and that is all. It can also be far more accurate to measure, say, 5ml of a solution than 0.5 gram of powder.

A 10 per cent solution, for example, has 10 grams of solid chemical dissolved in 100ml of water. This means that each 10ml of the solution contains 1 gram of the chemical. So if a formula calls for 2.5 grams of the chemical you add 25ml of the 10 per cent solution.

Similarly, a one percent solution contains 1 gram of solid chemical in 100ml of water; so each 10ml of solution contains 0.1 gram of the chemical. For a formula requiring 0.15 gram of the chemical you would therefore add 15ml of the one per cent solution.

The important thing to remember is that the *total* amount of the solution must be 100ml. What this means is that you dissolve the appropriate amount of dry chemical in about 75ml of water, then add more water to make a total of 100ml. If you start with 100ml of water and add the dry chemical to that, you will not have an accurate percentage solution. For instance, 10 grams of dry chemical added to 100ml of water produces a nine percent solution, not 10 per cent.

Taking the Trevor Jones bleach-tan formula as an example. Mixed with percentage solutions the working solution would be:

Copper sulphate, 10% solution	35 ml
Potassium bromide, 10% solution	35 ml
Potassium dichromate, 1% solution	15 ml
Water to	500 ml

Glossary

Bleach – A chemical solution that converts the silver image of a print into a virtually colourless silver compound. In bromoil printing, the bleach is usually combined with a tanning solution to form the matrix ready for inking.

Bromoil – One of a number of processes using an oily ink to form an image on a matrix. In bromoil, the starting point is a bromide print.

Bromoil transfer – A secondary process whereby the image forming an inked bromoil is transferred by pressure to a sheet of support paper, usually some kind of artists' watercolour or etching paper.

Bromotype – An oil-reinforcement process, also known as Bromaloid, which uses the bromoil technique to strengthen tones in bromide prints. It differs from the bromoil process as the silver image is redeveloped after bleaching and tanning.

Characteristic curve – A graphical illustration of how light acts on the emulsion of a film or paper to produce density during development.

Chromogenic film – A monochrome film that is processed in C-41 colour negative chemicals. A typical chromogenic film is Ilford XP2 Plus.

Compensating developer – A developer with a very low concentration of developing agent that slowly builds up shadow detail in the negative while limiting the density of highlight areas to prevent them burning out when printed.

Dabbing action – A light, rapid vertical movement of the bromoil brush to clear muddy highlights and strengthen shadows after initial inking.

Developer – A chemical solution that converts the latent image formed during exposure into a visible image by converting the silver halide compounds in the exposed film or paper that have been affected by exposure to light into black metallic silver.

Fixer – A chemical solution that removes unexposed and undeveloped silver halides in a film or paper to stabilize the image and make it insensitive to white light. It is achieved by dissolving the silver halides in a solution that forms soluble silver salts, which are subsequently removed during washing.

Hopper – A simple tool that enables the bromoilist to use a very light touch when applying ink or cleaning up the image in the later stages of inking.

Hopping action – The final stage of the inking process where the brush handle is allowed to slide through the fingers and bounce off the surface of the print and the handle caught on the rebound. This cleans up the highlights in the print and reveals any hidden detail in the shadows.

Lith film – A high-contrast graphic arts film that can be developed in print developer to produce high-quality continuous tone images suitable for enlarged negatives.

Matrix – What the bromide print is known as after being treated in a bleach and tanning solution. It is a virtually colourless relief gelatin image which, when soaked, will accept bromoil inks in direct proportion to the tones in the original print.

Oil print process – The process from which bromoil evolved. It uses dichromate sensitized gelatin-coated paper which is exposed in contact with a negative to sunlight or ultraviolet radiation. This eliminates the need for a bromide print as a starting point and the bleaching and tanning stages.

Oleobrom – A very similar process to bromoil, but the bleached and tanned matrix is first inked using a roller, then soaked and excess ink removed under water with another roller. This procedure can be repeated several times or the print can be finished by brush inking in the usual way.

Orthochromatic – Film that is sensitive to the whole visible spectrum except deep orange and light red, used almost exclusively now for graphic arts applications. Orthochromatic films can be processed by the light of a red safelight.

Panchromatic – Film that is sensitive to the entire visible spectrum and must therefore be processed in total darkness. Almost all modern camera films are panchromatic.

Stiffening – Using pigment, resin or candle wax to make bromoil ink harder or stiffer. This is another degree of control offered by the process.

Stop bath – A chemical solution, usually acidic in nature, used to halt the action of the developer on a film or paper. It does this by immediately neutralizing the alkalinity of the developer and, therefore, its activity.

Supercoat – A coating of unsensitized gelatin on top of the sensitized layer or layers to protect the emulsion from abrasion and other physical damage. Traditionally, papers for bromoil have no supercoating, but many modern papers that have this layer are also suitable for the bromoil process.

Tan – The stage that hardens the bleached silver image in proportion to the density of the original image. The tanning solution often forms part of the bleach, although separate formulas are available.

Thinning – Adding linseed oil, turpentine or stand oil to the bromoil ink to make it softer and capable of producing denser shadows.

Two-bath development – A technique for controlling negative contrast and particularly suitable for negatives that will be made into bromoil prints. In the first bath, containing a developing agent and preservative, the film absorbs developer and begins development. It is then transferred to the second bath, containing alkali, where the bulk of development takes place. The solution in the dense highlight areas quickly becomes exhausted and development ceases, but in thin shadow areas it continues, building up density.

Variable contrast paper – Printing paper coated with two layers sensitive to light of different colours. Images of different contrasts can be produced by filtering the amount of each colour.

Walking action – The first stage of inking a bromoil is performed using a brush placed down on the matrix, pushed gently and dragged a little before being allowed to spring up again.

Wash aid – A chemical solution that helps remove fixer from the emulsion of a film or paper and thus reduce washing time.

Wetting agent – A chemical rather like a weak detergent that reduces the surface tension of water. It is used in very low concentration.

Further Reading

At the time of writing there are, in addition to this book, only two others that I know of currently in print devoted exclusively to the bromoil process. They are:

Laughter, Gene, *Bromoil 101*, self-published, 1997

Lewis, David W., *The Art of Bromoil and Transfer*, self-published, 1995

Plus a booklet:

Hooper, Gilbert; McDougal, Maija and Atherton, Dennis, *An Introduction to Bromoil*, Bromoil Circle of Great Britain, 1998

There are also a few general books in print on historic processes in general that include chapters on the bromoil, bromoil transfer and oil processes:

Crawford, William, *The Keepers of Light*, Morgan and Morgan, 1979

Farber, Richard, *Historic Photographic Processes*, Allworth Press, 1998

Reed, Martin and Jones, Sarah, *Silver Gelatin*, Working Books, 1995

Webb, Randall and Reed, Martin, *Spirits of Salts*, Argentum, 1999

Other books, no longer in print, which are worth reading if you can locate them include:

Cox, Bertram and Tilney, F.C., *The Art of Pigmenting*, Henry Greenwood & Co, 1924

Gabriel, Leonard, *Bromoil and Transfer*, Sir Isaac Pitman & Sons, 1930

Hawkins, G.L., *Pigment Printing*, Henry Greenwood & Co, 1933

Mortimer, F.J. and Coulthurst, S.L., *The Oil and Bromoil Processes*, Hazell, Watson & Viney, 1912

Mayer, Emil, *Bromoil Printing and Transfer*, American Photographic Publishing Co, 1923

Mayer, Emil, *A Manual of Bromoil and Transfer*, American Photographic Publishing Co, 1927

Sinclair, James A., *Bromoil and Oil Prints*, James A. Sinclair & Co, 1920

Sinclair, James A., *An Introduction to Bromoil and Transfer*, James A. Sinclair & Co, date unknown

Symes, Chris J., *Perfection in the Pigment Processes*, The New Photographer, 1924

Symes, Chris J., *Bromoil and Transfer*, Fountain Press, fourth edition, 1946

Whalley, G.E., *Bromoil and Transfer*, Fountain Press, 1961

There is also a video tape on the process which is well worth watching:

Westgate, Colin, *Gryspeerdt and the Bromoil Process*, Eastbourne Photographic Society, 1995

For further information on specific topics that are covered in this book, refer to:

Anchell, Stephen G., *The Darkroom Cookbook*, Focal Press, 1994

Burkholder, Dan, *Making Digital Negatives for Contact Printing*, Bladed Iris Press, c.1998

Clerc, L.P., *Photography: Theory and Practice*, Sir Isaac Pitman & Sons, 1930

Coote, J.H., *Ilford Monochrome Darkroom Practice*, Focal Press, Third edition, 1996

Hutchings, Gordon, *The Book of Pyro*, Bitter Dog Press, 1992

Wall, E.J. and Jordan, F.I., *Photographic Facts and Formulas*, Amphoto, 1975

There are many other articles and other publications on the bromoil processes available on the Internet, some old and some more modern. Just type 'Bromoil' into any one of the Internet search engines and be prepared to be overwhelmed with sources of information.

Useful Contacts

The following list of suppliers is by no means exhaustive. It includes only those companies from which I have either purchased personally or know someone who has. They all offer a mail-order service.

United Kingdom

L Cornelissen & Son Limited,
105 Great Russell Street,
London WC1B 3RY
Tel: 020 7636 1045
Fax: 020 7636 3655
e-mail: info@cornelissen.com
Website: www.cornelissen.com

Brushes, inks and watercolour papers

Fotospeed,
Jay House Limited, Fiveways House, Rudloe, Corsham,
Wiltshire SN13 9RG
Tel: 01225 810596
Fax: 01225 811801
e-mail: info@fotospeed.com
Website: www.fotospeed.com

Chemicals, bromoil kits, brushes, inks and photographic papers

Intaglio Printmakers,
62 Southwark Bridge Road,
Play House Yard,
London SE1 0AS
Tel: 020 7928 2633

Brushes, inks and watercolour papers

Kentmere Limited,
Staveley, Kendal, Cumbria LA8 8BR
Tel: 01539 822322
e-mail: sales@kentmere.co.uk
Website: www.kentmere.co.uk

Photographic papers and chemicals

T N Lawrence & Son Limited,
208 Portland Road, Hove,
East Sussex BN3 5QT
Tel: 01273 260260
Fax: 01273 260270
e-mail: sales@lawrence.co.uk
Website: www.lawrence.co.uk

A huge variety of artists' and printmakers' equipment and materials from brushes, rollers and inks to a range of etching presses suitable for bromoil transfer. Excellent on-line catalogue

Also at: 38 Barncoose Industrial Estate, Pool, Redruth, Cornwall TR15 3RQ
Tel: 01209 313181 – ring to check they are open before making a long journey

Nova Darkroom Equipment Limited,
Unit 1A, Harris Road,
Wedgnock Industrial Estate,
Warwick CV34 5JU
Tel: 01926 403090
Fax: 01926 499992
e-mail: sales@novadarkroom.com
Website: www.novadarkroom.com

Deep slot processors, archival washers, photographic papers and chemicals

Silverprint Limited,
12 Valentine Place,
London SE1 8QH
Tel: 020 7620 0844
Fax: 020 7620 0129
e-mail: sales@silverprint.co.uk
Website: www.silverprint.co.uk

Wide range of raw chemicals, photographic papers and chemicals, liquid emulsion, coating rods, brushes, inks and bromoil kits. Excellent on-line catalogue

United States and Canada

Bostick & Sullivan,
PO Box 16639, Sata Fe,
New Mexico 87506, USA
Tel: (505) 474-0890
Fax: (505) 474-2857
e-mail: orderinginfo@earthlink.net
Website: www.bostick-sullivan.com

Wide range of chemicals, photographic papers, brushes and inks

Freestyle,
5124 Sunset Boulevard,
Los Angeles, California 90027, USA
Tel: (800) 292-6137
Fax: (800) 616-3686
e-mail: info@freestylecamera.com
Website: www.freestylesalesco.com

Graphic Chemical & Ink Co,
728 N Yale, Villa Park, Illinois 60181, USA
Tel: (630) 832-6004
Fax: (630) 832-6064
e-mail: graphchem@aol.com

Full range of printmakers' supplies and equipment, particularly inks including litho inks

Luminos Photo Corp,
PO Box 158, Yonkers, New York 10705, USA
Tel: (800) 431-1859
Fax: (914) 965-0367
e-mail: luminos@worldnet.att.net

Photographic papers, chemicals and liquid emulsion

David Lewis,
PO Box 254, 457 King Street,
Callander, Ontario, Canada P0 1H0
Tel: (705) 752-3029

Photographic papers, chemicals, brushes, inks and transfer presses

About the Author

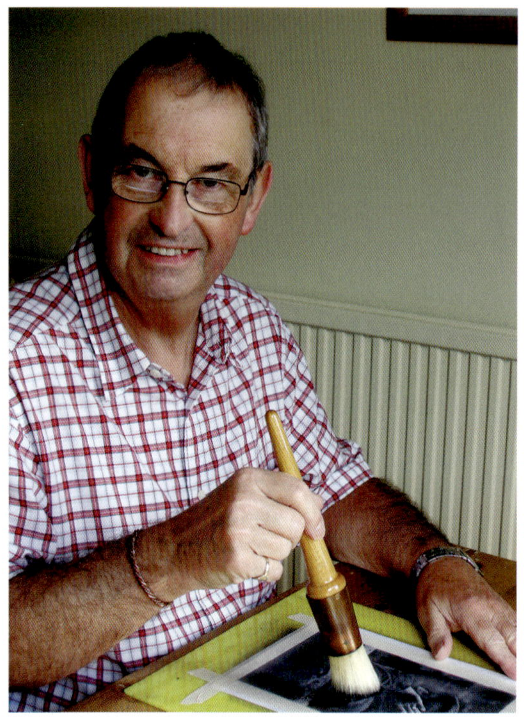

Derek Watkins has been a freelance writer and photographer for over 25 years, and before that worked as a copywriter for advertising and public relations agencies. He has had a lifelong interest in photography and has written eight previous books on the subject and two on other topics. In addition, he has written for a wide range of British, Australian and American photographic journals.

His interest in bromoil and other historic photographic processes stems from a disenchantment with the 'automatic everything' philosophy of modern photography. He has found that these old processes have given him a new approach to picture making and a better understanding of the history of photography.

Derek Watkins is a member of Coventry Photographic Society and the International Society of Bromoilists, and a former member of the Bromoil Circle of Great Britain. He is married with a married son and lives in Coventry, Warwickshire, England.

ACKNOWLEDGEMENTS

I would like to thank my fellow member of Coventry Photographic Society, Colin Ivison, for kindly allowing me to use some of his beautiful bromoils in this book. And I would also like to thank Durst UK Limited, T. N. Lawrence & Son Limited, Nova Darkroom Limited, and Paterson Products Limited for supplying photographs of some of their products to illustrate the book.

Derek Watkins, Coventry, September 2005

Index

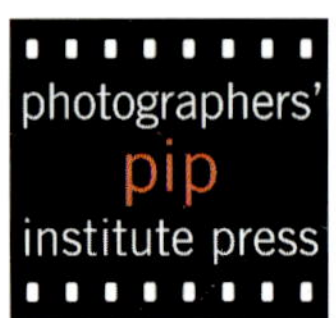

Photographers' Institute Press an imprint of The Guild of Master Craftsman Publications Ltd, 166 High Street, Lewes, East Sussex BN7 1XU
Tel: 01273 488005 Fax: 01273 402866
www.pipress.com